Political
Participation
in the
United States

Political Participation in the United States

THIRD EDITION

M. Margaret Conway

University of Florida

CQ PRESS

A Division of Congressional Quarterly Inc.

Washington, D.C.

CQ Press
A Division of Congressional Quarterly Inc.
1414 22nd Street, N.W.
Washington, D.C. 20037

202-822-1475; 800-638-1710
www.cqpress.com

Political Participation in the United States, Third Edition, was designed and
typeset by Blue Heron Typesetters, Inc., Lawrence, Kansas.

Cover by Rich Pottern Design

Printed and bound in the United States of America

04 03 02 01 00   5 4 3 2 1

Library of Congress Cataloging-in-Publication Data

Conway, M. Margaret (Mary Margaret), 1935–
Political participation in the United States / M. Margaret Conway.—3rd ed.
p.   cm.
Includes bibliographical references and index.
ISBN: 0-87187-792-9 (paperback)
1. Political participation—United States.   2. Political participation—
United States—History.   I. Title.

JK1764.C548   2000
323'.042'0973—dc21   00-025713

Contents

Tables

Preface

L ow levels of political participation are one of the paradoxes of political behavior in the United States. Voting turnout has ebbed significantly since 1960, and there is scant evidence of a compensating increase in other forms of participation. This decline has occurred despite the penetration of television network and cable news into almost every household, significantly higher levels of educational attainment than ever before, increased levels of employment among all groups in American society, and the spread of unprecedented affluence across the nation.

Thus, some important questions about political participation require analysis: Who takes part in American politics, and in what types of political action do they engage? How can we explain why political participation in some forms has not increased and in others has actually declined? *Political Participation in the United States* examines the nature and extent of political participation in the United States and offers explanations for the patterns of participation. In addition, it assesses the effects that those patterns have on citizens and on public policy.

Chapter 1 traces historical trends in political participation. Chapter 2 considers the effects of selected life-experience variables on political participation. These variables include age, education, gender, ethnicity, race, region, and employment.

Patterns of political participation also vary with the attitudes, beliefs, and values held by citizens. Chapter 3 examines trends in attitudes and beliefs, such as political trust, efficacy, interest in politics, and concern with the outcome of elections and their relationships with various forms of political participation.

Chapter 4 discusses the many aspects of the political system that affect patterns of political participation. These include the political party system; political movements such as those concerned with civil rights, women's rights, and the Vietnam War; and the coverage of politics by the mass media.

Chapter 5 examines the effects of the legal structure on suffrage in America. The histories of the United States and many other nations demonstrate that access to effective participation in the political system can be limited or shaped by a number of legal means, such as election laws and procedures of election administration, and sometimes by illegal means.

When so many citizens are eligible to participate, is participation by any one citizen a rational act? How can one person have any influence on the political system and its policies? That important issue is addressed in Chapter 6.

In Chapter 7 all the elements discussed in the previous chapters—who participates, in what way, and to what effect—are examined in relation to one another. Finally, Chapter 8 considers whether political participation has an instrumental effect on public policy and governance, or whether it is merely a symbolic action that provides support and legitimation to the structures of government, certain political leaders, and the political system as a whole. It also addresses the changing ways in which citizens pursue their interests through various forms of political participation.

This third edition benefited from the valuable suggestions of Paul R. Abramson of Michigan State University and Melissa R. Michelson of the University of Illinois at Chicago. Some of the data used in this book were made available by the Inter-University Consortium for Political and Social Research. Data for the American National Election Studies were collected by the Center for Political Studies, Institute for Social Research, at the University of Michigan, under grants from the National Science Foundation. Neither the original data collectors nor the consortium bears any responsibility for the analyses or interpretations presented here.

My thanks go to Brenda Carter, Gwenda Larsen, Ann Davies, Belinda Josey, and Julie Rovesti of CQ Press for their guidance and support and to Lydia Jeanne Duncan for her superb edit of the manuscript.

Chapter 1

Introduction

Describing what most impressed him during his visit to the United States in 1831, Frenchman Alexis de Tocqueville singled out politics as the American passion: "[T]he political activity that pervades the United States must be seen in order to be understood. No sooner do you set foot upon American ground than you are stunned by a kind of tumult."[1] Is that widespread passion for politics still present? One political contest suggests a possible answer. In 1990, Texas held a primary election for governor, in which well-known candidates were vying for both the Democratic and Republican nominations; nominations for many other offices were being made at the same time. The gubernatorial candidates alone spent a record $28 million in the primary contests, which were marked by numerous accusations and countercharges, frequently traded in rancorous formal debates; they were given extensive news coverage. Yet only three out of ten eligible Texans bothered to vote. Why was turnout so low? In postelection interviews, journalists sought to answer that question. Suggested answers elicited by the reporters from the nonvoting public ranged from "cynicism to ignorance to contentment to laziness."[2]

Although primary turnout is always lower than that for general elections, the 1990 Texas primary illustrates a more general pattern. Voting participation in presidential elections has declined significantly since the late 1960s; in 1996, voter turnout for the presidential election was the lowest it has been since 1948.[3]

How can nonvoting be explained? Do people who do not vote engage in other forms of political participation? Who engages in political action, and how can patterns of political participation be explained? This book addresses these and many other questions about the causes, patterns, and consequences of political participation.

What is the role of citizen participation in a democracy? Classical democratic theory assumes that citizens in a democratic state are interested in and participate in politics, are knowledgeable about the process of government and the proposed alternative solutions to public problems, and vote in accordance with a set of values or principles.[4] Studies of the electorate in democratic nations, however, indicate that these assumptions are unrealistic. For example, in the United States, many citizens are not interested in public affairs. Voting participation rates are low. Only a small proportion of the electorate (defined as those eligible to vote) has much knowledge about the structure and functions of government, and the general public is often unaware of even the major policy problems being considered by federal, state, or local governments. Many voters cast their votes on the basis of retrospective evaluations of the party of the incumbents, or their expectations of what candidates would do if elected to office.[5]

Revisionists of classical democratic theory argue that low levels of political participation and interest in politics actually contribute to governmental stability.[6] Furthermore, some revisionists contend that because many people are not interested in most issues before the government, it is easier for those who are concerned to work out compromises on divisive issues. Low levels of political interest and participation in public affairs are interpreted as reflecting satisfaction with the operating processes of the political system and the consequent policy outputs.[7]

Perhaps, then, the requirements for a stable democracy specified by classical democratic theory are not met. And yet stable democracies, such as the United States and Great Britain, do exist. Scholars have therefore suggested an alternative set of conditions. They include: (1) social pluralism; (2) diverse and competing elites that are circulating and accessible; (3) a basic consensus, at least among the elites, as to the rules of democratic competition; and (4) elections that provide regular opportunities for citizens to participate in the selection of public officials.[8]

Nevertheless, the belief that widespread popular participation is necessary for the effective functioning of a stable democracy continues to find support, partly because participation is viewed as necessary to maintain open access to the system. If the system is open to participation, then those who want to participate can do so in the event that an issue arises which is sufficiently important to motivate their participation. This raises the question of the extent to which barriers to political participation exist. These barriers may be structural, such as voter registration laws and election administration procedures, or they may be psychological, created by political learning processes that fail to encourage in some segments of American society an orientation toward political participation.

The revisionist view of democratic theory implies that political participation is instrumental to achieving preferred policy outcomes. To what extent does popular participation, when it occurs, have an impact on public policy, and to what extent is it merely ritualistic—that is, habitual? This question can be expressed differently: Under what conditions is political participation rational? A decision to participate is rational if a citizen (1) has specific preferences for certain policy outcomes, (2) can rank outcomes in an order of preference, (3) has a set of rules by which he or she can link preferences to actions that will contribute to obtaining the desired outcomes, and (4) chooses those alternatives that can contribute to obtaining the preferred outcome.[9] This last requirement raises a particular problem. Suppose a citizen is only one of nine million people who are eligible to vote, and five million are expected to vote on election day. Is participation rational when the chance that one citizen's vote will have an impact on the outcome is extremely small?

The Meaning of Political Participation

The term *political participation* as used here means those activities of citizens that attempt to influence the structure of government, the selection of government officials, or the policies of government. These activities may be supportive of the existing structure, officials, or policies, or they may seek to change any or all of these. This definition emphasizes active involvement that is assumed to be instrumental or goal oriented. However, political participation also includes passive kinds of involvement, such as attending ceremonial or supportive activities, or paying attention to what is happening in the government or in politics. Thus, following the coverage of political campaigns by the mass media, and paying attention to the activities and policy decisions of a city council, state legislature, or federal agency, can be classified as passive forms of political participation.

A distinction can be made between conventional and unconventional political participation.[10] *Conventional participation* refers to those activities that are accepted as appropriate by the dominant political culture. Voting, seeking elective office, working for a candidate or a political party, writing a letter to a public official—these are examples of conventional forms of political participation. Some conventional political participation is organizational—it consists of working with others to obtain a particular outcome. The full range of public policies can be the focus of such activities, and organized groups try to influence policy at all levels of government. Examples of organizational activity include advocacy of a nuclear weapons freeze, efforts to end pollution of rivers, and the attempt to prevent the closing of a local school.

Certain forms of political participation—which can be labeled *unconventional*—are not accepted as appropriate by the dominant political culture, even though they may be legal. A march by students in a college town to protest redrawing of boundary lines for city council districts to weaken the students' political power would be legal, but the local residents might regard it as inappropriate. Some forms of political participation are both unconventional and illegal. For example, during the Vietnam War, a small group of radicals planted a bomb in a building that housed classrooms and laboratories at the University of Wisconsin, killing one student, because they believed that some of the research conducted in the building contributed to the war effort. Political protest in this form goes beyond what is acceptable to Americans and violates the law as well. Unconventional political behavior can be viewed as a continuum, ranging from participating in peaceful protest marches to engaging in terrorist violence or civil war.

Another form of political participation is activity aimed at the repression of either conventional or unconventional political participation.[11] Repression is most frequently aimed at protest behavior. During the 1950s and 1960s, sit-ins and other demonstrations were staged in many areas of the United States in support of civil rights for black citizens who were being denied them. Countermeasures were taken, sometimes by private citizens and sometimes by law enforcement authorities, in an attempt to halt these protests, even when they took the form of peaceful, lawful demonstrations.

Measurement of the frequency with which citizens engage in different types of political activities presents a number of problems. Voting is the simplest form of activity to measure, but even that is not without difficulty. *Voter turnout* is the percentage of the voting-age population that actually voted. One way of measuring it is to add up the number of votes cast for a particular office, such as the presidency, and divide the total by the number of people of voting age. Some citizens vote but cast invalid ballots, however; others vote for some offices but not for a presidential candidate. Furthermore, it is generally recognized that the census undercounts the population; since a census is taken only once every ten years, the size of the population in the intervening years must be estimated. The census count also includes resident aliens (citizens of other countries) who are legally living in the United States, as well as some proportion of illegal aliens. The voting-age population also includes those in prison, and in all states except Massachusetts where prisoners are ineligible to vote. Furthermore, persons convicted of certain crimes are ineligible to vote in many states after being released from prison. Despite these problems with measuring the voting age population, the percentage of the voting-age population that actually voted is probably the best estimate of voter turnout available.

Another method of calculating voter turnout is to draw a representative sample of the voting-age population and interview it. The Bureau of the Census uses this method, with a sample of 50,000 or more households. The person interviewed in each household is asked whether each voting-age person in the household voted. The Bureau of the Census estimates that, because interviewees overreport the frequency of voting, turnout measured in this way is 5 to 12 percent higher than the true figure.[12] Other estimates of voter turnout are derived from much smaller representative samples, ranging from 1,500 to 3,500 people, drawn from the voting-age population by the University of Michigan's Center for Political Studies for the American National Election Studies—in-depth research on the beliefs, attitudes, and political participation of the American electorate. These surveys are a major source of information about other forms of political participation as well.[13]

Problems also exist in measuring other forms of political participation. Our knowledge of citizens' engagement in forms of political action other than voting depends on their responses to survey questions about various kinds of political activity. National surveys conducted in election years frequently ask about campaign-related activities; however, collection of information about other kinds of participation, such as contacting public officials or engaging in political protest activities, is done much less frequently.

Trends in Political Participation

During the American Revolution, the colonists expressed their belief that those who are governed have a right to be represented in the governmental decision-making process in the slogan, "No taxation without representation." The usual mechanism for providing popular representation is an election. However, in eighteenth-century England, the right to vote was sharply limited.[14] In the American colonies, the right to participate in elections to the colonial legislatures was limited to adult males; and because of additional restrictions, such as "good character," property ownership, and payment of taxes, less than half of even the adult males were eligible to vote in colonial America.[15]

After the Revolution, most members of the electoral college (which actually chooses the president of the United States) were elected by the state legislatures, but by 1832, they were elected by popular vote in all but one of the states. Only 22 percent of the adult male population participated in the election that year, however.[16] (Nonwhite citizens were not allowed to vote in most states, and women did not have the legal right to vote in any state.) Voter turnout increased gradually thereafter, reaching 37.6 percent of the adult male population in the election of 1876. Turnout averaged 36.1 percent in the presidential elections held between 1876 and 1896, but it then began to decline. After the Nineteenth Amendment to the federal Constitution, granting women the right to vote, was ratified in 1920, turnout increased to 42.5 percent. Voter turnout attained a post–World War II high in 1960, but declined between 1960 and 1980. In 1984, it increased slightly, with 59.9 percent of the voting-age population participating, but decreased again in 1988, to 57.4 percent. In 1992 turnout in the presidential election increased to 61.3 percent, but in 1996 it declined again, to 54.2 percent.[17]

Table 1-1 is a comparison of voter turnout in elections of presidents with voter turnout in elections of members of the House of Repre-

TABLE I-I

Voter Registration and Turnout as a Percentage of the Voting-Age
Population, Presidential and Midterm Elections, 1960–1996

	Presidential elections			Midterm elections		
Year	Percent registered	Percent Voting for president	Percent Voting for House of Representatives	Year	Percent registered	Percent voting
1960	—	62.8	58.5	1962	—	46.3
1964	—	69.3	57.7	1966	70.3	55.4
1968	74.3	67.8	55.0	1970	68.1	54.6
1972	72.3	63.0	50.7	1974	62.2	44.7
1976	66.7	59.2	48.9	1978	62.6	45.9
1980	66.9	59.2	47.4	1982	64.1	48.5
1984	68.3	59.9	47.8	1986	64.3	46.0
1988	66.6	57.4	44.7	1990	62.2	45.0
1992	68.2	61.3	50.8	1994	62.5	45.0
1996	65.9	54.2	45.8			

SOURCES: Bureau of the Census, "Projections of the Voting Age Population for States, November 1990," Bureau of the Census, *Current Population Reports*, ser. P-25, no. 1029 (Washington, D.C.: Government Printing Office, April 1990), Table 5; Lynne M. Casper and Loretta E. Bass, "Voting and Registration in the Election of November 1996," Bureau of the Census, *Current Population Reports*, ser. P-20, no. 504 (Washington, D.C.: Government Printing Office, July 1998), Table 1; Historical Voting Tables, Table 1, at http://www.census.gov/population/socdemo/voting/history/htable01.txt; U.S. Dept of Commerce, *Statistical Abstract of the United States* (Washington, D.C.: Government Printing Office, 1998), 297, Table 485.

sentatives from 1960 to 1996. It shows that fewer people cast votes in the congressional elections than in the presidential elections held at the same time. An even smaller proportion of the voting-age population voted in the congressional elections held in the middle of the president's four-year term of office (with the exceptions of 1982 and 1990).

Politicians often interpret their electoral victories as a "mandate from the people," but such claims should be viewed with considerable skepticism. The winning candidate usually receives the vote of substantially less than 50 percent of the voting-age population. In the presidential elections held since 1920, the candidate who received the largest percentage of the popular vote was Lyndon Johnson, and he received the votes of only 37.8 percent of the voting-age population in 1964. The president with the lowest level of popular support during that period is Calvin Coolidge, who was elected by the votes of 23.7 percent of the voting-age population in 1924. He is closely followed

TABLE 1-2

Reported Participation in Election-Related Activities, Presidential and Midterm Elections, 1952–1998 (in percent)

Presidential elections

Form of campaign activity	1952	1956	1960	1964	1968	1972	1976	1980	1984	1988	1992	1996
Tried to persuade others how to vote	28	28	34	31	33	32	37	36	32	27	37	28
Attended campaign rallies or political meetings	7	7	8	9	9	9	6	8	8	7	8	6
Worked for political party or candidate	3	3	6	5	6	5	4	6	4	3	3	3
Wore campaign button or put bumper sticker on car	—	16	21	16	15	14	8	7	9	9	11	10
Gave money to a party or candidate	4	10	12	11	9	16	8	8	8	9	7	9

Midterm elections

Form of campaign activity	1954	1958	1962	1966	1970	1974	1978	1982	1986	1990	1994	1998
Tried to persuade others how to vote	—	17	18	22	27	15	22	22	21	17	23	19
Attended campaign rallies or political meetings	—	—	8	—	9	6	10	9	7	6	6	5
Worked for political party or candidate	—	—	4	—	7	5	6	6	3	3	3	2
Wore campaign button or put bumper sticker on car	—	—	10	—	9	5	9	8	7	7	7	6
Gave money to a party or candidate	—	—	9	8	—	8	13	9	10	7	7	6

SOURCES: American National Election Studies Cumulative File, 1948–1996; 1998 American National Election Study.
NOTE: Percentages have been rounded to whole numbers.

by Harry Truman in 1948 (25.3 percent), Jimmy Carter in 1976 (27.2 percent), and Ronald Reagan in 1980 (27.3 percent). Bill Clinton was elected by the vote of 43.0 percent of the registered voters in 1992, but by only 23.9 percent of the voting-age population. In 1996, he received the vote of 49.2 percent of the registered voters but only 24.1 percent of the voting-age population.[18]

Survey research conducted since 1952 indicates that citizen participation in other forms of election-related activity is low (see Table 1-2). The most common of these other forms is trying to persuade others how to vote. From 1952 to 1998, the proportion of the electorate reporting that they engaged in that activity ranged from 28 percent to 37 percent in presidential election years and from 17 percent to 27 percent in midterm election years. Substantially lower proportions of the electorate reported participating in other ways in political campaigns. Between 6 percent and 10 percent attended campaign rallies or political meetings in this period. The proportion who wore campaign buttons and displayed bumper stickers on cars, which never exceeded 21 percent, appears to have declined to 11 percent or less since the middle 1970s. That may be attributable to changes in federal campaign finance laws, which in 1976 began requiring more rigorous accounting for campaign receipts and expenditures. The decline may also in part reflect the increased emphasis on radio and television advertising in political campaigns. The cost of buttons and bumper stickers and doubts about their effectiveness make campaign managers reluctant to expend limited funds on these types of advertising.

The proportion of the electorate that contributes money to political campaigns varies over time (see Table 1-2). This may reflect changes in the use of targeted direct mail by both candidates and political parties, to solicit small political contributions from a larger proportion of the electorate, as well as the tax deductibility of small contributions during the late 1970s and early 1980s.

A more passive form of political participation is a general interest in politics and political events. As Table 1-3 indicates, general political interest and concern with the outcome of political campaigns was higher from the 1960s to the mid-1970s than either before or since. The political environment of that period included the 1964 presidential campaign—a contest between Barry Goldwater, a conservative Republican, and Lyndon Johnson, the first southerner nominated as a

Midterm Elections, 1958–1998 (in percent)

	1958	1962	1966	1970	1974	1978	1982	1986	1990	1994	1998
Reported general interest in politics											
Most of the time	—	16	35	—	39	23	29	26	28	30	27
Some of the time	—	43	30	—	36	34	36	35	33	34	37
Said they were interested in the current campaign											
Very much	26	36	30	33	—	21	26	23	21	28	31
Somewhat	33	38	40	43	—	45	44	44	46	47	48
Not much	41	26	30	24	—	34	30	33	33	25	21
Said they "care a good deal" which party wins the elections to the House of Representatives	—	—	—	65	57	43	56	53	47	59	62

SOURCES: American National Election Studies Cumulative File, 1948–1996; 1998 American National Election Study.

presidential candidate by either major political party since the Civil War. The candidates differed sharply on both foreign and domestic policy issues: Goldwater advocated a greater American involvement in the war in Vietnam and a more confrontational policy toward communist nations. By 1966, the United States had half a million military troops in Vietnam, and the controversy over U.S. involvement there generated substantial political interest. Another stimulus to political interest at the time was the set of events generally referred to as "Watergate," beginning in June 1972 with the arrest of four persons inside the Democratic Party national headquarters in the Watergate office building in Washington and ending, after the initiation of impeachment proceedings in the House of Representatives, with the resignation of President Richard M. Nixon on August 9, 1974.[19] In general, political interest continued at a high level until 1976 and then began to decline. It was also higher during the 1992 and 1996 presidential election campaigns when measured by the proportion who reported they "care a good deal" about the outcomes of those elections.

The proportion of respondents who said they care about which party wins the election remained relatively stable in presidential elections until 1972, when it began to decline. But concern with the election outcome increased slightly in the 1984 and 1988 presidential elections. The fact that fewer people of voting age care who wins in congressional elections than in presidential elections corresponds to the lower voter turnouts in midterm election years.

Symbolic and Instrumental Participation

In considering the various forms of political participation, the question arises: To what extent is engaging in political activity a symbolic act? Some types of political acts are easily recognized as symbolic: saluting the flag, singing the national anthem, reciting the pledge of allegiance. Performing symbolic acts may serve to reduce citizens' resentments and doubts about government institutions and policies, may reaffirm citizens' beliefs and attitudes that support governing institutions, and may increase the likelihood that citizens will accept as legitimate the political institutions and the policies they develop.[20] Of course, citizens may also engage in symbolic acts that express their disapproval of government policies, leaders, and institutions.

Voting in an election can be a symbolic act. By voting, an individual expresses support for the prevailing political system and may also give expression to feelings of support for or opposition to a candidate, a party, or certain policies. Some voters in effect keep a political "hit list"—a list of candidates they want to vote against. Many politicians believe that the vote *against* is more strongly motivated than the vote *for* a candidate; they therefore try very hard not to give citizens any cause for placing them on a hit list. Sometimes voting may be used to express general disapproval, as when the citizens of São Paulo, Brazil, elected a rhinoceros in the city zoo to the city council in 1959.[21] In countries where citizens were required to vote but were given no choices among candidates, opposition could be expressed by casting a blank ballot.[22] Obviously, such voting behavior is also a symbolic act.

Political participation regarded as instrumental action is performed with a view to obtaining a specific personnel or policy outcome. For example, some citizens may be quite aware of the policy views and past legislative voting record of a congressional candidate on a particular issue, and when they decide how to vote in the congressional election, they decide on the basis of that issue. If these "instrumental" voters join with enough others who vote the same way on the basis of the same or other policy issues, they may have a decisive impact on the outcome of the election. Thus, some forms of political participation can be both symbolic and instrumental.

If political action proves to be instrumental (is effective), then patterns of political participation will determine the distribution of the goods and services available through the political system. If political action is symbolic, we must consider how and why it is used both by those who seek to stimulate it and by those who engage in it, and what the consequences are.

Notes

1. Alexis de Tocqueville, *Democracy in America*, ed. Phillips Bradley (New York: Vintage, 1957), 1:259.
2. David Maraniss, "Cynical or Lazy, Majority Didn't Vote," *Washington Post*, March 15, 1990, A3.
3. Charles E. Johnson Jr., "Nonvoting Americans," Bureau of the Census, *Current Population Reports*, ser. P-23, no. 102 (Washington, D.C.: Government Printing Office, April 1980), 2, Table A; and Lynn M. Casper and Loretta E. Bass, "Vot-

ing and Registration in the Election of November 1996," Bureau of the Census, *Current Population Reports,* ser. P-20, no. 504 (Washington, D.C.: Government Printing Office, July 1998), 1–2, Tables 1 and 2.

4. Bernard R. Berelson, "Democratic Theory and Public Opinion," *Public Opinion Quarterly* 16 (1952): 313–330; G. Bingham Powell Jr., *Contemporary Democracies: Participation, Stability, and Violence* (Cambridge: Harvard University Press, 1982); Carole Pateman, *Participation and Democratic Theory* (Cambridge: Cambridge University Press, 1970), chap. 1; Robert A. Dahl, *Democracy and Its Critics* (New Haven: Yale University Press, 1989); and Michael X. Delli Carpini and Scott Keeter, *What Americans Know about Politics and Why It Matters* (New Haven: Yale University Press, 1996).

5. Bernard R. Berelson, Paul F. Lazarsfeld, and William N. McPhee, *Voting: A Study of Opinion Formation in a Presidential Campaign* (Chicago: University of Chicago Press, 1954), chap. 14; Lester W. Milbrath and M. L. Goel, *Political Participation,* 2d ed. (Chicago: Rand McNally, 1977); Angus Campbell et al., *The American Voter* (New York: Wiley, 1964); Ivor Crewe, "Electoral Participation," in *Democracy at the Polls,* ed. David Butler, Howard R. Penniman, and Austin Ranney (Washington, D.C.: American Enterprise Institute, 1981); Paul R. Abramson, John H. Aldrich, and David W. Rohde, *Change and Continuity in the 1996 and 1998 Elections* (Washington, D.C.: CQ Press, 1999); Morris P. Fiorina, *Retrospective Voting in American National Elections* (New Haven: Yale University Press, 1981); and Delli Carpini and Keeter, *What Americans Know about Politics,* chap. 2.

6. Seymour Martin Lipset, *Political Man: The Social Bases of Politics* (Baltimore: Johns Hopkins University Press, 1981); and Berelson, Lazarsfeld, and McPhee, *Voting,* chap. 14.

7. See, for example, Berelson, Lazarsfeld, and McPhee, *Voting,* chap. 14.

8. Roger W. Cobb and Charles D. Elder, *Participation in American Politics: The Dynamics of Agenda-Building,* 2d ed. (Baltimore: Johns Hopkins University Press, 1983). See also Berelson, Lazarsfeld, and McPhee, *Voting,* chap. 14; Gerald M. Pomper, with Susan S. Lederman, *Elections in America,* 2d ed. (New York: Longman, 1980), chaps. 2 and 10; and, for a comparative analysis of the role of political participation in contributing to political stability, see Powell, *Contemporary Democracies.*

9. Norman Frohlich and Joe A. Oppenheimer, *Modern Political Economy* (Englewood Cliffs, N.J.: Prentice-Hall, 1978), 6–13.

10. For discussions of conventional and unconventional political activities, see Samuel H. Barnes and Max Kaase, eds., *Political Action* (Beverly Hills, Calif.: Sage, 1979).

11. Ibid., 87–92.

12. Casper and Bass, "Voting and Registration in the Election of November 1996," 2, fn. 1.

13. In checking the turnout reported by persons interviewed against that certified in local election board records, the Center for Political Studies, like the Census Bureau, has found that citizens tend to overreport their voting participation. They are less likely to falsely report other forms of political participation, because they are not under the pressure of cultural norms to engage in them. For discussions of overreporting of voting participation and its consequences for political analysis, see Aage Clausen, "Response Validity: Vote Report," *Public Opinion Quarterly* 32 (1968): 588–606; and John P. Katosh and Michael W. Traugott, "The Consequences of Validated and Self-Reported Voting Measures," *Public Opinion Quarterly* 45 (1981): 519–535. See also the following works by Paul R. Abramson and William H. Claggett: "Race-Related Differences in Self-Reported and Validated Turnout," *Journal of Politics* 46 (November 1984): 719–738; "Race-Related Differences in Self-Reported and Validated Turnout in 1984," *Journal of Politics* 48 (May 1986): 412–422; and "Race-Related Differences in Self-Reported and Validated Turnout in 1986," *Journal of Politics* 51 (May 1989): 397–408.

14. Kenneth Mackenzie, *The English Parliament* (Harmondsworth, England: Penguin Books, 1959), 97–102. The efforts of the British Parliament to levy direct taxes on colonial commercial activities, to tax trade between the colonies and British merchants, and even to grant trade monopolies to British merchants (most notoriously, trade in tea, which led to the Boston Tea Party), aroused outrage among the colonists. They considered themselves British subjects and therefore to have the legal rights of Englishmen. These rights included the right not to be taxed unless they or their legally elected representatives consented to the tax. Since the colonies were not represented in the British Parliament, the colonists felt Parliament had no right to tax them.

15. Dudley O. McGovney, *The American Suffrage Medley* (Chicago: University of Chicago Press, 1949), chap. 1. See also Kirk Harold Porter, *A History of Suffrage in the United States* (New York: AMS Press, 1971).

16. Johnson, "Nonvoting Americans," 2, Table A.

17. Ibid., 5, Table B. The Census Bureau reports that in 1996, 54.2 percent of the electorate voted, whereas the election results filed with the clerk of the House of Representatives indicate that 49.8 percent voted. See Table 1 and footnote 1, page 2, in Casper and Bass, "Voting and Registration in the Election of November 1996."

18. Johnson, "Nonvoting Americans," 5, Table B, and 7, Fig. 4; "Voting and Registration in the Election of November 1988," Bureau of the Census, *Current Population Reports,* ser. P-20, no. 440 (Washington, D.C.: Government Printing Office, 1989), Table A; and Bureau of the Census, *Statistical Abstract of the United States 1982–1983* (Washington, D.C.: Government Printing Office, 1982), 489, Table 801. Data for 1992 and 1996 were calculated from Bureau of the Census, *Statistical Abstract of the United States 1998,* 297, Table 485; and 281, Table 462.

19. It was learned that the activities of these four persons were funded by Republican President Nixon's campaign committee, the Committee to Re-elect the President. Other illegal activities, conducted by Nixon's campaign committee or by the White House itself, included unauthorized wiretappings, other burglaries sponsored by White House staff members, illegal contributions to Nixon's campaign committee, and illegal expenditures on its behalf. For a full history of these events, see William B. Dickerson Jr., ed., *Watergate: Chronology of a Crisis* (Washington, D.C.: CQ Press, 1973, reprint 1999).

20. For discussions of the roles of symbols and rituals in politics, see Murray Edelman, *The Symbolic Uses of Politics* (Urbana: University of Illinois Press, 1964); Murray Edelman, *Politics as Symbolic Action* (Chicago: Marham, 1971); and Charles D. Elder and Roger W. Cobb, *The Political Uses of Symbols* (New York: Longman, 1983).

21. Alexander T. Edelman, *Latin American Government and Politics* (Homewood, Ill.: Dorsey, 1969), 377.

22. Ibid.

Chapter 2

Social Characteristics and
Patterns of Political Participation

The extent to which citizens participate in politics and the ways in which they do so are determined by their social circumstances, which include the kinds of neighborhoods they live in, how much and what kinds of education they have, the kinds of work they do and how much they earn, the opportunities they have for improving their lives, and the social networks in which they are involved. Social circumstances affect the level and type of resources available for political participation, the skills that citizens can apply to political activities, and the extent of their political involvement. They also foster or inhibit development and maintenance of the attitudes and beliefs that underlie various types of political participation. Indicators of social circumstances include age, race, gender, ethnicity, the social class and educational attainment level of individuals and their parents, place of residence including region of the country, length of residence in the community, and marital status—these are also referred to here as social characteristics.[1]

Life experiences also influence citizens' patterns of political behavior. For example, those who have been poor are likely to value economic security more than those who have never known poverty.[2] Life experiences, which color an individual's evaluations of the past and expectations about the future, also vary according to social circumstances such as social class, race, gender, ethnicity, level of educational attainment, employment patterns, and career opportunities and choices.[3]

Life experiences are not constant over time; they differ between generations as well as within individual lifetimes. After enactment of the 1972 amendments to the Higher Education Act, which required nondiscrimination on the basis of gender in scholarships and admissions to college and university programs, women in much greater numbers entered many types of academic programs, such as business, law, medicine, science, and engineering, their admission to which had previously been limited. As a consequence, the range of occupations open to women increased dramatically, expanding their career opportunities and increasing their families' income levels. Passage of the act has thus affected many facets of women's lives, including their social roles and their status in society.[4]

The life experiences that are particularly important to large segments of the electorate determine the prevailing political issues. Moreover, as citizens' life experiences change with economic and social conditions, their political views and incentives to engage in political activity frequently also change.

There are several possible explanations for the effects of social characteristics on political participation. First, the variables that influence socioeconomic status help to determine the social roles that people play, influencing their expectations both for others and for themselves.[5] Second, socioeconomic status helps to determine the flow of political communications and explains why some individuals receive more political stimuli than others. Exposure to increasing amounts of political information can stimulate political interest and desire for involvement and usually increases political activity.

A third possible explanation is that socioeconomic status affects both citizens' stakes in political outcomes and their perceptions of those stakes. Although all citizens are affected by governmental decisions, not all perceive equally clearly the extent to which those decisions affect their interests. Middle-income citizens receive many direct benefits from government programs, such as insured mortgage loans, grants and low-interest loans to help pay their children's college expenses, and income tax deductions for such things as interest payments on mortgage loans, real estate property taxes, and contributions to retirement pension plans. Lower-income people also benefit from a number of government programs: for example, they may receive housing subsidies and assistance in the purchase of food and other necessities and in the payment of medical expenses. Both middle-income and lower-income citizens also receive benefits from the government that are provided to the community as a whole—public elementary and secondary schools, public safety services, transportation facilities (roads, highways, and public transit), and parks and recreation facilities. However, awareness of the connection between political participation and government programs, as well as the quantity and quality of benefits and services provided, is lower among lower-income groups. Groups conducting voter registration and mobilization drives among citizens of lower socioeconomic status often find that political education is necessary to help them see the connections between political activity and benefits received.[6] To summarize, one lens through which patterns of political participation can be viewed is that of social characteristics; the characteristics of those who participate can be compared with the characteristics of those who do not.[7]

The basic socioeconomic status model of participation tells us *who* participates and who does not, but critics argue that it is inadequate in explaining *why* people do or do not participate in politics. One alternative model builds on the basic model by attempting to explain how socioeconomic status and other sociodemographic characteristics are linked to political participation. This alternative—the Civic Volunteerism Model—suggests that people do not participate because they lack the necessary resources of time, money, and skills; because they do not want to (they lack political engagement); or because no one asked them to (they were not recruited by others to be politically active).[8] Some aspects of individuals' socioeconomic status, such as their occupation or their workplace responsibilities, may result in the development of resources such as organizational or leadership skills that can be employed in political activities. The importance of education, income, and occupation in generating resources such as politically relevant skills, time to be politically active, and money to support political campaigns and causes varies with the type of political activity.

Sidney Verba, Kay Lehman Schlozman and Henry E. Brady, the creators of this explanatory model of political participation, point out that a significant path for resource development is through parental education, for that can affect the child's educational attainment and subsequent life opportunities and resources. However, the skills that facilitate political activity can be acquired through participation in organizations affiliated with religious institutions and in civic and social organizations, as well as in the workplace.

The political attitudes that citizens have also vary with their social characteristics, and certain attitudes are closely related to political participation. Citizens who have higher levels of political interest and involvement, who believe that politicians and the government are responsive to citizens' wishes, who are more trusting of public officials, and who perceive the government as being responsive to their demands are more likely to participate in politics.[9] Those who identify with a political party are also more likely to participate.[10]

In the remainder of this chapter we examine in detail the relationships between several social characteristics and forms of political participation.

Age and Its Correlates

Age differences in political participation can be examined in several ways. One is to look at differences among age groups at a single point in time. Another is to compare the political behavior of different generations, either at one point in time or across time.[11] Sociologist Karl Mannheim distinguished between a "generation as actuality" and "generation-units." He suggested that a generation as actuality is created when individuals of the same age group during a period of social or political turmoil "participate in the characteristic social and intellectual currents of their society and period, and . . . have an active or passive experience of the interactions of forces which made up the new situation." Members of the same generation may react differently to their experiences, however, resulting in generation-units, defined as "groups within the same actual generation which work up the material or their common experience in different specific ways."[12]

Sometimes the term *generation* is used to refer to people who were born within a certain time span. Much attention has been paid in discussions of American politics to the baby boomers, those born between the mid-1940s and the mid-1960s. In both attitudes and behavior they are perceived as significantly different from earlier and subsequent generations, and because of the size of the baby boomer generation, it has the potential to have a very substantial impact on political outcomes. Alternatively, a political generation can be defined in terms of when it becomes eligible to vote. Those who came of political age during the Vietnam War are sometimes referred to as the Vietnam generation. However a generation is defined, the underlying assumption is that the political attitudes, beliefs, and values of its members have been significantly and lastingly affected by their experiences.

The downward trend of voter turnout since 1960 begs for explanation. One approach to such an explanation is to examine differences in turnout by generation and by age cohorts within generations. Thus, the decline in turnout may be a result of generational differences in political socialization and the effects of generational replacement on the composition of the electorate. Using data from the 1952 to 1988 American National Election Studies, Warren E. Miller and J. Merrill Shanks divide the electorate into three generations based on the first presidential election in which individuals were eligible to vote.[13]

Members of the pre–New Deal generation entered the electorate in 1928 or earlier; New Deal generation members became eligible to vote in presidential elections between 1932 and 1964, and those belonging to the post–New Deal generation were first eligible to vote in presidential elections between 1968 and 1988. As the pre–New Deal generation left the electorate, political participation patterns changed because the post–New Dealers were significantly less likely to vote than were the New Deal generation or the pre–New Dealers they were replacing. This decline in turnout occurred despite the higher levels of formal education attained by the post–New Deal generation, and it occurred within each level of educational attainment.[14]

An increase in voting participation does occur between the first election in which members of a generation become eligible to vote and the second or third election, but then the level of turnout stabilizes until the fifteenth or later election, when turnout begins to drop.[15] On average, the turnout rates at the time of first eligibility to vote are lower in the post–New Deal generation than in the New Deal generation for each level of educational attainment.[16] This pattern leads to the conclusion that differences in voter turnout are indeed associated with generational differences and cannot be attributed to an individual's point in the life cycle.

One explanation for these patterns is that members of the post–New Deal generation are less likely to acquire the social connections that both facilitate the acquisition of information and are a conduit for political mobilization efforts. Among the factors contributing to this generations' decline in voter turnout were lower levels of involvement by its members in social institutions such as the church, synagogue, or mosque where those in attendance could be exposed to informal political discussions, the distribution of political information, and even efforts to recruit them to participate politically. Furthermore, not only did attendance at religious services decline; the voter turnout levels of those who were regular attendees at those services also declined.[17] Scholars disagree about the extent to which there has been a decline in the social connectedness that contributes to social capital and the maintenance of a civil society.[18]

Differences in sex-role socialization cause political participation to vary more among women of different ages than among men. Women who became eligible to vote when the Nineteenth Amendment to the Constitution was ratified (1920) or shortly afterward tended to have much lower voting rates than women who became eligible to vote later.[19] Persons living with a spouse are more likely to vote than those who are single, divorced, or widowed; and because elderly men are more likely to be living with a spouse than are elderly women, elderly men have a higher voting rate. The effects of sex and marital status are thus confounded with those of age.

A "life-cycle effects" theory offers one explanation for why voter turnout does not decline with age when marital status and gender are held constant. Those who earlier were occupied with jobs and raising families are free of these burdens during their retirement years. Thus, many interests and distractions that existed earlier are eliminated or reduced, and these citizens can devote more of their attention to politics.

There is evidence that refutes this explanation, however. The explanation implies that housewives would be less likely to vote than employed women in the same age category, since working women would be expected to be better informed and to perceive more clearly the impact of government policies on their interests. Some studies report this to be the case,[20] but a study using a survey by the Bureau of the Census, based on a very large survey sample, found that during the 1970s housewives had the same voting rates as women who worked outside the home. Furthermore, the study reported that differences in turnout levels among different occupational groups (including housewife) are influenced more by their levels of educational attainment than by their occupation.[21]

The attitudes that are significant in motivating voting participation also vary significantly by age group. Older persons are more likely to perceive the government as being responsive to citizens,[22] and they are more likely to identify strongly with one of the two major political parties.[23] Compared with their opposites, persons who do not perceive the government as responsive are less likely to vote, but persons with strong party identification are more likely to vote.[24]

Older citizens as a group have lower levels of education. Individuals who are more educated are more likely to vote and to engage in other forms of political activity. Therefore, on the basis of educational attainment level we would expect older citizens to have lower levels of political participation. However, among those with less than a high school education, the oldest generation of citizens (pre–New Deal) are more likely to vote than are members of younger generations.[25]

The effects of age on political participation can be seen in a study of parents of former high school students, who were interviewed in 1965 and reinterviewed in 1973 and again in 1982. At the beginning of the seventeen-year period, the parents' average age was fifty-three; in 1982 the average age was seventy. In 1982 the parents' level of political knowledge remained approximately the same as in 1965, but their sense of political effectiveness and frequency of reading about politics in newspapers had declined, whereas their ideological sophistication had increased. The proportion of this group who engaged in most forms of active participation declined in this period; fewer reported trying to influence others how to vote, attending political meetings, displaying signs or wearing campaign buttons, and engaging in other political activities. Most of the groups' decline in political participation can be accounted for by a decrease in participation by those over the age of sixty-five and by a disenchantment with politics that occurred between 1973 and 1982. Many of the political activities in which older citizens participated were of specific interest to them, such as attending meetings related to senior citizens' problems, reading a newspaper column for senior citizens, and going to a senior citizens' center.[26]

Younger citizens are less likely to participate politically than are middle-aged citizens. Several social characteristics interact with age to produce this effect. One is marital status: only a small proportion of those under the age of twenty-five are married, and persons who are not married are less likely to be involved in politics. Interpersonal influences have a significant impact on voting participation among those who are less interested in politics; the influence of one's spouse is particularly important.[27] A second social characteristic that explains why younger citizens participate less in politics is their high rate of mobility. Individuals who have lived in an area for a relatively short time are less likely to vote, and younger citizens move more frequently than do older citizens.[28] As we have seen, however, the post–New Deal generation is also less likely to be politically active.

The legal consequences of mobility are potentially less important with regard to voting than they were in the past. Many states had lengthy residency requirements for eligibility to vote, but in the aftermath of several court decisions, such requirements are no longer a serious obstacle to voting. Many states do close their voter registration books before elections, and this could be a problem for those who have very recently moved to those states. No state closes its registration books more than fifty days before an election, however. Furthermore, the National Voter Registration Act (NVRA), passed in 1993 and first implemented in 1995, has made registering to vote a much easier task. This law specifies that, in states that require citizens to register to vote, a motor vehicle license application or renewal serves as a voter registration application for the purposes of voting in a federal election. Each state must also establish procedures whereby citizens can register to vote by mail, and must designate voter registration agencies, which are to include all state agencies that provide public assistance, unemployment compensation, or disability services, as well as certain other state and local government offices and, with their agreement, federal and nongovernmental offices. The law also prohibits removal of the name of any individual from the voter registration list for a federal election for failure to vote in previous elections. (See the discussion of the NVRA in Chapter 5.)

It is the social consequences of mobility, rather than the legal consequence, that are now important. Those who have not lived in a community very long usually have fewer social and organizational ties, less information about local issues, and fewer political contacts, and they are less interested in and involved in the local community. The effects of these consequences of mobility are greater for middle-aged persons who move, but those who are younger move more frequently.[29]

Political participation increases markedly among persons who have lived in a community for three to five years. It may be that such a length of residence is necessary for acclimation to the community and for development of an interest in its problems and politics. Another explanation is that events concerned with national politics, such as a presidential election campaign, stimulate sufficient political interest among community newcomers that they will register to vote and become more politically active in other ways.[30]

The influence of community ties on political participation is evident when voter turnout rates of college students are compared with those of nonstudents of the same age group. Norms within the college student community usually promote voting participation; social interaction and integration into the campus community further encourage student participation. Special efforts may be made to register students at a location on campus, thereby lowering their costs of registering, in terms of time and effort. Among nonstudents, community norms and peer pressure are frequently less supportive of participation, and voter registration may require more individual initiative and effort. After students leave the college environment, there is a drop in political participation rates.[31]

The impact of the assumption of adult roles on the political participation rates of younger citizens is a matter of debate. One view is that participation increases as young people assume adult roles and responsibilities. Young parents would be expected to become concerned with the schools, recreational facilities, and other community amenities as their children reach school age, and their increased concern would lead to more participation. A related hypothesis is that married younger citizens would thus have higher rates of voter turnout than would single people, and in fact voter turnout is higher (by 3 to 10 percent) among young married people than among single people of the same age.[32]

In summary, patterns of political participation by citizens of different ages are influenced by other social characteristics that reflect variations in life experiences. Among older citizens, women and those who are single and who have lower levels of educational attainment are less likely to participate in politics. Among younger citizens, those who have moved more recently, are not currently in college, and are not married are less likely to participate.

Components of Socioeconomic Status

In the United States, socioeconomic status is of paramount importance to both the type of political activities engaged in by citizens and the frequency of such participation. Citizens of higher socioeconomic status are more likely to engage in several different kinds of political activity, such as attending organizational and campaign functions, contacting public officials, and voting in elections, and to do so more frequently.[33] This pattern of more frequent participation in several types of political activity by persons of higher socioeconomic status does not occur in all developed democracies. In some countries, social and political organizations mobilize individuals of lower socioeconomic status and increase their levels of political activity to equivalence with those of the middle class.[34]

One reason for the more frequent political activity by persons of higher socioeconomic status is that they have higher levels of politically relevant resources, such as education and income.[35] Other explanations are more access to political information, a greater capacity to process that information, and a keener awareness of the impact of political decisions on their interests. Persons of higher socioeconomic status are also more likely to have the civic orientations—such as perception of government responsiveness and sense of obligation to participate—that motivate individuals to participate in politics.[36]

What is it about higher socioeconomic status that makes it predictive of higher rates of political participation? Socioeconomic status is usually measured by an index that combines two or three of the main components of socioeconomic status—education, income, and occupation. It may help us to understand how socioeconomic status affects political participation if we analyze each of these three components separately.

Education

Education is the most important component of socioeconomic status in influencing political participation in the United States.[37] Individuals who have higher levels of educational attainment not only vote more often (see Table 2-1) but also participate more in campaigns and in organizational and other activities. Even within the same income level, individuals who have more education participate more.

TABLE 2-1

Reported Voter Turnout by Level of Educational Attainment, Presidential and Midterm Elections, 1952–1998 (in percent)

Presidential elections

Level of educational attainment	1952	1956	1960	1964	1968	1972	1976	1980	1984	1988	1992	1996
Grade school	66.1	63.3	68.9	69.4	64.0	59.3	58.5	56.5	57.0	49.9	50.7	56.5
High school	85.0	79.0	87.3	81.9	83.8	75.3	69.8	69.7	69.7	62.2	71.4	72.7
Some college	86.6	90.5	88.8	88.6	79.2	83.9	83.2	75.8	81.5	78.4	83.5	81.0
College degree	93.3	88.7	93.0	87.7	89.4	89.9	87.1	90.7	90.6	92.4	92.5	89.9

Midterm elections

Level of educational attainment	1954	1958	1962	1966	1970	1974	1978	1982	1986	1990	1994	1998
Grade school	—	49.6	52.7	52.3	47.6	41.1	43.5	42.7	37.9	26.9	35.9	49.3
High school	—	59.9	63.0	67.1	60.9	51.8	51.1	59.1	47.5	43.5	53.2	44.1
Some college	—	70.1	72.1	69.5	71.3	58.9	62.3	66.6	56.4	52.8	61.0	59.8
College degree	—	76.6	71.8	81.1	82.8	75.4	72.4	76.6	72.1	66.7	78.5	72.5

SOURCES: American National Election Studies Cumulative File, 1948–1996; 1998 American National Election Study.

There are several explanations for the importance of education with regard to participation. Those who have more education generally know more about how the political system works; therefore, they are more aware of the consequences of government actions for their lives. Those who are more educated are also more likely to have an environment in which considerable social pressure exists to be politically active, at least to the extent of voting. These social norms may also have been instilled by parents; those who have attained higher levels of education tend to come from families in which the parents attained higher levels of education as well.[38]

Education encourages the development of certain skills that facilitate participation in politics, such as running for office, serving as a political party official, assuming a leadership role in a political campaign, or serving as an officer in an organization (union or local civic group) that becomes involved in campaigns or lobbying activity. Moreover, anyone who has dealt successfully with the bureaucratic structure and procedures of a large university has developed the skills necessary to handle successfully the bureaucratic tasks involved in voter registration.

Education involves the acquisition of the kinds of cognitive skills that facilitate political activity. These include the reading and analytical skills that enable individuals to understand complex events and problems and the connections among them. Higher levels of educational attainment may also stimulate increased political interest, which can lead to increased participation.[39] Individuals who are interested in politics are more likely to care about the outcome of elections and also to vote and to engage in political activities.

Citizens who have attained higher levels of education are more likely to follow political events in the mass media, especially the print media (newspapers and magazines).[40] The print media can present more information about national political events than can be covered in a half-hour television newscast. Comprehensive coverage of local and state political events and policy decisions is usually provided only by a local newspaper, although the quality of coverage varies substantially from one paper to another.

Those who have higher levels of educational attainment are more likely to have opinions on a wide range of subjects and to be more easily stimulated to engage in political activity. They are also more likely to discuss politics with others, and to feel confident in discussions with a more diverse group of people. More educated citizens are more likely to believe that they can, through their actions, have an impact on government.

Educational attainment level affects attitudes toward others, such as political and social tolerance, and participation in organized groups. Citizens with more education are more likely to express satisfaction with their societal environment and confidence in their ability to have an impact in changing elements of their environment with which they are not satisfied.[41] They are also more likely to perceive the government as responsive to their interests and their activities in this regard.[42] The percentage of the electorate included in each level of educational attainment has varied since the 1950s, but the relationship between education and voter turnout has not changed.

Differences exist in the extent to which citizens overreport voting. The expectations that individuals believe others have about them influence their reports. For example, individuals who are more highly educated, have a stronger sense of civic duty and party identification, feel more politically effective, and are more concerned about election outcomes are more likely to overreport voting, because they are more likely to believe that others expect them to vote. Black citizens who live in predominantly black areas and who are interviewed by black interviewers are also more likely to overreport voting than are white citizens. When reported voting is validated by checking it against local election board records, differences in the turnout rates of whites and blacks remain, even in comparisons within the same level of education and controlling for the region in which the citizens live.[43] Thus, in addition to the other factors discussed, perceptions of others' expectations influence levels of political participation.

Education is the key element in the theory of democratic citizenship developed by Norman H. Nie, Jane Junn, and Keith Stehlik-Barry. Education appears to affect two important dimensions of citizenship, which they label political engagement and democratic enlightenment. They define *political engagement* as those "behaviors and cognitions that enable citizens to pursue and protect self-interest in politics" and *democratic enlightenment* as "those qualities of citizenship that encourage understanding of and adherence to norms and principles of democracy."[44] Political engagement is largely competitive. There is a limit to the number of persons who can engage in most forms of political activity, because of limits on either resources or opportunities to become involved—for example, serving in elected or appointive positions. (Obviously, the limit on available opportunities does not apply to voting.) Whereas political engagement is for the most part competitive, democratic enlightenment is consensual. All citizens may increase their levels of social and political tolerance, but only a limited number may serve on the city council or in the state legislature or Congress.

Formal education acts as a sorting mechanism in its influence on political engagement; in effect, it assigns citizens to positions of social and political advantage on the basis of their relative educational attainment. It is not the absolute level of educational attainment that determines such assignment but rather how much education an individual has compared to others. In contrast, the effects of education on democratic enlightenment are cumulative and noncompetitive. The absolute levels of individuals' educational attainment contribute to democratic enlightenment in a society.

One element of the "puzzle of political participation" is why such participation has not increased as absolute levels of educational attainment have increased. The research by Nie, Junn, and Stehlik-Barry helps us solve that puzzle. Those who are most likely to participate in politics are those who have the most education compared to others. The consequence of educational attainment as a mechanism for sorting individuals into social classes and occupations is to privilege some citizens and not others. Those most privileged are most likely to participate.

Income

Within each level of educational attainment, those who have higher incomes tend to participate more in politics.[45] The socioeconomic class bias in voter turnout has remained relatively stable in both presidential elections[46] and midterm congressional elections since 1948.[47] Three explanations can be offered for the effects of income. First, the poor must focus a disproportionate amount of their attention on obtaining the necessities of life, which means they have less time and energy for politics. For those in lower income brackets, political activity might be regarded as a "luxury" item.

Second, citizens who have higher incomes are likely to have environments that stimulate interest in politics and that create social pressures for, and provide opportunities for, political participation.[48] Political interest is for many individuals in higher income groups stimulated by the information made available to them at their place of employment. That information may include political knowledge as well as details of how government activity and policies affect the business or the sector of the economy in which they are employed, as well as various aspects of their personal life, such as tax obligations, employment conditions, and environmental quality.

Third, some effects of higher income on political participation are related to personal characteristics. Individuals who succeed financially (especially those who have not attained higher levels of education) may have personal attributes that might be expected to be consistent with political activity—personality traits reflecting an emphasis on purposive activity and personal competence, and a tendency to pay attention to events outside their immediate environment.[49]

Occupation

When differences in political participation attributable to education have been taken into account, few effects of occupation remain. However, for three occupational categories, participation rates are higher than what might be predicted by educational level: farm ownership, government employment, and clerical and sales work.[50]

The income and job security of farm owners are directly and significantly affected by governmental activities. Most farmers produce commodities that, until very recently, received some form of subsidy or were grown under some form of quota system. Such changes in the federal government's price support policy substantially alter the level of farm incomes. In addition, a substantial proportion of American agricultural production is exported, and export levels are strongly influenced by international trade agreements, foreign-exchange rates, and governmental regulation of trade in agricultural products. Many American farmers borrow money to finance their operations. Interest rate levels thus have a major effect on their ability to make a profit—

and interest rates are largely determined by the government's monetary and fiscal policies. Farm owners are well aware of these facts; consequently, their rates of political participation are much higher than might be predicted on the basis of their other sociodemographic characteristics.[51]

Those government employees for whom forms of political participation other than voting are not prohibited under civil service and merit systems are likely to have participation rates higher than might be predicted by their levels of education.[52] Government employees tend to have high levels of political interest, to be knowledgeable about politics, to follow politics in the mass media, and to have a strong sense of civic duty. Those who are not covered by merit systems are sometimes expected to engage in political activity as a condition of continued employment, although some research suggests that such expectations are not as important as they were in the 1950s and 1960s.[53]

One explanation for the higher participation rates of clerical and sales workers is that their jobs require them to deal with abstractions and to cope with bureaucratic forms. They either have or develop the verbal and communications skills that facilitate their understanding of political events and their participation in political activities.[54]

Some have argued that one major difference in occupations that affects participation is the amount of free time they allow for following political events and for participating in political activities. Analyses of the time demands of different occupations and the use of leisure time in the United States do not sustain such an argument: neither blue-collar workers who work a forty-hour week nor the unemployed are more likely to participate than are those whose occupations demand substantially more than forty hours.[55]

Indeed, unemployment seems to have a negative effect on political participation. Individuals who are unemployed tend to focus their attention on personal economic concerns and to withdraw from politics.[56] Financial resources that could be allocated to political activity are not likely to be available.[57] When other variables—such as age, gender, level of education, usual occupation, and length of residence at the current address—are controlled, those who are unemployed (or who, for whatever reason, feel that they are financially worse off than they have been in the past) are less likely to vote.[58]

Other Social Characteristics

Race

Equal access to the ballot box and equal opportunity to participate in politics in ways other than voting did not effectively exist for members of minority races in many areas of the United States until the mid-1960s. Voter registration laws and procedures in some states discouraged political participation in general but usually had the strongest impact on these citizens. Voter registration books were closed months before an election; hours for registration were irregular; there was no evening or Saturday registration; and inadequate provisions were made for absentee registration. It has been estimated that in 1972, improvements in these procedural aspects alone would have increased voter turnout in the South by 14.5 percent among blacks and 12.4 percent among whites.[59] In addition to these procedural obstacles, political participation by minority-race members was inhibited, especially in some areas of the South, by discriminatory administration of the laws and even by threats of physical violence or economic retaliation against African Americans who attempted to register to vote. Since 1957, the enactment of a number of civil rights laws, the rendering of several important court decisions, and passage of the Twenty-Fourth Amendment (abolishing poll-tax requirements) have gone a long way toward ensuring access to the ballot box for all citizens in all areas of the United States.[60] The NVRA further facilitates citizens' access.

Racial patterns of reported registration and voter turnout in the seventeen elections from 1966 to 1998 are shown in Table 2-2. Black citizens were less likely than white citizens to report being registered and voting in the general election. A decline in voter turnout among both groups occurred after the midterm elections of 1966.

Black citizens were less likely than whites to vote before enactment of the Voting Rights Act of 1965. In 1952, only 4 percent of southern blacks of voting age voted, compared with 64 percent of nonsouthern blacks of voting age. Turnout among southern blacks increased to 31 percent in 1960 and to 63 percent in 1968. Among nonsouthern blacks, 83 percent voted in 1964, but turnout in this group declined slightly thereafter. Among both southern whites and nonsouthern whites, turnout increased between 1953 and 1960,[61] then declined

TABLE 2-2

Reported Registration and Voter Turnout by Race, Presidential and Midterm Elections, 1966–1996

	Presidential elections					Midterm elections			
	Percent registered		Percent voting			Percent registered		Percent voting	
Year	White	Black	White	Black	Year	White	Black	White	Black
1968	75.2	66.2	69.1	57.6	1966	71.7	66.2	64.5	52.1
1972	73.4	65.5	64.5	52.1	1970	69.1	60.8	56.0	43.5
1976	68.3	58.5	60.9	48.7	1974	63.5	54.9	46.3	33.8
1980	68.4	60.0	60.9	50.5	1978	63.8	57.1	47.3	37.2
1984	69.6	66.3	61.4	55.8	1982	65.6	59.1	49.8	43.0
1988	67.9	64.5	59.1	51.5	1986	65.3	64.0	47.0	43.2
1992	70.1	63.9	63.6	54.0	1990	63.8	58.8	46.7	39.2
1996	67.7	63.5	56.0	50.6	1994	64.6	58.5	47.3	37.1

SOURCES: Bureau of the Census, "Voter Participation in November 1972," *Current Population Reports,* ser. P-20, no. 144 (Washington, D.C.: Government Printing Office, December 1972), Tables A and B; "Voting and Registration in the Election of November 1988," *Current Population Reports,* ser. P-20, no. 440 (Washington, D.C.: Government Printing Office, October 1989), Tables A and B; http://www.census.gov/population/socdemo/voting/history/htable01.txt.

through 1996; the decline was greater among northern whites than among those residing in the South. Whites are more likely to register and to vote than African Americans in both the South and the rest of the United States, a pattern that has continued from the 1960s to 1996. The difference between whites and blacks in both registration and turnout rates has been declining since the mid-1960s in both regions of the country, however.[62]

Because of previously restricted educational opportunities, a smaller proportion of minority-race citizens have completed college or high school. Controls for the effects of level of education and region reduce the disparity in voter turnout between blacks and whites; nevertheless, black citizens are less likely to vote than are white citizens of the same socioeconomic status.[63]

Among younger black voters (ages eighteen to twenty-four), voter turnout was at its highest level in 1964. Turnout declined from 1968 through 1980, then increased in 1984. In that year, 40.6 percent of this group reported voting, partly as a consequence of presidential candidate Jesse Jackson's voter mobilization efforts in his unsuccessful pursuit of the Democratic Party's nomination. In 1988, young

black citizens' turnout declined again; only 35 percent reported casting a vote for president in that year.[64] In 1996, turnout among those
aged eighteen to twenty was 32 percent for whites, 28 percent for
blacks, and 16 percent for Hispanics. Among those aged twenty-one
to twenty-four, voting participation rates in 1996 were 34 percent for
whites, 36 percent for blacks, and 14 percent for Hispanics.[65]

Groups differ in the extent to which their members identify with
them; moreover, higher levels of group consciousness stimulate higher
levels of voter turnout among the members of some groups but not
others. For example, research suggests that in 1984, high levels of
group consciousness stimulated higher rates of voting participation
among older black southerners than among white southerners of the
same age groups.[66] Those who have a higher level of group consciousness are more likely to be active in political campaigns, however.[67]

Ethnicity

Latino citizens have lower rates of voter registration and turnout
and of engagement in other forms of political participation than do
either white citizens or black citizens. Among the explanations offered
is the language barrier. Another factor may be the age distribution of
Latinos. Chicano (Mexican-American) and Puerto Rican groups have
a relatively high proportion of younger citizens, and as already noted,
younger citizens are less likely to participate in politics. Levels of educational attainment are also lower among Latinos than among the
rest of the population. Within the same socioeconomic levels, however, Chicanos are slightly more likely to vote than are the members
of other Latino groups.[68] Puerto Ricans are slightly less likely to vote,
however. One explanation given for this difference is that many
Puerto Ricans intend to return to Puerto Rico and view their stay on
the U.S. mainland as temporary. As a consequence, they do not become involved in politics.[69] In contrast to these two Latino groups,
Cuban Americans tend to be older, better educated, and more affluent, and they have higher rates of political participation.[70]

Research conducted in California in the 1980s shows that Latino
and Asian-American citizens are less likely to engage in all forms of
political participation than either white citizens or black citizens. Political participation among Asian-American citizens varies by nation-
ality: Japanese Americans, Korean Americans, and Filipino Ameri-

cans are less likely to register and vote than are white Americans; Chinese Americans are equally as likely to register and vote as are white Americans. Members of Asian-American ethnic groups are less likely to contact public officials than are white Americans, but Japanese Americans are more likely to contribute money to political organizations and campaigns than are whites. When controls are applied for sociodemographic characteristics and group identification, ethnicity remains an important variable for Asian Americans but not for African Americans or Latinos. In other words, sociodemographic variables account for differences in political participation between whites and blacks and between whites and Latinos.[71]

In an extensive comparative analysis of the political participation of whites, African Americans, Latinos, and Asian Americans in 1984 and in 1989–1993, Pei-te Lien found that Asian Americans participate less than might be predicted on the basis of socioeconomic status, demographic characteristics, sociopsychological attitudes, and legal constraints. Socioeconomic status does not predict participation among Asian Americans as well as it does for members of other racial and ethnic groups. In part this can be attributed to their relatively recent immigration and attainment of citizenship. Length of stay in the United States does not predict political participation among the entire Asian-American group, but it does contribute to explaining participation patterns among Korean Americans. Lien's research indicates that how individuals construe their ethnic identity is important in understanding the disparities in participation between non-Hispanic whites and Asian Americans. Among Asians, being concerned about group status, perceiving themselves as the most generally deprived group, and supporting group intermarriage are associated with high rates of voter turnout. Being victimized by hate crimes increases the probability of voter participation in other political activities as well. Lien concludes that "the factors influencing participation which structure the models of political participation derived from studying the American mainstream are not suitable for predicting or explaining the political behavior of Asian Americans."[72]

Lien also found that noncitizens (both Asian Americans and Hispanics) engage in political participation to a limited extent by working in groups (11 percent), contacting the media (5 percent), and contacting public officials (18 percent); length of time spent in the United

States is the most important factor in accounting for such participation. Noncitizens are more likely to participate politically in a group if they believe they have a problem related to their ethnicity, such as access to the educational system or perceived inadequacy of public services available in their residential area.[73]

Gender

In the past, women have participated in politics less than men, regardless of whether participation was measured in terms of voting, campaign and political party work, running for public office, or involvement in community-oriented activities. However, when age and level of educational attainment are held constant, studies show that by the late 1970s college-educated women, particularly those in their thirties and younger, were as likely to vote as were their male counterparts.[74] By 1980, women were as likely as men to vote in presidential elections, and beginning in 1986 their turnout rates in midterm elections equaled those of men (see Table 2-3).[75]

Surveys conducted in 1967 and 1976 indicate that women are becoming more active in local politics—joining with others to form or run an organization seeking to solve a local problem, attending school board and city council meetings, and contacting local public officials. In 1967, only college-educated women tended to participate in such activities to the same extent as men with the same level of educational attainment. By 1976, women with a high school education were also as likely as men with a high school education to participate in these activities.[76]

Gender differences in campaign activity are also diminishing, but they remain substantial. Comparison of the average number of campaign-related activities engaged in shows that women were less active than men in every presidential election from 1952 to 1996.[77] An examination of involvement in specific campaign activities in 1988 indicates that statistically significant gender differences exist in making a campaign contribution, working informally in the community, contacting a public official, and becoming affiliated with a political organization.[78] Several explanations can be offered for the lower rates of such participation by women. Women pay less attention to politics; for example, they are much less likely to follow politics in the mass media.[79] Leisure-time studies suggest that working women have less

TABLE 2-3

Reported Voter Turnout by Gender, Presidential and Midterm Elections, 1964–1996 (in percent)

Presidential elections			Midterm elections		
Year	Men	Women	Year	Men	Women
1964	71.9	67.0	1966	58.2	53.3
1968	69.8	66.0	1970	56.8	52.7
1972	64.1	62.0	1974	46.2	43.4
1976	59.6	58.8	1978	46.6	45.3
1980	59.1	59.4	1982	48.7	48.4
1984	59.0	60.8	1986	45.8	46.1
1988	56.4	58.3	1990	44.6	45.4
1992	60.2	62.3	1994	44.7	45.3
1996	52.8	55.5			

SOURCES: Lynn M. Casper and Loretta E. Bass, "Voting and Registration in the Election of November 1996," Bureau of the Census, *Current Population Reports*, ser. P-20, no. 504 (Washington, D.C.: Government Printing Office, July 1998), Table 1; http://www.census.gov/population/socdemo/voting/history/htable01.txt.

time to keep up with political news because they usually have almost total responsibility for household tasks and family care.[80] Women are also less likely to be members of organizations that take stands in politics. When women are active in voluntary organizations, they do contribute more time than men, but they contribute less money.[81]

Women are less likely to have certain attitudes and beliefs that are associated with political participation. These include confidence in one's ability to understand politics and government and the belief that governmental activities can be influenced by the activities of individuals like oneself (*internal political efficacy*), as well as the belief that public officials are responsive to the interests of individuals like oneself and that governmental and political institutions, such as legislatures and political parties, help make the government responsive to people like oneself (*external political efficacy*). An attitude that is significantly related to levels of political participation is a belief in *governmental attentiveness*: the expectation that various governmental and political institutions will respond favorably to the policy preferences of the general public. Women tend to have levels of external political efficacy equivalent to those of men, but women have substantially lower levels of internal political efficacy—that is, they are less likely to perceive that individuals like themselves can influence the activities of government. Women also perceive the government as less attentive and responsive to citizens' needs and preferences than do men.[82]

There are three possible explanations for these attitudes. The first may be women's childhood socialization to the view that an interest in politics and political activity are more appropriate for men. Research conducted in the 1950s and 1960s found that girls were both less interested in politics and less knowledgeable about governmental and political processes and events than boys. Some later studies have reported fewer and smaller differences between boys and girls in both political knowledge and attitudes, so if there is a link between childhood socialization and adult levels of political participation, higher rates of political participation may be expected among women reaching adulthood in the 1980s and thereafter. The evidence on this question is not conclusive, however.[83]

The second explanation may be women's traditional adult roles. Women who are not employed outside the home may be less interested in politics, acquire less politically relevant information, be less likely to perceive the consequences of political events for their own well-being and that of their family, and be less likely to develop the skills necessary for successful political participation. Even when women have been employed outside the home, their occupations were traditionally restricted to a few categories, such as teaching, secretarial and clerical work, and nursing; only infrequently were they employed in fields such as business and law, from which political officials are often recruited. The barriers to employment in these fields were lowered during the 1970s, however, and more women are now employed in them.[84] Some research supports the view that women who are employed outside the home are more likely to participate in politics,[85] although employment patterns may not be related to voter turnout.[86]

Third, women may have lower rates of political participation because the men who serve as gatekeepers in the political process have negative attitudes toward women's participation. Although women's willingness to perform the menial tasks of campaign work made them an important part of the campaign work force, only recently has their involvement in higher-level political and campaign activities been more favorably received.[87]

Disagreement exists about the extent to which women are disadvantaged as candidates for public office. Some studies of women as congressional candidates have concluded that women win as often as male candidates in similar situations. Thus the reason why few women candidates have won is that few women have run.[88] But at least one study supports the argument that women are not as likely as men to be elected to powerful political offices and that their access to political office is hindered by the public's stereotypes about the appropriate roles for women and about the effectiveness of women as candidates. The news media coverage of female women candidates tends to focus less on their issue agendas and issue stands (except to echo the opposing male candidates' distorted messages about them) and more on who is winning the electoral contest.[89] Supporting evidence is provided by a study of congressional contests in California in 1992 and 1994, which also concluded that there are small but important differences in the behavior and experiences of men and women candidates: "Women and men have different experiences with the media, the party structure, and the voters. Men and women also waged their campaigns differently, stressing different campaign messages employing different campaigning styles, and relying on different strategies. . . . Most of these gender differences were not overpowering, but they were subtle and pervasive. Many of them indicate a lack of fairness toward women in the electoral arena."[90]

Increases can be expected in all forms of political participation by women. Changes in women's level of educational attainment, in their employment, in their occupational and other roles, in their attitudes, and in the attitudes of the public all predict a trend in that direction. Media attention to women who are active in politics presents younger women with political role models. Women in increasing numbers will also learn the skills necessary to engage in political activity and acquire the necessary resources as more of them enter the fields of business and law, from which elected public officials are frequently recruited.

Summary

Patterns of political participation vary with an individual's life experiences. Political participation varies widely with socioeconomic status, the most important component of which is level of educational attainment. Those who have more years of formal education are more likely to engage in all forms of political activity. Occupation also has an impact; individuals in certain occupations are more likely to participate than might be predicted on the basis of level of educational attainment or income alone. These occupations are either directly affected by government policies or provide the skills necessary for political participation. There have also been gender differences, but they are gradually decreasing because changes in the life circumstances of women since the mid-1960s, particularly in their levels of educational attainment and patterns of employment, are being accompanied by changes in their patterns of political participation. Racial and ethnic differences have also existed; minority-group members participate less than members of the white majority. In large part these differences can be explained by lower levels of educational attainment and by deliberate efforts in the past to discourage political participation by minority-group members. The legal barriers to their political participation have largely been removed, however, and increases in levels of educational attainment and other changes in their life circumstances have been accompanied by increased rates of political participation. Thus, it is reasonable to expect increasing similarities in patterns of political participation among members of different racial and ethnic groups in the future. Gender differences in political participation can also be expected to decrease. Differences in participation patterns based on socioeconomic status, age, and marital status do not appear likely to change, however.

One question that should be addressed is why voter turnout has declined since 1960, even though for a large proportion of the American electorate, the main components of socioeconomic stats—level of educational attainment, income, and occupational status—have improved substantially since then, and positive changes in these components would be expected to be associated with higher levels of political participation and voter turnout. One answer is that there have been changes in other characteristics of the American electorate. Although more citizens are better educated, have higher-status occupations, and have higher levels of income, a larger proportion of the electorate is concentrated in younger age groups, which are more geographically mobile and have lower levels of voter turnout. In addition, the prevalence of certain sociopolitical characteristics—such as having a party identification, strongly identifying with one party, reading newspapers frequently to keep abreast of events in politics and government, and having a strong sense of political efficacy—has declined. These changes have more than offset the changes in components that are associated with higher levels of voter turnout.[91] In chapter 3 we examine the patterns of change in attitudes, beliefs, and values that are related to political participation.

Notes

1. See Sidney Verba and Norman H. Nie, *Participation in America* (New York: Harper and Row, 1972), chap. 1. For a different formulation of the link between social circumstances and political participation, see William Mishler, *Political Participation in Canada* (Toronto: Macmillan, 1979), 104–108.
2. See the following works by Ronald Inglehart: *The Silent Revolution* (Princeton: Princeton University Press, 1977); "The Changing Structure of Political Cleavages in Western Society," in *Electoral Change in Advanced Industrial Democracies,* ed. Russell Dalton, Scott Flanagan, and Paul Allen Beck (Princeton: Princeton University Press, 1984); "Aggregate Stability and Individual-Level Change in Mass Belief Systems: The Level of Analysis Paradox," *American Political Science Review* 79 (1985): 79–116; "New Perspectives on Value Change," *Comparative Political Studies* 17 (1985): 485–532; and *Culture Shift in Advanced Industrial Societies* (Princeton: Princeton University Press, 1990).

   For a criticism of Inglehart's methods and measures, see Scott Flanagan, "Changing Values in Advanced Industrial Societies," *Comparative Political Studies* 14 (1982): 403–444; and "Measuring Value Change in Advanced Industrial Societies," *Comparative Political Studies* 15 (1982): 99–128. For a debate over the appropriateness of Inglehart's conclusions about value change in western democracies, see Ronald Inglehart and Scott Flanagan, "Controversies: Value Change in Industrial Societies," *American Political Science Review* 81 (1987): 1289–1319.
3. See, for example, Robert E. Lane, *Political Life* (Glencoe, Ill.: Free Press, 1959), and the works cited in note 1, *supra.* See also William H. Chafe, *Women and Equality* (New York: Oxford University Press, 1977); Paul C. Light, *Baby Boomers* (New York: Norton, 1988); Kay Lehman Schlozman and Sidney Verba, *Insult to Injury* (Cambridge: Harvard University Press, 1979); and Reeve Vanneman and Lynn Weber Cannon, *The American Perception of Class* (Philadelphia: Temple University Press, 1987).
4. Barbara Sinclair Deckard, *The Women's Movement,* 3d ed. (New York: Harper and Row, 1983), chaps. 6, 7, 11, and 12; Nancy McGlen and Karen O'Connor, *Women, Politics, and American Society* (Englewood Cliffs, N.J.: Prentice-Hall, 1995); and M. Margaret Conway, David W. Ahern, and Gertrude A. Steuernagel, *Women and Public Policy,* 2d ed. (Washington, D.C.: CQ Press, 1999).
5. For example, individuals of higher socioeconomic status are expected to vote. When they do not, they have contradicted the role expectations that they and others hold. Thus, when interviewed after an election, citizens of higher socioeconomic status who have not voted are more likely to claim that they have voted than are citizens of lower socioeconomic status. See Kenneth Grant and L. John Roos, "Measuring Participation Using Public Opinion Surveys: Who Lies and Why" (paper delivered at the annual meeting of the Midwest Political Science Association, Chicago, 1983).

6. See the manual written for this purpose by Debra R. Livingston, *Power at the Polls* (Silver Spring, Md.: National Association of Social Workers, 1983), 21.

7. Raymond E. Wolfinger and Steven J. Rosenstone, *Who Votes?* (New Haven: Yale University Press, 1980); and Jan E. Leighley and Jonathan Nagler, "Socioeconomic Class Bias in Turnout, 1964–1988: The Voters Remain the Same," *American Political Science Review* 86 (1992): 725–736.

8. Henry E. Brady, Kay Lehman Schlozman, and Sidney Verba, "Beyond SES: A Resource Model of Political Participation," *American Political Science Review* 89 (1995): 271–294; and Sidney Verba, Kay Lehman Schlozman, and Henry E. Brady, *Voice and Equality* (Cambridge: Harvard University Press, 1995), 15–16. "Political engagement" refers to political interest and involvement, concern with political outcomes.

9. Warren E. Miller, "Disinterest, Disaffection, and Participation in Presidential Politics," *Political Behavior* 26 (1980): 7–32; and Carol A. Cassel and David B. Hill, "The Decision to Vote," in *Public Opinion and Public Policy,* ed. Norman R. Luttbeg (Itasca, Ill.: Peacock, 1981), 46–53.

10. Paul R. Abramson and John H. Aldrich, "The Decline of Electoral Participation in America," *American Political Science Review* 76 (1982): 502–521. On the relationship between political attitudes and social characteristics, see Warren E. Miller and J. Merrill Shanks, *The New American Voter* (Cambridge: Harvard University Press, 1996); and Paul R. Abramson, John H. Aldrich, and David W. Rohde, *Change and Continuity in the 1996 and 1998 Elections* (Washington, D.C.: CQ Press, 1999).

11. See, for example, analyses of the political attitudes and behavior of "Generation X," the group born during and since the early 1960s, in Stephen C. Craig and Stephen Earl Bennett, *After the Boom: The Politics of Generation X* (Lanham, Md.: Rowman and Littlefield, 1997).

12. Karl Mannheim, "The Problem of Generations," in *The New Pilgrims,* ed. Philip G. Altbach and Robert S. Lauder (New York: McKay, 1972), quoted in M. Kent Jennings and Richard G. Niemi, *Generations and Politics* (Princeton: Princeton University Press, 1981), 331–332.

13. Miller and Shanks, *New American Voter,* chaps. 3, 4, and 5.

14. Ibid.

15. Ibid., 67.

16. Ibid. See 64, Table 3.6; and 66, Table 3.7.

17. Ibid., 76, Table 4.2.

18. See Robert D. Putnam, "Bowling Alone: America's Declining Social Capital," *Journal of Democracy* 6 (1995): 65–78; and Robert D. Putnam, "Tuning In, Tuning Out: The Strange Disappearance of Social Capital in America," *PS: Political Science & Politics* 28 (1995): 664–683.

   Social capital refers to the aspects of social life that enable citizens to cooperate effectively to try to achieve shared objectives. These aspects include being a part of social networks, accepting social and political norms, and having trust in others and confidence in political leaders and in the operation of the political system.

   Civil society, also referred to as civic community, is the complex web of intermediary institutions, clubs, religious institutions, unions, charities, and a myriad of other voluntary and nonvoluntary associations that, together with the media and the family, instill in citizens the culture of their society by facilitating development of the skills, trust, and familiarity with norms that constitute social capital. The assumption is that these groups contribute to the sustenance of a democratic society. The possibility exists, however, that some of them, such as radical citizen militias and other antidemocratic organizations, contribute to the development of norms and behavior that are destructive of a democratic system of government. See Francis Fukuyama, *Trust: The Social Virtues and the Creation of Prosperity* (New York: Free Press, 1996); Nancy L. Rosenblum, *Membership and Morals: the Personal Uses of Pluralism in America* (Princeton: Princeton University Press, 1998); Michael Walzer, "The Idea of Civil Society, *Dissent* 38 (spring

1991): 213–215; Krishan Kumar, "Civil Society: An Inquiry into the Usefulness of an Historical Term," *British Journal of Sociology* 44, no. 3 (1993): 397. For a discussion of civic community, see Putnam, *Making Democracy Work* (Princeton: Princeton University Press, 1993), 86–91.

19. John J. Stucker, "Women as Voters: Their Maturation as Political Persons in American Society," in *A Portrait of Marginality*, ed. Marianne Githens and J. L. Prestage (New York: McKay, 1977), 264–283; McGlen and O'Connor, *Women's Rights*, chap. 4; and Virginia Sapiro, *The Political Integration of Women* (Urbana: University of Illinois Press, 1983).

20. Kristi Andersen, "Working Women and Political Participation, 1952–1972," *American Journal of Political Science* 19 (1975): 439–454.

21. Wolfinger and Rosenstone, *Who Votes?*, 49.

22. Paul R. Abramson, *Political Attitudes in America* (San Francisco: Freeman, 1983), 185; and analysis of data in the American National Election Studies Cumulative File, 1948–1996 (variables: belief in government attentiveness, age in years).

23. Analysis of data in the American National Election Studies Cumulative File, 1948–1996 (variables: party identification, age in years).

24. Abramson and Aldrich, "Decline of Electoral Participation," 506–510.

25. Wolfinger and Rosenstone, *Who Votes?*, 37–41; and Miller and Shanks, *New American Voter*, 66, Table 3.7.

26. M. Kent Jennings and Gregory Markus, "Political Involvement in the Later Years: A Longitudinal Survey," *American Journal of Political Science* 32 (1988): 302–317.

27. Wolfinger and Rosenstone, *Who Votes?*, 44–46.

28. Ibid., 50–54.

29. Ibid., 51; Peverill Squire, Raymond E. Wolfinger, and David P. Glass, "Residential Mobility and Voter Turnout," *American Political Science Review* 81 (1987): 45–65; and Ann R. Kendrick, "Group Economic Interests and Black Turnout in the 1984 Election" (paper presented at the annual meeting of the American Political Science Association, Atlanta, August 31–September 3, 1989).

30. Wolfinger and Rosenstone, *Who Votes?*, 53.

31. Ibid., 56–57.

32. Ibid., 56. In the 1990s, those who were married and aged twenty-eight or younger were 10 percent more likely to vote. Based on analysis of data in the American National Election Studies Cumulative File, 1948–1996 (variables: marital status, age in years).

33. Verba and Nie, *Participation in America*, 132, Fig. 8.4; Norman H. Nie et al., "Participation in America: Continuity and Change" (paper presented at the annual meeting of the Midwest Political Science Association, Chicago, April 14–16, 1989).

34. See, for example, Sidney Verba, Norman H. Nie, and Jae-on Kim, *Participation and Political Equality* (Cambridge: Cambridge University Press, 1978); Ivor Crewe, "Electoral Participation," in *Democracy at the Polls*, ed. David Butler, Howard R. Penniman, and Austin Ranney (Washington, D.C.: American Enterprise Institute, 1981), 251–253; G. Bingham Powell Jr., *Contemporary Democracies: Participation, Stability, and Violence* (Cambridge: Harvard University Press, 1982), 117–120; G. Bingham Powell Jr., "American Voter Turnout in Comparative Perspective," *American Political Science Review,* 80 (1986): 17–43; and Russell J. Dalton, *Citizen Politics,* 2d ed. (Chatham, N.J.: Chatham House, 1996), 45, Table 3.2.

35. Powell, "American Voter Turnout," Ibid. Verba, Nie, and Kim, in *Participation and Political Equality,* chapters 4 and 5, examine how political institutions modify the relationships between resources, motivations, and participation.

36. Richard A. Brody, "The Puzzle of Political Participation," in *The New American Political System*, ed. Anthony King (Washington, D.C.: American Enterprise Institute, 1978), 287–324.

37. Wolfinger and Rosenstone, *Who Votes?*, 23–26. Although higher levels of educational attainment are related to increased likelihood of voting participation in other developed democracies as well, the effects of education on turnout are not as great in these countries as in the United States. See, for example, Powell, "American Voter Turnout," 28, Table 3; and Norman H. Nie, Jane Junn, and Kenneth Stehlik-Barry, *Education and Democratic Citizenship in America* (Chicago: University of Chicago Press, 1996).
38. Gabriel A. Almond and Sidney Verba, *The Civic Culture: Political Attitudes and Democracy in Five Nations* (Princeton: Princeton University Press, 1963), 379–381.
39. Brody, "Puzzle of Political Participation," 299–301.
40. Based on analysis of data in the American Election Studies Cumulative File, 1948–1996. In the 1990s, the proportion of citizens in the highest category of media use declined (variables: news media index, educational attainment).
41. Almond and Verba, *Civic Culture*, 315–318.
42. Based on analysis of data in the American Election Studies Cumulative File, 1948–1996 (variables: belief in government attentiveness, educational attainment).
43. See the following studies by Paul R. Abramson and William H. Claggett: "Race-Related Differences in Self-Reported and Validated Turnout," *Journal of Politics* 46 (August 1984): 719–738; "Race-Related Differences in Self-Reported and Validated Turnout in 1984," *Journal of Politics* 48 (May 1986): 412–422; and "Race-Related Differences in Self-Reported and Validated Turnout in 1986," *Journal of Politics* 51 (May 1989): 397–408. See also Barbara Anderson, Brian D. Silver, and Paul R. Abramson, "The Effects of Race of the Interviewer on Measures of Electoral Participation by Blacks in SRC National Election Studies," *Public Opinion Quarterly* 52 (1988): 53–83.
44. Nie, Junn, and Stehlik-Barry, *Education and Democratic Citizenship in America*, 5–6.
45. Wolfinger and Rosenstone, *Who Votes?*, 23.
46. Leighley and Nagler, "Socioeconomic Bias," 725–736.
47. Todd G. Shields and Robert K. Goidel, "Participation Rates, Socioeconomic Class Biases, and Congressional Elections: A Cross-validation," *American Journal of Political Science* 41 (1997): 683–691.
48. Lester W. Milbrath and M. L. Goel, *Political Participation*, 2d ed. (Chicago: Rand McNally, 1977), 96–98; Lane, *Political Life*, 326–327; Seymour Martin Lipset, *Political Man: The Social Bases of Politics* (Baltimore: Johns Hopkins University Press, 1981), chap. 6; and Giuseppe Di Palma, *Apathy and Participation* (New York: Free Press, 1970), chap. 6.
49. This conjecture is offered in Wolfinger and Rosenstone, *Who Votes?*, 21–22.
50. Ibid., 28–34.
51. Michael Lewis-Beck, "Agrarian Political Behavior in the United States," *American Journal of Political Science* 21 (1977): 543–565.
52. Wolfinger and Rosenstone, *Who Votes?*, 95.
53. Frank J. Sorauf, "State Patronage in a Rural County," *American Political Science Review* 50 (1956): 1046–1056; and Michael Johnston, "Patrons and Clients, Jobs and Machines: A Case Study of the Uses of Patronage," *American Political Science Review* 73 (1979): 385–398.
54. Wolfinger and Rosenstone, *Who Votes?*, 95.
55. For an analysis of time demands, see John Robinson and Philip E. Converse, "Social Change in the Use of Time," in *The Human Meaning of Social Change*, ed. Angus Campbell and Philip E. Converse (New York: Russell Sage, 1972), 17–86; and John P. Robinson and Geoffrey Godbey, *Time for Life: The Surprising Ways Americans Use Their Time* (University Park: Pennsylvania State University Press, 1997).
56. Richard A. Brody and Paul M. Sniderman, "From Life Space to the Polling Place:

The Relevance of Personal Concerns for Voting Behavior," *British Journal of Political Science* 7 (1977): 344. However, in *Insult to Injury*, Kay Lehman Schlozman and Sidney Verba compared employed and unemployed citizens and found that the unemployed were more likely than the employed to follow politics in the electronic media but less likely to read news about politics in print media. When employment status was included with education, occupation level, race, age, and gender, employment status was not statistically significant in explaining participation (247, Table 9.2) or voter turnout (250, Table 9.3). The unemployed were, however, significantly less likely to be registered to vote, even when the effects of other sociodemographic variables were taken into account (253, Table 9.5).

57. Schlozman and Verba, *Insult to Injury*, 88.
58. Steven J. Rosenstone, "Economic Adversity and Voting Turnout," *American Journal of Political Science* 26 (1982): 33, Table 1.
59. Wolfinger and Rosenstone, *Who Votes?*, 76–79.
60. Richard P. Claude, *The Supreme Court and the Electoral Process* (Baltimore: Johns Hopkins University Press, 1970).
61. Carol A. Cassel, "Change in Electoral Participation in the South," *Journal of Politics* 41 (1979): 910.
62. Lynn M. Casper and Loretta E. Bass, "Voting and Registration in the Election of November 1996," Bureau of the Census, *Current Population Reports,* ser. P-20, no. 504, (Washington, D.C.: Government Printing Office, July 1998), 1–2, Tables 1 and 2.
63. Abramson and Claggett, "Race-Related Differences," *Journal of Politics* 46: 719–738.
64. Bureau of the Census, "Voting and Registration in the Election of November 1988," *Current Population Reports,* ser. P-20, no. 440 (Washington, D.C.: Government Printing Office, October 1989), 6, Table F.
65. Casper and Bass, "Voting and Registration in the Election of November 1996," 4–13, Detailed Table 2.
66. Kendrick, "Group Economic Interests."
67. Katherine Tate, *From Protest to Politics: The New Black Voters in American Elections.* (Cambridge: Harvard University Press, 1993), 90–92.
68. Wolfinger and Rosenstone, *Who Votes?*, 91–93. See also Nicholas Lovrich Jr. and Otwin Marenin, "A Comparison of Black and Mexican American Voters in Denver: Assertive vs. Acquiescent Political Orientations and Voting Behavior in an Urban Electorate," *Western Political Quarterly* 29 (1976): 284–294; F. Chris Garcia and Rudolph O. de la Garza, *The Chicano Political Experience* (North Scituate, Mass.: Duxbury Press, 1977), 94–110; Susan MacManus and Carol A. Cassel, "Mexican-Americans in City Politics: Participation, Representation, and Policy Preferences," *Urban Interest* 4 (1982): 57–69; Rodolfo O. de la Garza and Louis DeSipio, "Latinos and the 1992 Election: a National Perspective," in *Ethnic Ironies,* ed. Rodolfo O. de la Garza and Louis DeSipio (Boulder, Colo.: Westview Press, 1996), 3–49; Rodolfo O. de la Garza and Louis DeSipio, eds., *From Rhetoric to Reality: Latino Politics in the 1988 Elections* (Boulder, Colo.: Westview Press, 1992); Rodolfo O. de la Garza et al., *Latino Voices: Mexican, Puerto Rican, and Cuban Perspectives in American Politics* (Boulder, Colo.: Westview Press, 1992); and Rodney E. Hero, *Latinos and the U.S. Political System: Two-Tiered Pluralism* (Philadelphia: Temple University Press, 1992).
69. Wolfinger and Rosenstone, *Who Votes?*, 93.
70. Ibid., 141.
71. Carole Jean Uhlaner, Bruce E. Cain, and D. Roderick Kiewiet, "Political Participation of Ethnic Minorities in the 1980s," *Political Behavior* 11 (1989): 199, 225.
72. Pei-te Lien, *The Political Participation of Asian Americans* (New York: Garland, 1997), 130.
73. Ibid., 213.

74. Sandra Baxter and Marjorie Lansing, *Women and Politics,* rev. ed. (Ann Arbor: University of Michigan Press, 1983), chap. 2. See also McGlen and O'Connor, *Women's Rights,* 99.
75. M. Margaret Conway, Gertrude A. Steuernagel, and David W. Ahern, *Women and Political Participation* (Washington, D.C.: CQ Press, 1997), 79–80, Tables 5.1 and 5.2.
76. McGlen and O'Connor, *Women's rights,* 105–106.
77. Calculated from data in the American National Election Studies Combined File, 1948–1996 (variables: number of campaign acts performed, gender).
78. Verba, Schlozman, and Brady, *Voice and Equality,* 254–255.
79. Women in 1992 and 1996 scored lower on the political media use index. Calculated from data in the American National Election Studies Cumulative File, 1948–1996 (variables: news media index, gender).
80. Jonathan Gershuny and John P. Robinson, "Historical Changes in the Household Division of Labor, *Demography,* 25, no. 4 (November 1988): 537–552; John P. Robinson and Melissa Milkie, "Dances with Dust Bunnies: Housecleaning in America," *American Demographics* 19, no. 1 (January 1997): 37–40, 59; John P. Robinson and Melissa A. Milkie, "Back to the Basics: Trends in and Role Determinants of Women's Attitudes toward Housework," *Journal of Marriage and the Family* 60, no. 1 (February 1998):" 205–218; and Robinson and Godbey, *Time for Life.*
81. Verba, Schlozman, and Brady, *Voice and Equality,* 259–260.
82. Conway, Steuernagel, and Ahern, *Women and Political Participation,* chap. 3.
83. Declining gender differences were found in studies by Richard M. Merelman, *Political Socialization and Educational Climates* (New York: Holt, Rinehart, and Winston, 1971); and Anthony Orum et al., "Sex, Socialization, and Politics," *American Sociological Review* 39 (1974): 197–209. In contrast, Jennings and Niemi found that gender differences within a subsample of young adults increased from 1965 to 1973, even though such differences decreased among their parents in a number of measures of political involvement and activity; see M. Kent Jennings and Richard G. Niemi, *Generations and Politics: A Panel Study of Young Adults and Their Parents* (Princeton: Princeton University Press, 1981), chap. 9.
84. Francine D. Blau, "Women in the Labor Force: An Overview," in *Women: A Feminist Perspective,* 3d ed., ed. Jo Freeman (Palo Alto, Calif.: Mayfield, 1984), 302, Table 1, and 307, Table 3; Debra Renee Kaufman, "Professional Women: How Real Are the Recent Gains?"; in Freeman, *Women,* 355, Table 1; Rita Mae Kelly, *The Gendered Economy* (Newbury Park, Calif.: Sage, 1991), chap. 3; and Cynthia B. Costello, Shari Miles, and Anne J. Stone, eds., *The American Woman 1999–2000* (New York: Norton, 1998), 285, Table 4.13.
85. Andersen, "Working Women," 442–443, 446–451; Kathleen McCourt, *Working Women and Grass-Roots Politics* (Bloomington: Indiana University Press, 1977); and Susan Welch, "Women as Political Animals? A Test of Some Explanations for Male-Female Political Participation Differences," *American Journal of Political Science* 21 (1977): 724. See also Eileen McDonagh, "To Work or Not to Work: The Differential Impact of Achieved and Derived Status upon the Political Participation of Women, 1956–1976," *American Journal of Political Science* 26 (1982): 280–297. McDonagh reports that derived status (acquired by virtue of husband's status) is more strongly associated with the number of campaign-related acts performed than is employment or (self-) achieved status based on occupational prestige measures. However, Table 3 (p. 290) indicates that the pattern of relationships between the measures of employment and status and the number of campaign-related acts performed has varied substantially in this twenty-year period. Furthermore, the relationship between derived status and number of campaign-related acts performed may be a function of the leisure time available for campaigning.

86. Wolfinger and Rosenstone, *Who Votes?*, 43.

87. See Ellen Boneparth, "Women in Campaigns: From Lickin' and Stickin' to Strategy," *American Politics Quarterly* 5 (1977): 289–300; Albert K. Karnig and B. Oliver Walter, "Election of Women to City Councils," *Social Science Quarterly* 56 (1976): 605–613; Kristi Anderson, *After Suffrage* (Chicago: University of Chicago Press, 1996); and Charles D. Hadley and Lewis Bowman, eds., *Party Activists in Southern Politics: Mirrors and Makers of Change* (Knoxville: University of Tennessee Press, 1998). See also Robert Darcy and Sarah Slavin Schramm, "When Women Run against Men," *Public Opinion Quarterly* 41 (1977): 1–12; Ruth Mandel, *In the Running* (Boston: Beacon Press, 1981); and Jeane J. Kirkpatrick, *Political Women* (New York: Basic Books, 1974). For research that tests several alternative explanations, see Cal Clark and Janet Clark, "Models of Gender and Political Participation in the United States," *Women and Politics* 6 (1986): 5–25; and Carol Christy, *Sex Differences in Political Participation* (New York: Praeger, 1987).

88. Barbara C. Burrell. *A Woman's Place is in the House* (Ann Arbor: University of Michigan Press, 1997), chap. 7; Sue Thomas, "Introduction: Women and Elective Office: Past, Present, and Future," in *Women and Elective Office*, ed. Sue Thomas and Clyde Wilcox (New York: Oxford University Press, 1998), 1–14; Georgia Duerst-Lahti, "The Bottleneck: Women Becoming Candidates," in Thomas and Wilcox, *Women and Elective Office*, 15–25; and Richard A. Seltzer, Jody Newman, and Melissa Voorhees Leighton, *Sex as a Political Variable: Women as Candidates and Voters in U.S. Elections* (Boulder, Colo.: Lynne Rienner, 1997), chap. 4.

89. Kim Fridkin Kahn, *The Political Consequences of Being a Woman* (New York: Columbia University Press, 1996).

90. Richard Logan Fox, *Gender Dynamics in Congressional Elections* (Thousand Oaks, Calif.: Sage, 1997), 185.

91. Ruy A. Teixeira, *Why Americans Don't Vote* (Westport, Conn.: Greenwood Press, 1987), chap. 5.

Chapter 3

The Psychology of Political Participation

Patterns of political participation are significantly influenced by peoples' psychological orientations—their beliefs, attitudes, and values. Also relevant to an understanding of political participation is the study of personality, especially the motives underlying participation in certain kinds of political activities and the characteristic behavior patterns of politicians who have certain types of personalities.

Beliefs, Attitudes, and Values

Beliefs can be classified into three types: (1) *descriptive,* a person's observation of the way things are (for example, "the U.S. Congress has 535 voting members"); (2) *evaluative,* a person's judgment of people or events ("Franklin Roosevelt was a very skilled political leader"); and (3) *prescriptive,* a person's opinion concerning preferred courses of action or modes of behavior ("nuclear war should be avoided"). Beliefs have three components: cognitive (based on knowledge), affective (emotion-arousing), and behavioral (action-stimulating). Each belief is a predisposition that, when activated, leads to some preferential response.

An attitude is a "relatively enduring organization of interrelated beliefs that describe, evaluate, and advocate with respect to an object or situation."[1] Attitudes may focus on either objects (including people) or situations, and both are important in influencing political participation. For example, citizens frequently evaluate presidential candidates (the objects) in terms of how they might perform in different situations (setting budget priorities, managing routine foreign policy matters, handling an international crisis). Such evaluations might be instrumental in determining a citizen's decision whether and how to vote.[2]

Values are statements of what are considered "good"—situations or objects that are preferred to other situations or objects. Values can be categorized as *instrumental* and *terminal*. Instrumental values are ideal forms of behavior, such as affectionate, intellectual, and imaginative; terminal values are idealized end states, such as equality, justice, freedom, peace, and happiness.[3] Terminal values can be either material or nonmaterial.[4]

Trends in Psychological Involvement in Politics

Psychological involvement refers to the possession of a complex structure of beliefs, attitudes, and values with respect to some object. It is a plausible expectation that those who have a greater psychological involvement in politics will be more active politically. Among the components of psychological involvement in politics (also called political engagement) are a perceived obligation to participate (sense of civic duty), interest in politics, interest in a current or upcoming political campaign, sense of personal political effectiveness (internal and external political efficacy), and identification with a political party.[5]

Those who hold these beliefs, attitudes, and values more strongly tend to engage in more political activity. A study of individuals registered to vote in ten elections held in the state of Kentucky from 1978 to 1982 indicated that their level of interest in politics, party identification, perception of party's ideological differences, and sense of civic obligation were related to the frequency with which the individuals voted in those elections.[6]

The sense of civic duty includes the belief that citizens ought to vote in elections. One measure of this belief is rejection of the idea that people should not vote if they do not care about the outcome of the election. In effect, people were being asked in this study if they should vote just to express support for the system. As Table 3-1 demonstrates, support for such ritualized voting has declined since 1980.

The level of general interest in politics has changed, but there has not been a consistent trend (see Table 3-2). Some people follow what is going on in politics and government most of the time, whereas others are only sporadically interested in politics. Political interest appears to have peaked during the tumultuous decade spanning the last half of the 1960s and first half of the 1970s, when the civil rights movement, the Vietnam War, the Watergate scandal with the subse-

TABLE 3-1

Sense of Civic Duty, Measured by Rejection of Belief that
Citizens Not Concerned about Election Outcome Should Not Vote

1952	1956	1960	1972	1976	1980	1984	1988	1992
46	54	56	54	55	59	43	37	42

SOURCE: American National Election Studies Cumulative File, 1952–1996.
Note: Percentages indicate respondents disagreeing with the statement on "Civic duty." (For its wording, see the Appendix.) This item was not included in the 1964 or 1968 surveys. Percentages have been rounded to whole numbers.

quent resignation of President Nixon and his pardon by President Gerald R. Ford, the recession of 1973–1974, and the first major energy crisis inflamed public passions. As these issues decreased in importance to the electorate during the late 1970s, political interest declined correspondingly.

Attention to politics can be measured by the level of interest in the current political campaign. As Table 3-3 demonstrates, interest in presidential campaigns varies with the election. When the presidential

TABLE 3-2

Level of General Interest in Government and Politics, Presidential and
Midterm Elections, 1960–1998

	Presidential elections									
	1960	1964	1968	1972	1976	1980	1984	1988	1992	1996
Said they follow government and public affairs										
Hardly at all	38	11	18	11	12	15	14	15	11	12
Only now and then	—	17	19	16	18	23	23	26	21	26
Some of the time	42	42	31	36	32	35	36	37	41	40
Most of the time	21	30	33	37	38	26	26	22	26	23

	Midterm congressional elections									
	1962	1966	1970*	1974	1978	1982	1986	1990	1994	1998
Hardly at all	42	17	—	11	18	15	15	16	13	12
Only now and then	—	18	—	14	25	21	24	23	23	26
Some of the time	42	30	—	36	34	36	35	33	34	40
Most of the time	21	35	—	39	23	29	26	28	30	22

SOURCES: American National Election Studies Cumulative File, 1948–1996; 1998 American National Election Study.
Note: Percentages indicate responses to the question on "Interest in public affairs/follow public affairs." (For its wording, see the Appendix.) Some column totals do not equal 100 percent because of rounding.
* This question was not included in the 1970 survey.

TABLE 3-3
Level of Interest in the Current Political Campaign, 1952–1998
(in percent)

	Presidential election campaigns											
	1952	1956	1960	1964	1968	1972	1976	1980	1984	1988	1992	1996
Not much	29	31	25	25	21	27	21	26	25	25	17	24
Somewhat	34	40	37	37	40	41	42	44	47	47	44	49
Very much	37	30	38	38	39	32	37	30	28	28	39	27

	Midterm congressional election campaigns										
	1958	1962	1966	1970	1974	1978	1982	1986	1990	1994	1998
Not much	41	26	30	24	21	34	30	33	33	25	31
Somewhat	33	38	40	43	42	45	44	44	46	47	48
Very much	26	36	30	34	37	22	26	22	21	28	21

SOURCES: American National Election Studies Cumulative File, 1952–1996; 1998 American National Election Study.
Note: Percentages indicate responses to the question on "Interest in current campaign." (For its wording, see the Appendix.) Some column totals do not equal 100 percent because of rounding.

election outcome is in doubt, more people say they are "very much" interested in the campaign. For example, the 1992 contest between then President George Bush and Arkansas Governor Bill Clinton was perceived to be close by many people, and campaign interest was higher than in the 1988 election. In contrast, the 1996 contest between President Bill Clinton and former senator Robert Dole was not viewed as a close race by many people, and fewer reported that they were very much interested in the campaign. Campaign interest tends to be less strong in midterm elections than in presidential elections. Vigorous campaigns in elections for governor or U.S. senator or other state offices or concerning ballot propositions can stimulate voter interest, however.

Psychological involvement in politics is also measured by an individual's sense of internal and external political efficacy. The proportion of survey respondents who were rated as having a low level of internal political efficacy—as measured by the belief that sometimes politics and government seems too complicated to understand— ranged from 59 percent to 74 percent between 1952 and 1998 (see Table 3-4).

The proportion of respondents with a high level of external political efficacy—the belief that public officials are responsive to the interests of individuals like oneself—declined significantly between 1952

TABLE 3-4
Perception of Government and Politics as Too Complicated to Understand, Presidential Elections, 1952–1998 (in percent)

Response	1952	1956	1960	1964	1968	1972	1976	1980	1984	1988	1992	1996	1998
Agree	71	64	59	68	71	74	73	71	71	70	66	61	73
Disagree	29	36	41	32	29	26	27	29	29	21	27	28	20
Neither	—	—	—	—	—	—	—	—	—	8	7	11	7

SOURCES: American National Election Studies Cumulative File, 1948–1996; 1998 American National Election Study.
Note: Percentages indicate responses to "Too complicated" item. (For its wording, see the Appendix.) Some column totals do not equal 100 percent because of rounding. In 1988 and subsequent years, response categories were: agree strongly, agree somewhat, neither, disagree somewhat, and disagree strongly. For those years, the two "agree" categories have been combined, as have the two "disagree" categories.

and 1998 (see Table 3-5). Although the decline stopped and levels of external political efficacy resumed their increase during the first Reagan administration (1980–1984), they began to decline again in the late 1980s.

Identification with a political party, another component of psychological involvement in politics, has been measured since 1952 with the same set of questions. Respondents are initially asked, "Generally speaking, do you usually think of yourself as a Republican, a Democrat, an Independent, or what?" Those responding "Democrat" or "Republican" are asked, "Would you call yourself a strong Republican (Democrat) or a not very strong Republican (Democrat)?" Those responding "Independent" are asked, "Do you think of yourself as closer to the Republican or the Democratic Party?" From these questions a seven-point scale of party identification is created, ranging from "Strong Democrat" to "Strong Republican," with "Independent" in the middle.[7] The proportion of respondents who call themselves Independent increased from 1952 to 1976, with corresponding decreases in the proportion who identify strongly with either party (Table 3-6). The decline in strong party identifiers from 1952 to 1998 was greater in the Democratic Party than in the Republican Party.

There are generational differences in party identification. The post–New Deal generation (those entering the electorate in 1968 and subsequent years) is less likely to identify with a party than the pre–New Deal generation (who entered the electorate in the years before 1928) and the New Deal generation (those entering the electorate

TABLE 3-5
Level of External Political Efficacy, 1952–1998 (in percent)

Presidential elections

	1952	1956	1960	1964	1968	1972	1976	1980	1984	1988	1992	1996
Low	20	16	15	21	30	31	34	31	25	42	37	53
Medium	27	22	22	25	24	28	28	33	25	27	31	32
High	53	62	63	54	46	41	38	36	50	30	30	15

Midterm congressional elections

	1966	1970	1974	1978	1982	1990	1994	1998
Low	24	27	32	35	37	59	58	49
Medium	26	31	31	30	21	25	26	31
High	51	42	37	35	42	16	16	20

SOURCES: American National Election Studies Cumulative File, 1952–1996; 1998 American National Election Study.
Note: Percentages indicate respondents at each level of external efficacy. (For wording of "External efficacy" item, see the Appendix.) Percentages have been rounded to whole numbers.

TABLE 3-6
Party Identification, 1952–1998 (in percent)

	1952	1954	1956	1958	1960	1962	1964	1966	1968	1970	1972	1974
Strong Democrat	22	22	21	26	20	23	27	18	20	20	15	18
Weak Democrat	25	26	23	22	25	23	25	28	25	24	26	21
Independent, leaning Democrat	10	9	6	7	6	7	9	9	10	10	11	13
Independent	6	7	9	7	10	8	8	12	10	13	13	15
Independent, leaning Republican	7	6	8	5	7	6	6	7	9	8	11	8
Weak Republican	14	14	14	16	14	16	14	15	15	15	13	14
Strong Republican	14	13	15	11	16	12	11	10	10	9	10	8
Apolitical	3	4	4	4	2	4	1	1	1	1	1	3

between 1929 and 1964). These differences exist within each level of educational attainment.[8]

Racial and regional differences also exist in patterns of party identification. African Americans have been more Democratic than whites since the 1950s; this reflects their perceptions of the policies promoted and enacted by Democratic presidents and Democratic-controlled Congresses. In 1952, 30 percent of African Americans in the South strongly identified with the Democratic Party; by 1996, 43 percent were strong Democratic Party identifiers. Outside the South, 32 percent of African Americans strongly identified with the Democratic Party in 1952; by 1996, the proportion had increased to 44 percent. Between 1952 and 1996, the proportion of African Americans throughout the United States who were strong Republican Party identifiers decreased. The proportion of whites in the South who identified themselves as strong Democrats dropped from 36 percent in 1952 to 16 percent in 1996, whereas the proportion of whites residing outside the South who identified themselves as strong Democrats dropped from 17 percent in 1952 to 15 percent in 1996.[9]

Several other changes are evident in patterns of party identification. Among white citizens, those who reached voting age after World War II are less likely to be strong Democrats and more likely to be either Independents who usually support one party or pure Independents,

TABLE 3-6
(continued)

	1976	1978	1980	1982	1984	1986	1988	1990	1992	1994	1996	1998
Strong Democrat	15	15	18	20	17	18	18	20	18	15	19	19
Weak Democrat	25	24	23	24	20	22	18	19	18	19	20	19
Independent, leaning Democrat	12	14	11	11	11	10	12	12	14	13	14	14
Independent	15	14	13	11	11	12	11	10	12	10	8	11
Independent, leaning Republican	10	10	10	8	12	11	13	12	12	12	11	11
Weak Republican	14	13	14	14	15	14	14	15	14	14	15	16
Strong Republican	9	8	9	10	12	11	14	10	11	16	13	10
Apolitical	1	3	2	2	2	2	2	2	1	1	1	—

SOURCES: American National Election Studies Cumulative File, 1948–1996; 1998 American National Election Study.
Note: Percentages indicate respondents in each category. (For wording of question on "Party identification," see the Appendix.) Some column totals do not equal 100 percent because of rounding.

and the proportion of Independents is greatest among the most recent entrants into the electorate.[10]

Gender differences also exist in patterns of party identification. From the early 1960s through the late 1990s, more women than men have been Democratic Party identifiers, and more men than women have declared themselves to be Independent. In contrast, men and women have been equally likely to identify with the Republican Party.[11]

To summarize, several changes have occurred over time in the components of psychological involvement in politics. A significant decline has taken place in the proportion of the electorate that scores high on the measure of external political efficacy used here—perception of the government as responsive to the interests of citizens like oneself. The proportion with a low level of internal political efficacy (the belief that sometimes government and politics seems too difficult to understand) has increased. Fewer citizens have a strong party identification and fewer identify with either the Democratic Party or the Republican Party. Generational, racial, regional, and gender differences are evident in party identification. General interest in politics and government has varied with the dominant issues and with electoral campaigns.

Trends in Other Attitudes and Beliefs

Whereas external political efficacy measures citizens' perceptions of government's responsiveness to the interests of people like themselves, another measure—belief in government attentiveness—indicates citizens' perceptions of the effectiveness of elections and political parties in facilitating that responsiveness. This measure shows a substantial decline since 1964: the proportion scoring in the two highest categories has dropped from 60 percent in 1964 to 41 percent in 1998 (see Table 3-7).

Also relevant to the explanation of patterns of political behavior are citizens' beliefs about the utility or futility of traditional forms of political participation in making the government responsive to their views. Two questions have been included in the biennial American National Election Studies surveys to examine these beliefs. The general trend from 1964 to 1980 was an increased perception of the government as not responsive and not very attentive to citizens' views and preferences. From 1964 to 1980, a majority of those surveyed believed elections contributed a great deal to making the government pay attention to what the people think. In 1988, however, the proportion dropped to 38 percent, but increased to 47 percent in 1992.[12]

Political participation can be affected by a citizen's calculations of its likely benefits and costs. According to rational choice theory, each citizen estimates the benefits likely to be derived from different policy outcomes and also takes into account the personal costs of attempting to influence these outcomes. Another variable in the calculation is the relative probability that different outcomes will result from varying levels of effort.[13] For example, an individual may conclude that a senatorial election is going to result in a landslide victory for the incumbent and that the probability of his or her vote influencing the outcome of the Senate contest is so small that casting a vote is not worth the effort. In contrast, when an election appears to be very closely contested, citizens may be more motivated to participate, believing that their votes and campaign activities may have an impact on the outcome. As would be expected, presidential elections vary considerably in the extent to which they are perceived as being close contests (see Table 3-8). The pattern of perceptions of presidential elections as

TABLE 3-7
Level of Belief in Government Attentiveness, 1964–1998

	1964	1968	1970	1972	1974	1976	1978	1980	1984	1988	1992	1996	1998
Low	5	7	6	5	7	8	7	10	14	13	8	10	9
2	10	12	14	13	17	16	14	19	15	14	12	13	15
3	25	29	27	33	32	33	32	34	34	39	39	38	35
4	29	30	33	33	34	34	35	31	24	23	30	25	26
High	31	22	20	16	10	9	12	7	13	11	10	14	15

SOURCES: American National Election Studies Cumulative File, 1948–1996; 1998 American National Election Study.
Note: Percentages indicate responses to the question on "Belief in government attentiveness." (For its wording, see the Appendix.) Some column totals do not equal 100 percent because of rounding.

being close parallels the election outcomes in terms of the popular vote (but not always the electoral college vote).

In 1960 and 1968, the presidential elections resulted in narrow victories in terms of popular votes. Only two-tenths of a percentage point separated the popular vote received by the Democratic and the Republican candidates in 1960, and voter turnout in that election was the highest in modern times: 60 percent of those eligible to vote cast ballots. In 1968, Republican candidate Nixon received 43.4 percent and Democratic candidate Hubert H. Humphrey received 42.7 percent of the popular votes cast; voter turnout was slightly lower than in the preceding election but more than 5 percent higher than in the next (1972).[14]

Citizens' responses to the question, "How much of the time do you think you can trust the government in Washington to do what is right—just about always, most of the time, or only some of the time?" changed substantially from 1958 to 1998. The proportion responding

TABLE 3-8
Expected Closeness of Presidential Election, 1952–1996 (in percent)

	1952	1956	1960	1964	1968	1972	1976	1980	1984	1988	1992	1996
Will win by quite a bit	24	31	16	51	25	64	16	17	49	26	18	47
Will be a close race	76	69	84	49	75	36	84	83	51	74	82	53

SOURCES: American National Election Studies Cumulative File, 1948–1996.
Note: Percentages indicate responses to the question on "Expected closeness of election." (For its wording, see the Appendix). Excludes those who responded "don't know," "depends," or "pro-con." Percentages have been rounded to whole numbers.

TABLE 3-9
*Level of Concern about Which Party Wins Presidential Election,
1952–1996 (in percent)*

Year	Don't care very much or don't know	Care a good deal
1952	33	67
1956	37	63
1960	35	65
1964	35	66
1968	35	65
1972	40	60
1976	43	57
1980	56	44
1984	34	66
1988	39	61
1992	25	75
1996	22	78

SOURCES: American National Election Studies Cumulative File, 1948–1996.
Note: Percentages indicate responses to question on "Care who wins presidential election." (For its wording, see the Appendix.) Percentages have been rounded to whole numbers.

"most of the time" or "just about always" reached 76 percent in 1964, but declined to 36 percent in 1974, reflecting reactions to the Vietnam War, domestic policy changes, and the Watergate scandal. The decline continued through 1980, when the proportion of respondents giving one of the two more trusting responses reached a low of 26 percent. A revival of trust began during the Reagan administration: in 1988, 41 percent of those surveyed gave one of the more trusting responses. By 1996, trust had declined again: the proportion of respondents who said they could trust the government to do what is right just about always or most of the time was down to 32 percent.[15]

One scholar of American political history has argued that during certain periods of American history, the gap between the fundamental ideals of the American political system and the actual performance of its institutions and leaders has become too large to be tolerated by a substantial number of citizens. The result was increased distrust of political leaders, demands for changes in the structures and operations of political institutions, and increased levels of political activity.[16]

Higher levels of interest in a campaign can stimulate political participation, but individuals are more likely to participate in an election if they also care about who wins it. That concern may focus on the outcome of a highly visible and nationally important contest, such as that for the presidency. Citizens may also be deeply concerned about the outcomes of mayoral and city council elections and even local political party committee offices in a city such as Chicago, with a tradition of a strong party organization and party influence in the distribution of patronage jobs and neighborhood services. A number of national surveys have asked citizens how much they personally care about which party wins the presidential election or, in midterm years, the congressional elections. About two-thirds of those surveyed between 1952 and 1968 indicated they cared "a good deal" about the outcome of the presidential election. The proportion declined steadily thereafter, and stood at only 44 percent in 1980, but then began to increase, reaching 78 percent in 1996 (see Table 3-9). The proportion expressing "a good deal" of concern about the outcome of congressional elections has tended to be smaller.[17]

Effect of Attitudes and Beliefs on Political Participation

The attitudes and beliefs that have been discussed vary in their relationship to political participation. We will examine here the bivariate relationships of some of these variables to patterns of political participation. In Chapter 7, we consider the effects of these variables on participation after controlling for other relevant variables. General interest in government and politics and interest in the current political campaign have maintained a stable, though moderate, relationship to voter turnout since 1952. For example, in 1952 and 1956, more than 87 percent of those who paid a high level of attention to the current presidential campaign reported voting, but 58 percent or less of those who paid a low level of attention to the campaign reported voting. In 1992 and 1996, more than 90 percent of those who paid high levels of attention voted. Of those reporting low levels of attention to the presidential campaign, 43 percent voted in 1992 and 51 percent voted in 1996.[18]

Those who identify strongly with one party have generally been more likely to vote (and to participate politically in other ways) than those who do not.[19] The effects are greater in midterm elections than in presidential elections; presidential elections receive more media coverage, thus stimulating more turnout by those who are not strong party identifiers. In terms of the party with which people identify, Republicans are more likely to vote than Democrats. That can be explained in part by other characteristics of party identifiers, such as occupation, income, and education.

The relationship of internal political efficacy to voter turnout can be described as weak to moderately strong; those having higher levels of internal political efficacy are at best 10 to 15 percent more likely to vote. When the effects of other variables are taken into account, however, the relationship between internal political efficacy and turnout becomes nonsignificant. Measures of external political efficacy are also moderately associated with turnout in presidential elections. The effects of trust in government on voter turnout, as measured by a question about how much one can trust the government to do what is right, vary over time.[20]

The patterns of relationships between other measures of psychological involvement and voter turnout have not been stable over time. In general, the relationship between the belief that the government is responsive and voter turnout has not shown a consistent pattern; the trend increased slightly from 1964 to 1974 and then began a decline that has continued since that time.[21] Perception of the closeness of the presidential election has had the widest variation in its effects on electoral activities. During the era of political turmoil from 1964 to 1972, perceived closeness had little impact on participation. Those who expected the election to be close were no more likely to participate than were those who expected one candidate to win by a landslide. Other factors, especially the level of satisfaction with the government's current economic, social, and foreign policies, were clearly more important. If their level of dissatisfaction is sufficiently high, citizens will engage in electoral activity regardless of their perception of the closeness of the outcome. Before 1964 and after 1972, beliefs about the closeness of the presidential contest did have a moderate effect, however, for those who expected it to be close participated somewhat more.[22] When other contests, such as those for seats in the House or the Senate, or for the state governorship, are held at the same time, they may stimulate voter turnout in the presidential election.

One element of the belief that the government is attentive to citizens is the belief that elections are an effective instrument for making the government pay attention to what citizens want. A statistically significant but weak relationship does exist between holding that belief and the probability of voting.[23]

Those who care about who wins the presidential election are more likely to vote. Though statistically significant, the actual effect of the relationship is weak. That is because such a large proportion of the potential electorate chooses to vote despite claiming that they do not care very much about who wins.[24]

The effect of values on voting has received less attention than the effects of attitudes and beliefs. Values are more difficult to measure using survey research methods. A substantial amount of research has focused on comparing the effects of materialist values versus nonmaterialist values on voting, with interesting but controversial results.[25]

The Acquisition of Political Orientations

Attitudes, beliefs, and values are learned predispositions, and the various forms of political participation are learned behaviors. The attitudes, beliefs, and values are developed in a political, legal, and social context. All influence patterns of political behavior (a political action "repertory"[26]). Behaviors can be learned but not used, however. For example, children learn to throw rocks and other objects, but that does not mean that as adults they will necessarily engage in rock-throwing demonstrations when political leaders implement policies with which they strongly disagree.

Studies of the learning of political orientations and behaviors provide some answers to questions about who engages in what forms of political action. Political education begins in early childhood. Children learn attitudes, beliefs, and values primarily by overhearing the conversations of family members about political subjects, such as institutions, policies, and events. Family discussions about public officials, such as a president, governor, mayor, police officer, or bureaucrat, create images of public authorities and of the political system. Occasionally a family member, in discussions aimed at adding to a child's knowledge, may deliberately try to inculcate particular political attitudes and beliefs.[27]

The family continues to be an important source of political education. Moreover, the widespread availability of television network news since the late 1950s has undoubtedly increased the importance of the mass media as an instrument of political learning for both children and adults. Television learning is accomplished most efficiently with frequent repetition; complex ideas may not be easily acquired by means of such a passive learning mechanism, but both beliefs and attitudes can be acquired or reinforced by all of the mass media.[28] By showing individuals engaging in both conventional and unconventional forms of political behavior and political leaders' responses to them, the mass media help children and adults learn about such forms of political activity and assess the effectiveness of these activities in obtaining desired results. By choosing to emphasize some problems and not others, the mass media also help establish the public policy agenda.

Some scholars have argued that television has contributed to lower levels of political participation. Studies of television news coverage of elections have concluded that it fosters a general bias against all major candidates while ignoring minor candidates. Television news conveys an image of a group of independent political entrepreneurs playing games in order to win particular political offices. The importance of policy differences between candidates and the role of institutions such as the political parties are ignored. In effect, they argue, television creates an image of politics as a horse race and fosters a set of negative attitudes toward politics and toward participation in politics.[29] It was noted earlier that among the major trends in political attitudes since the 1960s is a decline in party loyalty, trust in government, and external political efficacy. That this decline occurred during the rise of television as a major source of political information is probably not a coincidence.

An important and recurrent criticism of television is that it contributes to the decline in social capital, which pertains to relationships among individuals. James S. Coleman specified three forms of social capital: obligations and expectations, information flow, and norms and sanctions.[30] In the realm of politics, political trust is essential for the first of these. Certainly norms and sanctions also structure political behavior, and the flow of information through social organizations (such as sports clubs and neighborhood associations) can influence attitudes, beliefs, values, and behaviors that relate to politics. In an examination of social capital in the United States, Robert D. Putnam argues that social capital has declined, in part because citizen involvement in voluntary organizations has declined, and that television is to blame.[31] His argument has stimulated controversy and an extensive body of research.[32]

Another vehicle of political learning is the educational system. Formal schooling serves to inculcate political beliefs, attitudes, and values and to instill forms of political behavior in students in a number of ways. The school accomplishes this political socialization through its curriculum, classroom rituals, and the values and attitudes unconsciously transmitted by its staff. The way students are taught about political affairs and the governmental system can have effects that bear on political socialization.[33] The school's social climate, political and nonpolitical organizations, and extracurricular activities exert subtle socializing influences that can have lasting effects.[34]

Friends and acquaintances can also play a significant role in children's political socialization. Adolescents whose friends have political attitudes congruent with parental attitudes are more likely to have attitudes similar to their parents. Children whose parents' attitudes are dissimilar from those prevailing in the community are more likely to adopt attitudes different from their parents and similar to those of the community.[35]

Although childhood political socialization results in the acquisition of political orientations and the learning of forms of political action, political learning is a lifelong process. As life experiences change, so also do political orientations. A study of high school students and their parents, who were interviewed first in 1965 and again in 1973, found that changes in political attitudes, beliefs, and behavior occurred among both the parents and the children, following changes in their personal circumstances and in prevailing political conditions.[36]

Engaging in political activities influences subsequent attitudes and behavior. For example, participation in elections by either voting or engaging in campaign activities has a positive effect on citizens' later sense of internal political efficacy.[37] Participation in protest demonstrations can also have a liberalizing effect on other attitudes. Those who participated in protest demonstrations while they were college students during the Vietnam War were later more likely to be supportive of civil liberties, to oppose prayer in schools, and to support racial integration in schools than were those who had not protested. However, the protesters became significantly less liberal on most issues as they grew older, with the exception of support for women's equality.[38]

Political learning can be indirect or direct. Indirect political learning is the acquisition of orientations and organizational skills that are politically relevant even though they are not explicitly political.[39] For example, an individual might subconsciously transfer attitudes toward parents and school authorities to political officials.[40] Another form of indirect political learning is the apprenticeship, from which can be acquired useful skills such as public speaking and the ability to organize and run meetings. By participating in the activities of social organizations with hierarchical structures and formal rules, people learn to operate within organizational frameworks, and this pattern of behavior can be generalized to the political arena.[41]

Direct political learning can be accomplished when individuals adopt the political views and behaviors of others—for example, by adopting the political party identification of their parents. Direct learning can be anticipatory, as when individuals set out to learn the orientations and skills needed to fill a political role, such as candidate for public office. Direct learning can also occur through experience; for example, people's attitudes toward government authorities can be significantly altered as a result of their dealings with public officials, such as a police officer or a clerk in the state motor vehicle bureau office.[42]

Personality and Political Participation

Personality can be defined as "the pattern of traits characterizing an individual person, trait here meaning any psychological characteristic of a person, including dispositions to perceive different situations similarly and to react consistently despite changing stimulus conditions, values, abilities, motives, defenses and aspects of temperament, identity, and personal style."[43] Personality is basically a set of inferences that we make about individuals on the basis of a set of concepts. The set of concepts depends upon which personality theory we use (for example, Freudian, Jungian, Maslovian). If we assume that political activity is the consequence not only of the individuals' environment but also of the psychological predispositions they bring to a situation, then knowledge of personality characteristics can help account for both the level and the type of such activity.

There are a number of approaches that exist to the study of personality, but the concepts of motive and control are basic to all of them. One theory of motivation that can be used to explain patterns of political participation is Abraham Maslow's needs theory. Maslow suggests a hierarchy of five basic types of needs that stimulate human behavior: physical; security; affection, love, and a sense of belongingness; self-esteem; and self-actualization.[44]

The first need of individuals, according to Maslow, is a physical need, for the basic necessities of life—food, water, and shelter. Governments in developed democracies are expected to provide citizens with these necessities, and many programs at the local, state, and national levels are designed to do so. Citizen demands, which may take the form of both conventional and unconventional political action, focus on such issues as the adequacy of government programs (the quantity and quality of food provided through the food stamp and surplus food programs) and the extent of the programs (the proportion of the homeless population served by shelter programs).

Maslow ranks security second in his list of human needs. The absence of security in the natural order of relationships among human beings was seen by the political philosopher Thomas Hobbes as the stimulus for the formation of governments.[45] One factor contributing to the perception of a government as legitimate is its ability to provide citizens with security of person and property. The failure of a government to provide food, water, shelter, and security to some portion of the citizenry can lead to strident demands for government programs.

Maslow lists the need to be loved and to belong to a group as third in his hierarchy. Research suggests that persons who are relatively isolated from society are more likely to support extremist political movements.[46] Psychological profiles of political assassins also suggest that they are frequently socially isolated individuals.[47] It can be hypothesized that those who participate in forms of political activity other than voting, such as working in political organizations, seek to satisfy a basic need for a sense of belongingness. Considerable research suggests that political party activists who initially became involved for other reasons, such as concern with a particular issue or support for a candidate, report an important long-term satisfaction to be the social rewards of their involvement, such as group camaraderie and the social contacts they have made.[48]

The fourth need suggested by Maslow is the need for self-esteem or self-respect. If social norms emphasize that individuals should participate politically in a certain way, such as voting, then individuals' self-respect requirements would act as a stimulus for voting participation. Some researchers have argued that members of political elites may be motivated by a need for self-esteem; although politics is only one avenue for obtaining heightened self-esteem, it is one that can bring considerable psychic rewards to the individual.[49] If the drive for equality can be considered a component of the search for self-esteem, that need can be viewed as a stimulus to participation in the women's movement and the civil rights movement in the United States and participation in various anticolonial movements in many parts of the world during the twentieth century.

The fifth need in Maslow's hierarchy is self-actualization—the need to develop personal capabilities and to pursue one's interests to the fullest extent possible. The Declaration of Independence held the pursuit of happiness to be an "unalienable right" and the absence of this right was a justification for the American colonies' revolt against Great Britain. Those who perceive the government to be unduly inhibiting of their pursuit of happiness may take action against government policies, leaders, and institutions through demonstrations and other forms of public protest, even—as in the colonists' revolt—armed rebellion. Some government programs and activities can be viewed as mechanisms for enabling individuals to achieve self-actualization; these might include loans and grants to students to finance their college education.

Advocates of participatory democracy argue that the act of participation itself contributes to individuals' self-actualization and that therefore participatory decision-making processes should be used to the greatest extent possible. In this view, not only will the quality of decisions be improved when more individuals are actively involved in the process, but the individuals participating become better persons and better citizens as a consequence of their participation. In other words, human growth and development—that is, self-actualization—can be achieved as a result of involvement in politics and in governmental decision making.[50] Individuals acquire knowledge and develop more positive attitudes about themselves, the community, and the larger society, thereby reducing their negative attitudes such as political cynicism and mistrust and increasing the legitimacy they accord the political system and its institutions, leaders, and policies.[51]

Other theories of personality emphasize different types of needs. David C. McClelland specifies three basic needs: affiliation, power, and achievement.[52] One application of this theory to the study of political recruitment suggests that individuals with different types of need patterns are best recruited by different methods and behave differently in public office.[53] (Of course, individuals must first learn that they can satisfy various needs through political participation.) Research indicates that individuals with high affiliation needs tend to be recruited to run for office by others, rather than being self-recruited. Behavior in public office also varies with patterns of needs. Individuals who have a high need for power tend to focus on organizational maintenance and control; those who have a high need for achievement tend to emphasize policy concerns rather than organizational concerns. Individuals who have a continuing commitment to work toward the achievement of certain policy goals are high in both need for achievement and need for power.[54]

Personality theory has also been used to develop typologies of the behavior of various political actors, such as executives and legislators. In one study of presidential types, a president's style, world view, and character suggest personality patterns, which, in combination with the prevailing distribution of political power, create expectations about how the president will behave, ultimately predicting how presidents will carry out their obligations of office.[55] In this theory, presidential character is defined in two dimensions: energy level (Lyndon B. Johnson and John F. Kennedy were described as "active" types; Calvin Coolidge was a "passive" type) and affect, or the president's attitude toward his activity (Theodore Roosevelt and Franklin D. Roosevelt had positive attitudes and enjoyed being president; Woodrow Wilson was negative toward his job, viewing it as a great burden). This analysis leads to a fourfold typology: active-positive (the Roosevelts, Harry S. Truman, Kennedy); active-negative (Herbert Hoover, Wilson, Lyndon Johnson, Nixon); passive-positive (William H. Taft, Warren G. Harding); and passive-negative (Coolidge). Personality theories may be useful in understanding both who can be recruited to perform various types of political roles and how various individuals can be expected to perform in them.[56]

A number of other studies have examined the psychological traits and behavior of political leaders, using a variety of psychological theories. Many have focused on one political leader, examining how his personality traits have influenced his leadership and the policies he pursued while in office.[57]

Psychological Influences on Unconventional Forms of Political Participation

During the tumultuous period from the early 1960s through the mid-1970s, public opinion in the United States became more supportive of the use of unconventional means of expressing dissatisfaction with public policies and demanding change. Approval of participation in protests permitted by local authorities increased slightly in this period, reaching a high of 19 percent in 1968, during the public protest against the Vietnam War; disapproval of protest participation dropped from 49 percent to 40 percent in the early 1970s. Approval of refusing to obey a law the individual considers to be unjust also increased between 1968 and 1974; it reached 16 percent in 1972. However, the proportion disapproving of disobedience under any conditions dropped from 61 percent in 1970 to 43 percent in 1974, with a concomitant increase in the proportion saying that whether individuals should refuse to obey a law they consider to be unjust would depend on the circumstances. Approval of stopping government activity by means of such actions as sit-ins, mass meetings, and other demonstrations increased slightly, to 8 percent by 1974; while the proportion disapproving of such activity dropped from 74 percent in 1970 to 30 percent in 1974.[58]

A study of citizens in five countries conducted in 1974 examined their approval of ten types of unconventional political activity. In the United States, a majority approved of signing petitions, engaging in lawful demonstrations, and participating in boycotts, but only a minority approved of each of the other seven forms of behavior; personal violence, the least favored form, received the approval of only 2 percent of those surveyed. Petition signing was the only form that a majority (58 percent) reported having engaged in themselves; 20 percent indicated that they would be willing to sign petitions. Only 11 percent reported having engaged in lawful demonstrations, and 28 percent said that they would engage in them under some conditions. Participation in boycotts was reported by 15 percent, and 20 percent responded that they would participate in boycotts in certain circumstances. In the other four countries a majority approved only of signing petitions and lawful demonstrations but fewer respondents had actually engaged in these activities than had done so in the United States.[59]

Of those surveyed in the United States, 80 percent thought that petitions were effective in obtaining political change, and two-thirds credited lawful demonstrations and boycotts with effectiveness. No other form of unconventional behavior was assessed as being effective by as much as 40 percent of the sample; 11 percent evaluated personal violence as being either very effective or somewhat effective.[60] Support for unconventional forms of political action has increased substantially in both the United States and several West European nations since 1970.[61] Some forms of protest activity are more likely to be engaged in by younger citizens and by those with lower levels of education.[62]

Some beliefs, attitudes, and values contribute to participation in unconventional political behavior.[63] Participation is conditioned by an individual's beliefs about peer and community approval or disapproval of a certain form of political activity, positive or negative attitudes toward it, and assessments of the extent to which it is effective in achieving the individual's desired ends.[64] Certain forms of political protest are also more likely to be supported by individuals who place greater emphasis on nonmaterialistic values and who tend to think about politics in ideological terms rather than in terms of the nature of the times or political personalities.[65]

Alienation and Conformism

One explanation that has been offered for nonparticipation in American politics is that those who do not participate are "alienated" from the political system. As an objective condition, alienation is the absence of social norms as perceived by observers of a society; as a subjective condition, it is a feeling that a discrepancy exists between expectations and reality on the part of an individual or group of individuals.[66] Ada W. Finifter has described four ways in which political alienation may be expressed: (1) *political powerlessness,* the feeling of inability to affect the actions of the government—in effect, a low sense of internal and external political efficacy; (2) *political meaninglessness,* the view that political events are unpredictable and unpatterned; (3) *normlessness,* the perception that societal norms are not being observed and that the traditional social and political order has broken down; and (4) *political isolation,* the belief that no legitimate norms governing the political system exist.[67]

In a study of alienation as a subjective condition among younger citizens in the United States, Kenneth Keniston describes it as having four dimensions:

1. *Focus*—From what is the individual alienated?
2. *Replacement*—What replaces the previous relationship?
3. *Mode*—How is the alienation manifested?
4. *Agent*—What is the agent of alienation?[68]

These four dimensions can be variously combined, resulting in a large number of types of alienation.[69] In Keniston's analysis, alienation is contrasted with conformism. Whereas the alienated person rejects behavioral norms and cultural values, the conformist accepts them. Keniston emphasizes two loci of alienation—behavioral norms and cultural values. Behavioral norms are defined as "the common social expectations about the kind of behavior that is proper, appropriate, and legal in any society"; cultural values are "general conceptions of the desirable."[70] Such values might include achievement, progress, and peace. Keniston also emphasizes two modes of expression: the alloplastic mode is an attempt to change the world; the autoplastic mode is an attempt to change oneself. Alienation may be expressed through such diverse forms of behavior as terrorism, sedition, agitation, civil disobedience, social criticism, self-isolation, and delinquency or crime. Those who are alienated may withdraw, or they may become politically active, engaging in many different types of political activity. Vigilantism, patriotic acts, ritualism, and compliance can be manifestations of conformism.

This approach implies that a tendency toward alienation or conformism, in combination with other personality variables, influences the individual's political behavior. David C. Schwartz argues further that these tendencies interact with situational variables, such as media content, group orientations, and other aspects of the individual's political environment, to produce patterns of political behavior.[71] Keniston's approach accounts for the wide range of behaviors that can result from the interaction of attitudes, environmental stimuli, and environmental constraints.

Summary

Several psychological characteristics can affect who participates in politics and the extent to which they participate. Individuals vary in both the relative importance of different motives and the extent to which they seek to satisfy different motives through political activity. A number of theories of personality, with different conceptualizations of human motivation, have been developed by psychologists and can be used in explaining patterns of political activity.

Psychological involvement in politics (also called political engagement) influences who participates in politics and the forms and extent of that participation. It may include a sense of personal political effectiveness, a perceived obligation to participate, an interest in politics and in the current political campaign, and identification with a political party. The higher the level of citizens' psychological involvement, the greater the number and variety of political activities in which they can be expected to engage. Since the early 1950s, some components of psychological involvement (such as identification with a political party) have declined among American citizens, resulting in a decrease in political participation of the conventional type. The percentage of citizens who believe that government is attentive and responsive to citizen preferences has declined; the percentage expressing cynicism has increased. Some research suggests that value patterns influence types of political participation; those who have nonmaterialistic values tend to engage in its unconventional forms.

Parents, peers, the educational system, the mass media, and government officials all contribute to the formation of citizens' beliefs about and attitudes toward the political system. The learning of politically relevant attitudes, beliefs, values, and behaviors can occur through both direct and indirect processes of political socialization.

Notes

1. M. Margaret Conway and Frank B. Feigert, *Political Analysis,* 2d ed. (Boston: Allyn and Bacon, 1976), 130.
2. Warren E. Miller and J. Merrill Shanks, "Policy Direction and Presidential Leadership: Alternative Interpretations of the 1980 Presidential Election," *British Journal of Political Science* 12 (1982): 299–356.
3. Milton Rokeach, *The Nature of Human Values* (New York: Free Press, 1973), 5–11.
4. Ronald Inglehart, *The Silent Revolution* (Princeton: Princeton University Press, 1977), chap. 1.
5. See, for example, Richard A. Brody, "The Puzzle of Political Participation," in *The New American Political System,* ed. Anthony King (Washington, D.C.: American Enterprise Institute, 1978), 287–324.
6. Lee Sigelman et al., "Voting and Non-voting: A Multi-election Perspective," *American Journal of Political Science* 29 (November 1985): 749–765.
7. American National Election Studies Cumulative File, 1948–1996, Codebook. See Appendix for party identification variable.
8. Warren E. Miller and J. Merrill Shanks, *The New American Voter* (Cambridge: Harvard University Press, 1996), 96, Table 5.1. The generational categorization is in terms of the first presidential election in which individuals were eligible to vote.
9. Calculated from data in the American National Election Studies Cumulative File, 1948–1996.
10. Miller and Shanks, *New American Voter,* 96, Table 5.1.
11. Calculated from data in the American National Election Studies Cumulative File, 1948–1996, and the 1998 American National Election Study.
12. Ibid.
13. Anthony Downs, *An Economic Theory of Democracy* (New York: Harper and Row, 1957), chaps. 3 and 14; and Norman Frohlich and Joe A. Oppenheimer, *Modern Political Economy* (Englewood Cliffs, N.J.: Prentice-Hall, 1978), chap. 5.
14. Bureau of the Census, *Statistical Abstract of the United States 1998* (Washington, D.C.: Government Printing Office, 1998).
15. Calculated from data in the American National Election Studies Cumulative File, 1948–1996. See Appendix for variable used.
16. Samuel P. Huntington, *American Politics: The Promise of Disharmony* (Cambridge: Belknap Press, Harvard University Press, 1981).
17. Calculated from data in the American National Election Studies Cumulative File, 1948–1996, and the 1998 American National Election Study.
18. Calculated from data in the American National Election Studies Cumulative File, 1948–1996.
19. Paul R. Abramson, *Political Attitudes in America* (San Francisco: Freeman, 1983), chap. 16; data in American National Election Studies Cumulative File, 1948–1996, and the 1998 American National Election Study.
20. Calculated from data in the American National Election Studies Cumulative File, 1948–1996, and the 1998 American National Election Study. Each of the variables is an index created from two items. See the Appendix.
21. Ibid.
22. Calculated from data in the American National Election Studies Cumulative File, 1948–1996.

23. Calculated from data in the American National Election Studies Cumulative File, 1948–1996, and the 1998 American National Election Study.
24. Calculated from data in the American National Election Studies Cumulative File, 1948–1996.
25. Wendy M. Rahn and John E.Transue, "Social Trust and Value Change: The Decline of Social Capital in American Youth, 1976–1995," *Political Psychology* 19 (1998): 545–565. For research on materialist values versus nonmaterialist values and their effects on political behavior, see Ronald Inglehart, "Political Action: The Impact of Values, Cognitive Level, and Social Background," in *Political Action,* ed. Samuel H. Barnes and Max Kaase (Beverly Hills, Calif.: Sage, 1979), 370–377.
26. For a discussion of the concept of political action repertory, see Max Kaase and Alan Marsh, "Political Action: A Theoretical Perspective," in Barnes and Kaase, *Political Action,* 27–56.
27. See, for example, Richard E. Dawson, Kenneth Prewitt, and Karen S. Dawson, *Political Socialization* (New York: Praeger, 1973), chap. 4. For evidence of the important but limited effects of the family as an agent of political socialization, see M. Kent Jennings and Richard G. Niemi, *The Political Character of Adolescence* (Princeton: Princeton University Press, 1974); and Jennings and Niemi, *Generations and Politics: A Panel Study of Young Adults and Their Parents* (Princeton: Princeton University Press, 1981), chap. 4.
28. M. Margaret Conway et al., "The News Media in Children's Political Socialization," *Public Opinion Quarterly* 45 (1981): 164–178; and M. Margaret Conway, David Ahern, and Mikel L. Wyckoff, "The Mass Media and Changes in Adolescents' Political Knowledge during an Election Cycle," *Political Behavior* 3 (1981): 69–80.
29. C. Anthony Broh, "Horse Race Journalism: Reporting the Polls in the 1976 Campaign," *Public Opinion Quarterly* 44 (1980): 514–529; Thomas E. Patterson, *The Mass Media Election* (New York: Praeger, 1980), chaps. 3 and 11; Thomas E. Patterson, *Out of Order* (New York: Vintage, 1993), and Doris A. Graber, *Mass Media and American Politics* (Washington, D.C.: CQ Press, 1980), 178–180. The media may also be biased in their coverage of candidates based not only on their perceived electability but on their social characteristics. See C. Anthony Broh, *A Horse of a Different Color: Television's Treatment of Jesse Jackson's 1984 Presidential Campaign* (Washington, D.C.: Joint Center for Political Studies, 1987).
30. James S. Coleman, "Social Capital in the Creation of Human Capital," *American Journal of Sociology* 94 (1988): S95–S120. Robert D. Putnam, in *Making Democracy Work* (Princeton: Princeton University Press, 1993), defines social capital as "features of social organization, such as trust, norms, and networks, that can improve the efficiency of society by facilitating coordinated actions" (p. 167).
31. Robert D. Putnam, "Bowling Alone: America's Declining Social Capital," *Journal of Democracy* 6 (1995): 65–78; Robert D. Putnam, "Tuning In, Tuning Out: The Strange Disappearance of Social Capital in America," *PS: Political Science & Politics* 28 (1995): 664–683.
32. See, for example, John Brehm and Wendy M. Rahn, "Individual-Level Evidence for the Causes and Consequences of Social Capital," *American Journal of Political Science* 41 (1997): 999–1023; Pippa Norris, "Does Television Erode Social Capital? A Reply to Putnam," *PS: Political Science & Politics* 29 (1996): 474–480; Dhavan V. Shah, "Civic Engagement, Interpersonal Trust, and Television Use: An Individual-Level Assessment of Social Capital," *Political Psychology* 19 (1998): 469–496; Eric M. Uslaner, "Social Capital, Television, and the 'Mean World': Trust, Optimism, and Civic Participation," *Political Psychology* 19 (1998): 441–467; and Michael Schudson et al., "Controversy," *American Prospect* 25 (1996): 17–28.
33. Richard G. Niemi and Jane Junn, *Civic Education* (New Haven: Yale University Press, 1998).

34. Alfonso J. Damico, Sandra Bowman Damico, and M. Margaret Conway, "The Democratic Education of Women: High School and Beyond," *Women and Politics* 19 (1998): 1–31; M. Margaret Conway, Sandra Bowman Damico, and Alfonso J. Damico, "Democratic Socialization in the Schools," in *Democratic Education in Western Developed Societies,* ed. Russell Farnen (New York: St. Martin's, 1996); Lee Ehrman, "The American School in the Political Socialization Process," *Review of Educational Research* 50 (1980): 99–119; Cees Klassen, "The Latent Initiation: Sources of Unintentional Political Socialization in the Schools," *Politics and the Individual* 2 (1992): 41–65.

35. Martin Levin, "Social Climate and Political Socialization," *Public Opinion Quarterly* 35 (1961): 596–606.

36. Jennings and Niemi, *Generations and Politics.*

37. Steven E. Finkel, "Reciprocal Effects of Participation and Political Efficacy: A Panel Analysis," *American Journal of Political Science* 29 (November 1985): 891–913.

38. M. Kent Jennings, "Residues of a Movement: The Aging of the American Protest Generation," *American Political Science Review* 81 (June 1987): 367–382.

39. Dawson, Prewitt, and Dawson, *Political Socialization,* 99–100.

40. Dean Jaros, Herbert Hirsch, and Frederic J. Fleron Jr., "The Malevolent Leader: Political Socialization in an American Subculture," *American Political Science Review* 67 (1968): 564–575.

41. Dawson, Prewitt, and Dawson, *Political Socialization,* 99–105.

42. Ibid., 105–112.

43. Benjamin B. Woman, ed., *Dictionary of Behavioral Science,* 2d ed. (San Diego: Academic Press, 1989), 249.

44. See two works by Abraham Maslow, "A Theory of Human Motivation," *Psychological Review* 50 (1943): 370–396; and *Motivation and Personality* (New York: Harper and Row, 1954). For applications of Maslow's theory to political behavior, see Jeanne N. Knutson, *The Human Basis of the Polity* (Chicago: Aldine-Atherton, 1972); and Stanley Renshon, *Psychological Needs and Political Behavior* (New York: Free Press, 1974).

45. Thomas Hobbes, *Leviathan,* ed. Michael Oakeshott (Oxford: Basil Blackwell, 1946).

46. See, for example, Seymour Martin Lipset, *Political Man: The Social Bases of Politics* (Baltimore: Johns Hopkins University Press, 1981), 178–79.

47. Lawrence Z. Freedman, "Psychopathology of Assassination," in *Assassinations and the Political Order,* ed. William M. Crotty (New York: Harper and Row, 1971), 143–160.

48. See, for example, M. Margaret Conway and Frank B. Feigert, "Motivation, Incentive Systems, and the Political Party Organization," *American Political Science Review* 62 (1968): 1169–1183.

49. See the classic argument in Harold D. Lasswell, *Politics: Who Gets What, When, and How* (New York: Meridian, 1958), 13.

50. See Carole Pateman, *Participation and Democratic Theory* (Cambridge: Cambridge University Press, 1970); and Terrence C. Cook and Patrick Morgan, "An Introduction to Participatory Democracy," in *Participatory Democracy,* ed. Terrence C. Cook and Patrick Morgan (San Francisco: Canfield, 1971), 40.

51. The same logic can be extended to participation in decision making in the workplace. In some countries, such as Germany and Yugoslavia, this kind of participation is mandated by law. The expected result is greater job satisfaction and higher productivity.

52. David C. McClelland, *The Achieving Society* (New York: Free Press, 1961).

53. Rufus Browning, "The Interaction of Personality and Political System in Decisions to Run for Office: Some Data and a Simulation Technique," *Journal of Social Issues* 24 (1968): 93–109.

54. Ibid.; and James David Barber, *The Lawmakers* (New Haven: Yale University Press, 1965).

55. James David Barber, *Presidential Character* (Englewood Cliffs, N.J.: Prentice-Hall, 1972), 11.

56. For criticisms of Barber's theory, see Alexander L. George, "Assessing Presidential Character," *World Politics* 26 (1974): 234–282; Jeanne Knutson, "Personality in the Study of Politics," in *Handbook of Political Psychology,* ed. Jeanne N. Knutson (San Francisco: Jossey-Bass, 1973), 28–56; and James H. Qualls, "Barber's Typological Analysis of Political Leaders," *American Political Science Review* 71 (1977): 182–211. For Barber's reply to Qualls's criticisms, see "Comment: Qualls's Nonsensical Analysis of Nonexistent Works," *American Political Science Review* 71 (1977): 212–225.

57. See, for example, Alexander L. George, *Presidential Decisionmaking in Foreign Policy: The Effective Use of Information and Advice* (Boulder, Colo.: Westview Press, 1980); Betty Glad, "Black and White Thinking: Ronald Reagan's Approach to Foreign Policy," *Political Psychology* 4: (1983): 33–76. Margaret G. Herman, "Explaining Foreign Policy Using Personal Characteristics of Political Leaders," *International Studies Quarterly* 24 (1980): 7–46; and Paul A. Kowert, "Where Does the Buck Stop? Assessing the Impact of Presidential Personality," *Political Psychology* 17 (1996): 421–452.

58. Calculations based on data in the American National Election Studies Cumulative File, 1948–1996 (variables 601, 602, and 603).

59. Samuel Evans and Kai Hildebrandt, "Technical Appendix," in Barnes and Kaase, *Political Action,* 545, Table TA.2; and 548–549, Table TA.3.

60. Ibid., 552, Table TA.4.

61. Max Kaase and Alan Marsh, "Political Action Repertory: Change over Time and a New Typology," chap. 5 in Barnes and Kaase, *Political Action.*

62. Max Kaase and Alan Marsh, "Distribution of Political Action," in Barnes and Kaase, *Political Action,* Table 6.3.

63. Clark McPhail, "Civil Disorder Participation: A Critical Examination of Recent Research," *American Sociological Review* 36 (1971): 1058–1073.

64. Martin Fishbein, "Attitudes and the Prediction of Behavior," in *Attitude Theory and Measurement,* ed. Martin Fishbein (New York: Wiley, 1967), 477–492; and Alan Marsh and Max Kaase, "Measuring Political Action," in Barnes and Kaase, *Political Action,* 61–65.

65. Ronald Inglehart, "Value Priorities and Socioeconomic Change," in Barnes and Kaase, *Political Action,* 374, Fig. 12.8.

66. For more extensive discussions of the concept of alienation, see Ada W. Finifter, ed., *Alienation and the Social System* (New York: Wiley, 1972); and David C. Schwartz, *Political Alienation and Political Behavior* (Chicago: Aldine, 1973).

67. Ada W. Finifter, "Dimensions of Political Alienation," *American Political Science Review* 64 (1970): 390–391. A sense of political powerlessness would imply that the individual lacks a sense of control over the political sphere. One psychological need suggested as affecting political participation is the need for a sense of mastery or control, which varies among individuals in both level and scope. A sense of personal control can be defined as a belief in the individual's ability to control his or her own life. For a discussion of how the need for personal control affects political behavior, see Renshon, *Psychological Needs.*

68. Kenneth Keniston, *The Uncommitted: Alienated Youth in American Society* (New York: Harcourt, Brace and World, 1965), 453–454. Keniston defines alienation as "the explicit rejection, 'freely' chosen by the individual, of what he perceives as the dominant values or norms of his society" (455).

69. For a discussion of several types of alienation, see ibid., 455–465. See also Finifter, "Dimensions of Political Alienation," 389–410.

70. Keniston, *Uncommitted,* 466.

71. Schwartz, *Political Alienation,* esp. chap. 4.

Chapter 4

The Political Environment and Political Participation

The political environment can stimulate or inhibit citizen partici-pation in elections and in other political activities. The political context of elections includes the electoral system, with its various requirements for voter eligibility, and the election administration rules of a state or community, which govern voter registration proce-dures, the form of the ballot, and the conduct of the balloting on elec-tion day. The candidates and issues that are at the center of political conflict in a certain political era (such as the Great Depression and the New Deal) can also have an important impact on electoral and campaign participation,[1] as does the historical division of contending political, social, and economic forces in the community, state, and nation.[2]

Another aspect of the political environment is the development of direct-mail techniques of fund raising and changes in federal cam-paign finance laws, which have induced a larger proportion of citizens to give money for the support of political parties, candidates, and causes.[3] Republican Party organizations have been particularly suc-cessful in using direct-mail solicitations to obtain funds. Some of these funds are used to promote increased political participation in cam-paign activities, as well as to increase voter turnout. Political action committees, which have increased greatly in number since the mid-1970s, are another vehicle for channeling increased contributions by donors to political parties, candidates, and causes.[4]

A number of organizations of various types seek to promote and facilitate political participation. During the 1990s, for example, many organizations and coalitions of organizations conducted voter regis-tration and voter turnout drives.[5] The significance of organizations as stimuli to political action was even noted by Tocqueville in the early days of the republic.[6] Research comparing developed nations has demonstrated the importance of organizational membership and activity in increasing rates of political participation, particularly among low-income persons with a limited education. This research also suggests that social and political organizations may play a more important role in stimulating political activity in other advanced democracies than they do in the United States.[7] Even if not deliberately attempting to mobilize their members politically, organizations expose them to politically relevant stimuli and provide opportunities for political activity. Furthermore, organizations may contribute to the development of skills that facilitate participation in political activity.[8]

In this chapter we analyze the impact of several aspects of the political environment on political participation in the United States. They include changes in patterns of political conflict and political coalitions, reflected by the electoral party system; political movements; the mass media's presentation of politically relevant material; and organizational membership and activities. We also examine the impact of factors specific to particular elections, such as the closeness of the election and the conduct of the campaign.

An electoral party system differs from a party system, which can have different meanings. One definition is based on the number of political parties that control or contest for control of the government. Authoritarian systems usually have only one dominant party, such as the Communist Party, which controlled the former Soviet Union. The United States throughout most of its history has had only two major political parties, along with several minor parties. Many countries in western Europe have multiparty systems, in which three or more parties contest elections and contend to form governing coalitions. A party system can also be defined in terms of the form of organization used by the major political parties in the system (for example, Communist Party cell, Fascist militia, cadre parties' caucus).[9]

Electoral Party Systems

Political parties serve as vehicles for structuring conflict in society—conflict over both the goals to be achieved through public policy and the means used to achieve them. During any one era in a nation's political history, one set of issues tends to be the focus of conflict, and remains so until the underlying problems are resolved or alleviated, when it is replaced by another set. One perspective on American politics is that in each era there is an electoral party system, which differs from the others in terms of the issues that divide the contending political parties, the composition of the coalitions that form the parties' support base, and the "style" of politics prevailing at the time—which is defined by the political leaders, the sources of their power, and the bases for their decisions. Thus, an electoral party system "encompasses an historical era in which the political parties differ in several ways from those in the previous electoral party system and in the succeeding one."[10]

Critical Realignment

In the past, a new electoral party system was created—that is, there was a critical party realignment—as a result of either a converting election or a realigning election. In a *converting election,* the party that previously had a majority of support among the electorate wins, but the issues and coalitions are changed, and remain unchanged throughout the period of that party's dominance. In a *realigning election,* not only are the issues and coalitions changed, but a different party wins the support of a majority of the electorate and is able to retain it for a number of years. The average period of dominance for each majority party has been approximately three or four decades.[11] One party realignment, for example, occurred during the late 1920s and early 1930s and signaled the end of seventy years of Republican Party dominance (through two electoral party systems).

Six conditions have been suggested as bearing upon a critical party realignment—that is, one that occurs as a consequence of a converting election or a realigning election: (1) the breadth and depth of public concern with a major, critical problem; (2) the likelihood that the proposed remedies for the problem will stimulate substantial public opposition; (3) the motivation and ability of the party leaders to exploit the divisive issues; (4) the extent of existing divisions between the parties representing contending groups in society; (5) the strength of citizens' allegiances to the existing political parties; and (6) the ability of the party that won the election to govern effectively (as perceived by its supporters) after it takes control of the government.[12] In sum, a critical realignment can be expected to occur, creating a new electoral party system, if an issue arises that substantially affects a large number of people, if that issue divides the electorate differently than does the existing issue basis of societal conflict, and if the proposed solutions to the problem provoke strong resistance from a substantial number of citizens. If leaders exist who are skilled at exploiting the grievance and emphasizing its effects in their attempt to resolve the political conflict, and if there exists a large pool of weak party identifiers and political independents available to be attracted to a different party, then the potential for realignment is very great. Realignment will occur, however, only if the political leaders swept into power as a result of the new pattern of conflict are subsequently perceived by their supporters to be governing successfully.

Secular Realignment

Realignment can also occur in a gradual process, called *secular realignment*. In this case, one election is not the focal point for a sudden and intensely felt change concerning the issue basis of political conflict. Rather, realignment occurs over a period of years, as a result of changes in the distribution of public opinion on one or more issues.

Secular realignment may occur as a consequence of social changes that alter either the salience or the distribution of public opinion on a particular issue. It may also result from social changes that affect social groups. Changes of this type that have occurred since the realignment of the 1930s include the migration of farm workers to urban areas to obtain industrial jobs, the population shift from one region of the United States to another (for example, to the sunbelt areas), and the entry of a majority of adult women into the paid work force. Some scholars argue that a secular realignment also occurred in the United States during the 1970s and 1980s, when the South and intermountain West became more Republican, and the Northeast became more Democratic.[13]

Realignment and Political Participation

The change in patterns of voting support that results from a realignment may involve at least three different processes of social change. Realignment can be a result of increased levels of political participation, traceable to heightened citizen concern with one issue and more intense political and societal group conflict, as well as to the mobilization of nonvoters or of newly eligible voters who have not previously voted or participated in elections in other ways.[14] If a distinction is made between core voters (who vote regularly), marginal voters (who vote occasionally), and nonvoters (who almost never vote), then realignment can be said to occur because of the entry into the electorate of large numbers of previously marginal voters and nonvoters. Over time, these two types of voters give their support disproportionately to one of the two parties, thus changing the political balance of power between the parties. A variation of this interpretation is that a new party replaces one of the existing parties, as occurred during the 1850s with the rise to power of the Republican Party.[15]

Second, realignment comes about as a result of the conversion of a substantial number of core voters, from regular support for one party to regular support for the other. Although a reverse flow of support may also take place, it is not enough to maintain the formerly dominant party in power.[16]

Third, realignment is a consequence of the replacement of older members of the electorate by younger members who have different interests and experiences. For example, one-half of the eligible voters age thirty-four and younger in 1964 were Democratic Party identifiers, but four years later, as discontent with the protracted war in Vietnam increased, particularly among these younger voters, their support for the Democratic Party (which at that time controlled both houses of Congress and the White House) decreased. Although many older members of the electorate converted from Democrat to Republican during the 1980s, and there was some movement of Independents to the Republican Party, a significant proportion of the voters who identified themselves as Republicans were age thirty and younger.[17] By 1996, however, fewer younger citizens than older citizens identified with the Republican Party. In 1998, the trend reversed; the two age groups most likely to be Republican identifiers were those age twenty-four and younger and those age seventy-five and older.[18]

Under the first electoral party system, which lasted from the 1790s to 1828, voter eligibility requirements were relaxed substantially. Although voting participation increased during this period, there appears to have been a lag between eligibility to vote and exercise of the franchise. However, under the second electoral party system (1828–

1860), the political conflicts of the time did generate increased voter turnout.[19]

The conflicts that led to one of the most traumatic events in American history—the Civil War—stimulated the realignment that created the third electoral party system (1860–1896). The intensity of issue concerns and the citizens' strong emotional commitment to the contending parties resulted in levels of political mobilization that have not since been matched in the United States. In rural areas, party commitment and political participation were a consequence of the low degree of economic interdependence, the relative isolation of many small-town communities, social pressures for political conformity, and the effectiveness of familial political socialization.[20] In many urban areas, political machines were very effective in mobilizing support. Indeed, some scholars have suggested that the apparently high voter turnout rates found in many cities in that electoral era might have been due in part to extensive ballot-box stuffing.[21]

With the beginning of the fourth electoral party system in 1896, political participation in the United States began to decrease. Although voter turnout was 5 percent higher in 1896 than in 1892, turnout in subsequent elections declined significantly.[22] The political alignment of the fourth electoral party system, which lasted until 1932, produced a number of one-party states; the South was Democratic and many states in the North were Republican. One interpretation of this alignment is that both parties were captured by business and wealthy agrarian interests, but the interests of working-class citizens were not represented by either party, and as a consequence, political participation declined among the working class.[23] Also contributing to the low rates of political participation in the South was the systematic denial of the political rights of black citizens.[24]

A detailed analysis of the election of 1896 and subsequent elections under the fourth electoral party system does suggest that the political realignment and decline in political participation that occurred during this period were the result of (1) the entry of two groups into the electorate—women newly enfranchised by the Nineteenth Amendment to the Constitution (in those states where women did not already have the right to vote) and large numbers of immigrants—and (2) the withdrawal of working-class voters. It was not caused by the transfer of loyalties of one party's supporters to the opposition party.[25] The argument is that, since political participation is a habit acquired over time, participation was low because of the inadequate political socialization of women and immigrants. However, turnout had begun to decline from the high levels of the nineteenth century even before the women's suffrage amendment was passed (1920) and in areas where new immigrants rarely settled.[26]

The electoral demobilization that occurred under the fourth electoral party system was moderated by a political realignment and increase in voter turnout that began at the end of the 1920s and extended through the New Deal in the 1930s, marking the beginning of the fifth electoral party system. The realignment may have been generated in large part by the mobilization of nonvoters, either those who were newly eligible or those who had previously been eligible but had not voted. (One study suggests that half of those who became eligible to vote during the 1920s did not vote before the election of 1932.)[27] Another hypothesis is that the New Deal realignment occurred primarily as a result of the decision of large numbers of Republican Party supporters to join the Democratic Party.[28] In any case, voter turnout increased until 1960, then began to decline again.[29]

Some scholars argue that a sixth electoral party system began during the 1980s. They maintain that this change occurred not as a consequence of a critical election, such as triggered the creation of the previous electoral party systems, but rather because of secular realignment, which was a result of all three processes previously discussed—the decision of some Democrats to join the Republican Party, mobilization of some Independents to join the Republicans, and the replacement of older, Democratic cohorts by a cohort of citizens age thirty and younger, who were more likely to identify with the Republican Party.[30] If such a realignment in fact occurred, one would expect voter turnout rates to be higher. But turnout rates did not increase during the 1980s (see Table 1-1). Of course, younger citizens are less likely to vote than those who are older; turnout is substantially lower among members of the post-New Deal generation than among those of the pre-New Deal generation. Therefore, we should not expect an increase in turnout to occur as a result of realignment through generational replacement. Furthermore, although turnout was higher in 1992, it declined substantially in both 1996 and 1998. Thus, the suggested realignment may in fact have occurred, even without a resulting increase in voter turnout.[31]

The lines of conflict have stimulated or discouraged political participation by some segments of the electorate throughout American history. Thus, the particular issues at the center of political conflict and the variations in responsiveness to those issues by different groups in society affect both the patterns of political support and the levels of political mobilization. Political mobilization and demobilization, in turn, play an important role in structuring electoral party systems.

Political Movements

A functioning party system in a democracy requires some degree of consensus on basic values, such as freedom and equality of opportunity. Conflict occurs primarily over the degree of emphasis accorded various material values in the society, such as income level and social status—not over the basic values. If a society has a party system that does not adequately reflect all points of view, however, those who do not perceive their interests to be represented may decide that they have no effective means of participating and will simply not engage in any political activities. Alternatively, they may engage in political activities outside the party system.

One form of such activity is the political movement. A political movement arises when citizens who feel that the government is not responsive to their problems join together to express their concerns and needs. At first, these individuals may have perceived the problem as personal, but they subsequently realized that others had similar experiences and faced a similar problem. Slogans and logos representing a diagnosis of the problem's causes and prescriptions for its solutions evolve and are adopted by the disaffected citizens, who form organizations to work toward effecting these solutions. Their methods may include protest activities—either peaceful or violent—and more conventional forms of political activity.[32]

In the late 1970s, for example, some farmers perceived that their interests were not being adequately represented by either political party or by already existing interest groups. A group of these disgruntled farmers, meeting over coffee in a southern Colorado restaurant, decided to form what became known as the American Agricultural Movement. The farmers staged an "agricultural strike" that received national media coverage, and within a few weeks this national organization claimed to have more than forty state chapters and eleven hundred local chapters. Their protests against the farm policies of the Carter administration were expressed in such unconventional ways as a "tractorcade" to the nation's capital on January 18, 1978.[33] A second tractorcade in 1979 resulted in violent confrontations with the police and substantial property damage. But as a consequence of the organization's lobbying efforts, federal agricultural policies were modified.

Political movements may mobilize individuals who have not previously been active. They often draw individuals to forms of participation they have not engaged in before, such as attending rallies or marching in protest demonstrations. For example, the civil rights movement in the South during the 1950s and 1960s stimulated political activity among many black citizens who had been denied the right to vote, as well as other civil rights, because of discriminatory laws and election administration procedures, but who had not yet spoken out. Their activity was primarily in the form of peaceful protests. In March 1965, however, many of Alabama's black citizens marched from Selma to Montgomery to demand voting rights and were attacked by local and state police using nightsticks, cattle prods, and police dogs. Largely as a result of coverage of that violent confrontation on national television, Congress enacted the Voting Rights Act of 1965, which has been very effective in ensuring suffrage for all qualified citizens. Since its passage, supporters of the civil rights movement have encouraged the forms of activity associated with campaigns for elective office.

Many other political movements have arisen since the early 1960s. Those opposed to U.S. involvement in the Vietnam War frequently staged peaceful protest demonstrations, but they were also responsible for a few acts of violence aimed at symbols of economic and political authority or at institutions perceived as engaging in activities supportive of the war. More recently, movements that have been active nationally have focused on such issues as equal political and economic rights for women, abortion policy, a freeze on the production of nuclear weapons, gun control, the use of nuclear power for the production of electricity, adherence to traditional values, and protection of the environment and of endangered species. Proposed policy decisions have generated political movements in many communities. Particularly controversial are decisions related to industrial land use or road building that would affect already existing communities and subdivisions.

If a movement is successful in having its demands fulfilled, it may eventually die. Frequently, however, successful movements evolve into traditional interest groups, which engage in a wide range of lobbying and related activities and encourage their members to become involved in conventional politics. A new political party may even emerge from a political movement. The Republican Party, for example, originated with the antislavery movement. Several minor parties in American history also began as political movements.[34]

Some supporters of a political movement view acts of violence as merely symbolic, a forceful means of expressing a point of view in order to focus public attention. However, some others may believe that violent forms of political action are necessary for the attainment of a desired outcome. During the Vietnam War, a splinter group that broke off from the antiwar movement and came to be known as the Weathermen vandalized property, bombed government buildings, and attacked such symbols of the war as draft board offices.[35]

The anti-abortion movement is an example of a movement that has encouraged conventional forms of political activity. It has raised funds for political action committees that have run advertising campaigns calling for the electoral defeat of congressional incumbents who have not supported anti-abortion legislation, and it has conducted voter registration drives and voter mobilization campaigns. In 1978, the Iowa Pro-Life Action Council targeted the state's Democratic senator, Dick Clark, for defeat. The group distributed 300,000 leaflets urging a vote against him, placing most of them on the windshields of cars in church parking lots on the Sunday before the November election. Clark lost by a margin of about 3 percent of the total vote. A postelection poll conducted by his campaign pollster found that about 4 percent of Iowa's voters had been persuaded to change their vote by the leaflets,[36] although it does not necessarily follow that the activities of the Pro-Life Council were decisive in the election outcome. In 1980, the council adopted another tactic. Volunteers contacted registered voters to identify those holding anti-abortion views who were willing to cast a vote solely on the basis of a candidate's stand on the abortion issue. These potential single-issue voters were then asked to serve as volunteers in the movement's campaign against

Iowa's Senior senator (also a Democrat), John C. Culver. They distributed campaign literature and conducted a voter mobilization
drive. Culver, too, lost his bid for reelection, again by a margin of
about 3 percent. Efforts of this kind undoubtedly increased political
participation among those who supported the anti-abortion group's
position.[37]

Policy Agendas and Political Campaigns

Mobilization efforts to increase political participation can utilize
various tactics. Party organizations, candidates, and interest groups
seek to identify potential supporters, make sure they are registered to
vote, and get them to the polls on election day. The campaigns may
rely on phone banks, face-to-face contacts at shopping centers, and
door-to-door solicitations. In 1984, the Republican National Committee, using demographic data from the census and other data on
past voting patterns, identified precincts that contained large numbers
of unregistered voters who would be likely to vote Republican. Volunteers canvassed each of these precincts, either by making phone
calls or by going from house to house, and provided voter registration
information and registration forms to those who indicated they supported President Reagan's reelection and were interested in registering
to vote. The Republicans' goal was to register 2 million additional
Republican voters by November 1984. The goal was exceeded.[38]

Several studies indicate that even though these electoral mobilization activities may increase voter turnout by only 5 to 10 percent,
they can have a significant impact on both electoral participation and
choice of candidate.[39] Citizens who register in a group-based registration drive may be less likely to vote than those whose registration is
self-motivated, however.[40] The effectiveness of voter registration drives
is increased the closer to the election date that they are held.[41] The effect appears to be greater in primary elections than in general elections. The effectiveness of voter mobilization efforts also varies with
other circumstances of the election contest. For example, the proportion of registered voters among black residents of Chicago increased
substantially during the mayoralty campaign in 1983, in part because
there was a black candidate, Harold Washington, and because of the
mobilization activities of the candidates and organizations, as well

as coverage by the mass media.[42] Political participation has also increased in other cities as a consequence of the candidacy of minority or ethnic group members.[43] The inclusion of minority group candidates' names on the ballot for state offices can also stimulate voter registration. Contributing to the significant increase in Latino voter registration that occurred in California between 1996 and 1998 was the fact that Cruz Bustamente, a Democratic candidate for lieutenant governor, was the first Latino to run on the statewide ballot since the 1870s.

The closeness of a contest also appears to have an impact on voter turnout. Citizens who perceive an election for an important office as being close are more likely to vote than those who do not.[44] Those who are more interested in politics and more attentive are more likely to perceive an election as being close. Thus political interest and attentiveness seem to be mobilizing influences affecting voter turnout.[45] Turnout in state legislative elections is higher in contests that are decided by a small margin of votes.[46] When there is little consensus on the issue agenda and the preferred outcomes regarding the issues, and when one party's candidates are not assured of victory, there is a greater likelihood that citizen's efforts directed at a member of a legislature will have an effect on the outcome. Therefore, we would expect voter turnout to be higher in closely contested elections, and we would expect other forms of political participation, such as lobbying officials in the legislative and executive branches to be more extensive on issues when the probable outcome is in doubt.

The number and importance of offices being filled affect voter turnout. Turnout is highest in presidential elections and lowest in local elections not held concurrently with any national or state elections. Turnout is higher in gubernatorial elections when they coincide with elections to the U.S. Senate than it is when they coincide with other elections.[47]

Campaign spending by candidates, party organizations, and interest groups does have a substantial impact on voter turnout.[48] Robert A. Jackson has shown that if the extent of campaign activity is measured by the amount of campaign expenditures, then extensive campaigning has significantly affected turnout in gubernatorial and congressional elections. The greatest impact of campaigns is on more educated citizens with lower levels of income; campaigns have less effect on less educated citizens with higher levels of income.[49] However, studies of state legislative contests suggest that the impact of campaigns declines after a certain threshold is reached.[50]

Political mobilization efforts aimed at increasing voter turnout are facilitated when many of the citizens have a strong commitment to a mobilization organization, such as a political party. One measure of this commitment is the proportion of those registering to vote who declare a party affiliation at the time of registration. In state legislative elections, districts with a higher proportion of declared partisans have higher rates of turnout.[51] This outcome, of course, differs between states that encourage voter registration by party or use closed (party-registrant only) primaries, and states that do not.

One model describes patterns of turnout by the same voters over time. It shows the eligible electorate as constituting a series of concentric circles, with those who vote in the most elections in the center, and those who vote in no elections in the outermost ring. However, Lee Sigelman and Malcolm E. Jewell examined voting participation in ten Kentucky elections (five primaries and five general elections), held between 1978 and 1982, using a sample of 115,800 voters drawn from the state's voter registration records, and found this interpretation of electoral participation to be inaccurate. Only 3 percent of the electorate participated in all elections, and the mean voter turnout within the sample was four or five elections. The decision to vote depends on such considerations as the offices being contested; whether referendum measures are on the ballot, and if so, what the issues are; the candidates' characteristics, such as popularity and group identification; the proportion of offices being contested by incumbents; and the competitiveness of the contests.[52]

To what extent does competition between parties increase voter turnout? In states with more restrictive voter registration laws, interparty competition appears to increase statewide turnout. In states with less restrictive requirements, candidates' campaign expenditures and party ideology are more important in increasing voter turnout.[53]

Some research suggests that political activists who supported a losing candidate in a contentious nominating campaign or primaries withdraw from participation in the general election campaign, thus reducing voter turnout in the general election.[54] However, other research does not support this conclusion.[55]

Effects of the Mass Media on Political Attitudes

The impact of the mass media on political attitudes is a subject of continuing debate. One criticism is that there is no in-depth, continuing coverage of governmental activities and policy issues. A majority of Americans rely on television for political news.[56] But most local television stations present only limited coverage of state and local government activities,[57] and much of the national news coverage focuses on momentary controversies or crisis events.[58] Television news tends to concentrate on events that can be presented dramatically; news anchors mechanically reading the news ("talking heads") are considered to be relatively unappealing to the viewers. Thus, continuing coverage of less dramatic events is avoided, even though they may be more important in the long run.[59] For example, debates on budgetary allocations are usually given only superficial coverage, although they can have a greater impact on citizens' lives than many of the fleeting but more dramatic political incidents that receive more thorough coverage.

The style of media coverage, as well as the selection of stories covered, may foster negative perceptions and cynical attitudes about government and politics. Some scholars suggest that the result is to reduce citizens' involvement with government to the maximum possible in a modern society.[60] Surveys conducted since the 1950s show that the increase in television coverage of politics has been accompanied by a decline in political trust. The proportion of citizens who can be said to "trust" the government declined from 76 percent in 1960 to 32 percent in 1982; it increased to 44 percent in 1984 but declined to 32 percent in 1996.[61] In one series of surveys, 50 percent of those questioned in 1966 reported they had "a great deal" of confidence in "the people running" the Supreme Court, and 42 percent had a great deal of confidence in the people running Congress; by 1981, the proportion reporting a great deal of confidence had dropped to 29 percent for the Supreme Court and 16 percent for Congress. The executive branch of government fared almost as badly: 41 percent of the respondents had a great deal of confidence in 1966 but 24 percent did in 1981.[62]

Citizens' confidence in some political institutions has apparently begun to increase in recent years, however. The decline in citizens' confidence in Congress, but not the Supreme Court, is evident from the responses to a series of questions used by the Gallup Poll since 1973. In 1973, the Gallup organization reported that 44 percent of respondents expressed "a great deal" or "quite a lot" of confidence in the Supreme Court; by 1999, the proportion expressing that level of confidence had increased to 49 percent. In contrast, only 26 percent of the respondents indicated that level of confidence in Congress in 1999, compared to 42 percent in 1973. Confidence in the presidency can also be studied, but within a much shorter period. In March 1993, 43 percent of the respondents said they had a great deal or quite a lot of confidence in the presidency. By May 1996, the proportion had declined to 39 percent, but by June 1999, confidence in the presidency had increased to 49 percent. If we confine our analysis to the proportion of respondents who said they had a great deal of confidence in each institution in June 1999, we find that 20 percent reported a great deal of confidence in the Supreme Court, compared with 9 percent expressing that level of confidence in Congress and 23 percent in the presidency.[63]

Can the declines in trust and confidence that took place after 1960 be attributed to the mass media? Several researchers have concluded that they can be, and they put the principal blame on television. Analysis of data from a 1968 survey indicates that those who rely on television as their primary or only source of political news are more cynical and have less understanding of politics than those who rely on several sources, including the print media. This difference remains, although it is a slightly less, when comparisons are made among persons with the same level of education.[64] A study of the effects of a controversial 1971 CBS television documentary, "The Selling of the Pentagon," led to the conclusions that reliance on television as a primary source of political news increases "(a) social distrust, (b) political cynicism, (c) [perception of] political inefficacy, (d) partisan disloyalty, and (e) third party viability."[65]

The print media also have an impact. People who frequently read newspaper articles that give relatively more emphasis to political criticism and to political conflict and controversy have lower levels of political trust and political efficacy (sense of personal political effectiveness), although levels of trust appear to be affected more than levels of political efficacy.[66]

If both print media and television focus on political conflict and controversy and present criticisms of political leaders, why do we assign to television more of the blame for the decline in the attitudes that are important in stimulating mass political participation? The reason apparently is that exposure to political coverage on television is inadvertent; a person who watches a television news program sees whatever the television news editors have decided to present in that program. In contrast, print media can be selectively "edited" by the readers themselves. If they wish to read only the sports section and the comics, or only stories about political issues and events, they can do so.[67]

Of course, many of the events that have unfolded since television began to evolve as a mass medium for the presentation of news in the 1950s also account for the decline in public confidence in political leaders and the political process. The assassinations of a president and of other prominent figures, the long and ultimately unpopular Vietnam War, the resignation of a president in disgrace, cycles of economic recession and recovery, and a series of international economic and political crises—all have provided news that may be not only controversial or unpleasant but is often complex and confusing to the average American citizen. That exposure to political news has a depressant effect on those attitudes, such as political efficacy and party loyalty, which are important in stimulating political participation is thus not surprising. Most news media content, however important or trivial, is presented as significant and usually in a context of controversy and crisis. Furthermore, good news and positive outcomes receive far less coverage than the bad and the negative. In short, both the content of the news and the style of news coverage have had an important impact on citizens' political attitudes.

Effects of the Mass Media on Political Participation

The news media have a direct impact on one form of political participation—voter turnout. Citizens' perceptions and attitudes, and ultimately their decisions about whether to vote and for whom, can be influenced by the campaign coverage in news broadcasts, candidate-sponsored (and-financed) advertisements, and television programs devoted to debates among candidates or public forums. The media also affect turnout by predicting election outcomes before and on election day.

Editors make judgments about who are the more important candidates and how extensive the coverage of different candidates and contests should be. Reporters offer interpretations of candidates' actions and ideas. Potential presidential candidates must be considered "viable" by the media in order to get sufficient news coverage; if candidates are taken seriously by the media, they find it much easier to raise campaign funds and build an effective organization.[68]

Media requirements frequently determine the timing and staging of campaign events. An appropriate visual background for a presidential candidate's televised statement about farm policy may require rousing the candidate's media entourage for an early morning fifty-mile journey to the site of a picturesque barn.[69] The fact that only fifty seconds of the statement will be aired is not necessarily discouraging to the candidate's campaign managers, but it illustrates why news coverage often confuses or fails to inform citizens. Those fifty seconds may be all the television coverage that policy issue will receive during the entire campaign, despite the policy's importance and complexity.

The media tend to give unequal coverage to the candidates. In presidential primaries, for example, the general pattern is for the candidate judged by the media to have won one round of nominating caucuses and primaries to receive more than a proportionate share of television time and print column-inches during the period extending to the next round of caucuses and primaries. In 1976, Democratic presidential candidate Jimmy Carter was anointed by the media as the "winner" of the Iowa caucus and the New Hampshire primary, even though he received only about 28 percent of the votes cast in each case. Thereafter he benefited from a disproportionate amount of news coverage and went on to win the Democratic nomination.[70]

The conclusion of most research, however, is that media coverage does not change attitudes or beliefs during a campaign. Why, then, is the pattern of media coverage important? To answer that question we must consider the effects of campaigns. The first and probably most important effect is to structure citizens' perceptions of candidates, political parties, and the public policy agenda. Second, campaigns crystallize or sharpen and elaborate already existing cognitive and affective elements relating to candidates and parties in such a way as to increase consistency among already existing attitudes and beliefs. Third, they reinforce already existing attitudes and beliefs.[71] But even if the campaign does not change attitudes or beliefs, media coverage of it is the major communications mechanism by which the candidates and party organizations impress most citizens. Media coverage structures their perceptions of the candidates and the issues, and they interpret these perceptions in the context of existing attitudes and beliefs. If some citizens think that the need for a strong national defense is the most important problem facing the nation, and if one candidate is presented by the media as being more likely to support additional expenditures for national defense, that perception, structured by both what the candidates are saying and the media's coverage of them, will affect those citizens' choices of candidate as well as their probability of voting.

Candidates and party organizations also present information to citizens in the form of paid advertisements, especially thirty-second or one-minute television spots. These advertisements are apparently a major influence on the least informed and least interested citizens. They have a feature not found in television news—frequent repetition of a single theme, with the message being simply and vividly presented so that it becomes familiar to and is easily remembered by these potential voters.[72]

Some evidence suggests that these paid advertisements may be more influential in primary elections than in general elections. In the primaries, potential voters have less information about the candidates (except in the case of a popular incumbent) and few alternative sources of information. This type of media influence also appears to vary with the visibility of the office; it is greater in contests for less visible offices.[73]

The activities of candidates as presented by the mass media can have an impact on citizens' familiarity with the candidates. In a nationwide survey conducted in 1994, more than half the citizens in districts where an incumbent representative was seeking reelection reported having heard, seen, or read something about the incumbent in the mass media, whereas only 15 percent had personally talked with the incumbent or members of the incumbent's staff. Although a vigorous challenger to an incumbent can help stimulate electoral participation, the challenger is usually less visible; 93 percent of those interviewed recognized the incumbent's name but only 57 percent recognized that of the challenger. One-third of those surveyed reported having seen or read about the challenger in the mass media, so it would appear that about half the recognition received by a challenger is attributable to media coverage and campaign advertising.[74]

Political participation can be significantly affected by citizens' attentiveness to news coverage of the campaigns and by direct contacts with the candidates. The likelihood that citizens would vote in the congressional elections in 1978 could be predicted just as accurately from patterns of their contacts with the candidates and from the frequency of their exposure to the mass media in learning about the campaign as from their demographic characteristics and political attitudes.[75]

Studies of the news coverage of political campaigns indicate that the press concentrates on who is winning and losing (the horse race) and on the strategies pursued by various candidates, rather than on the candidates' issue stands and competence to govern.[76] But predictions by the mass media about the closeness of a contest can have significant impact on election day turnout. A prediction that the election will be close stimulates interest in the contest. The cost-benefit calculations of citizens are affected, for they sense an increased probability that their votes will affect the outcome. That such calculations influence the decision to vote has been demonstrated by several studies.[77]

Media predictions of the election outcome are made both early in the campaign and on election day. The latter especially have become quite controversial. Outcome projections used to be based on surveys of samples of voters taken days or even weeks before the election. Now, however, they can be based on interviews with randomly selected voters as they leave the voting place (exit polls), and predictions of the outcome can be broadcast on television on election day before the polling places have closed in some areas.

Several studies have examined the effects of these election day predictions. Three studies concerned the 1964 presidential election, when Lyndon Johnson achieved a landslide victory over Barry Goldwater. That outcome had been predicted long before election day, however, so the effects of the election day predictions were probably minimal. The first study reported no effects on voter turnout, the second reported a 1 percent change in choice of candidate, and the third reported a 3 percent change in choice of candidate.[78] Although the effects found in the latter two studies could have made a difference in a close presidential election, they had no impact on the outcome of the 1964 contest. In a study of the 1968 presidential election, 4 percent of those surveyed in the East and 7 percent surveyed in the West changed their intention to vote after hearing the election day outcome projections; 6 percent of those surveyed in the East and 7 percent of those surveyed in the West changed their choice of presidential candidate.[79] It should be noted that, in addition to their effects on the outcome of the presidential election, such projections can have a significant impact on the level of turnout in the concurrent congressional contests. A study of the effects of 1972 election day predictions concluded that they reduced voter turnout by 2.7 percent in the Pacific Coast states. That translates into 337,000 votes in California, for example, or an average of 7,800 votes per congressional district—enough to determine the outcome of a close congressional contest.[80]

An analysis of the effects of election day projections concerning the 1980 presidential contest provide support for the view that they can have a small but decisive influence on voting participation. Those projections, as well as President Carter's concession speech, both of which were made before the polls closed in many states, reduced voter turnout in both the East and the West below what had been predicted on the basis of preelection interviews of a sample of the voting-age population.[81]

The failure of some members of the electorate to vote in 1980 because of the supposedly clear outcome of the presidential contest could have significantly affected the outcomes of other contests. Two Democratic representatives who were defeated in 1980 blamed their loss on the failure of many Democratic voters to come to the polls after hearing the networks' presidential election outcome predictions and (or) Carter's concession speech. However, a study of the party affiliation of those who did not vote after hearing the projections or the Carter speech suggests that the reduction in turnout was greater among Republicans than among Democrats.[82]

Another study concludes that the early call of the 1980 election outcome had only a slight effect on turnout but a larger effect on the direction of the vote; Democratic candidates in both the presidential and the congressional elections were adversely affected. Contests in fourteen congressional districts were won by margins of victory smaller than had been estimated.[83]

Representatives of the television news media and some scholars dispute the conclusion that election day projections are a significant deterrent to voting participation. Admittedly, attempts to assess the effects of election projections on voter turnout and choice of candidate encounter certain problems. Because much of the research based on individual responses is conducted one to two months after the election has been held, citizens may have difficulty recalling if and when they heard election projections on election day. Improved research designs would greatly facilitate such studies. Researchers should also focus on various groups within the electorate to ascertain whether there are differential effects of hearing election day projections. For example, are Democrats and Republicans equally affected in various types of districts? Are individuals, classified by occupation, social class, race, and age group, similarly affected by hearing election day projections? Research suggests that people who hear election day projections and are making the decision whether and how to vote may also be influenced by various aspects of the political context—the number and level of offices being contested, traditional electoral outcomes, and the presence or absence of referenda measures on the ballot.[84]

Extensive media coverage of an election helps stimulate voter turnout by increasing the public's interest in the campaigns; scant or spotty campaign coverage may contribute to low turnout rates and also decrease other forms of political participation. The extent of coverage is in part a function of news editors' perceptions of the level of public interest. Competition for viewers among local television stations and between local stations and cable television is quite intensive, and if the news editors believe that the campaign is not interesting to the viewers, they will allow it only limited coverage. This explanation was offered for the limited television coverage of the 1974 gubernatorial contest in California.[85]

Do the mass media also have an impact on other forms of political participation? One argument is that by providing information about events, issues, and organizations, the media stimulate people to join or support organizations that engage in political activity (such as political action committees), to contact public officials, or to become involved in court suits to block government actions. For example, local and national media coverage might be responsible for the formation of chapters of Mothers Against Drunk Driving, first in one area of one state and then throughout the country.

Those skeptical of this function of the mass media argue that the political activities that receive extensive coverage are often remote from the average citizen, for they occur either in Washington or overseas. Coverage is intermittent and often after the fact; for example, important legislation may be reported on only after a crucial vote has been taken in the House or Senate. And those parts of the policy process that occur within the executive branch, such as the drafting of regulations concerning the implementation and enforcement of the policy, generally receive little publicity. Usually the issues are complex, the key actors unknown to ordinary citizens, and the relevant processes not sufficiently understood to facilitate effective participation. The elites most affected by the issue, if not already involved (their noninvolvement is unlikely), and perhaps also a small proportion of the population most likely to be attentive to the media's political content, may be mobilized by media coverage, but the mass public will usually not be induced to participate by the media's political coverage. If an issue (such as Medicare) has received continuing coverage over a long period and is thus highly salient to ordinary citizens, the media's coverage of it may have an impact. There are only a few such issues, however. Furthermore, the media usually do not provide information about how the public can become involved and whom should be contacted. One explanation for the success of some interest groups may be their effectiveness in putting their name before the public, so they become identified as the mechanism for getting action on particular issues.[86]

The Influence of Organizations

Organizations—both voluntary and involuntary—are an important source of political information, and through the formal and informal messages they present may contribute to motivating members to be politically active. They are also a training ground for the communications and organizational skills that facilitate engagement in political activity.[87]

Individuals have the opportunity to join and participate in many types of voluntary organizations at the national, state, and local levels. Those who are involved in their community are more likely to be exposed to the formal and informal messages that stimulate political activity. Studies of members of voluntary organizations indicate that unintentional mobilization for political activity occurs in both political and nonpolitical groups, regardless of individuals' incentives (such as issue interests, material gain) for being group members.[88]

Of course, citizens vary in the number and types of groups to which they belong, but even membership in just one group is related to an increase in voter turnout. In 1996, 52 percent of those individuals who were not a member of any group reported voting, compared with 70 percent of those who were a member of one group, 79 percent of those who were a member of two groups, 84 percent of those who were members of three groups, and more than 90 percent of those who were members of four or more groups. Clearly, those who were more active in groups were also more likely to vote.[89]

Summary

Aspects of the political environment can both encourage and inhibit various types of political participation. In the early stages of an electoral party system's evolution, participation in conventional political activities tends to increase; as the conflicts are alleviated or resolved and tensions in society decrease, such participation can be expected to decline. When new conflicts arise that are not adequately handled by the political system or by the government, participation in both conventional and unconventional political activities can be expected to increase.

One type of political participation that increases when certain groups perceive their problems as not being dealt with by the government is membership in a political movement. Many political movements have arisen in the United States since the 1950s. Some have evolved into organized interest groups that emphasize electoral and lobbying activities; some that have continued to function as political movements, have utilized such forms of action as protest marches and other types of public demonstration.

Political mobilization can be stimulated by such factors as the perceived closeness of the contest for political office; the appeal of the candidates; the perceived importance of an issue; and the activities of parties, candidates, and interest groups. The latter mobilization efforts can have a small but significant effect when elections are close; they can also influence legislative outcomes and the decisions of bureaucrats charged with implementing or enforcing a policy.

The mass media should also be recognized as a key element in the political environment. The increasing influence of television at the expense of newspapers' readership and changing patterns of print news accessibility (fewer afternoon newspapers) have had a significant impact on citizens' perceptions of government, politicians, and the political process.

Notes

1. Lester W. Milbrath and M. L. Goel, *Political Participation,* 2d ed. (Chicago: Rand McNally, 1977), 137–140; Angus Campbell, "The Passive Citizen," *Acta Sociologica* 6 (1962): 9–21; and Wayne Parent and Wesley Shrum, "Critical Electoral Success and Black Voter Registration: An Elaboration of the Voter Consent Model," *Social Science Quarterly* 66 (1985): 695–703.
2. Paul Kleppner, *Who Voted?* (New York: Praeger, 1982); and Thomas Jahnige, "Critical Elections and Social Change," *Polity* 3 (1971): 465–500.
3. In 1952, 4 percent of the citizens reported contributing funds to political campaigns, whereas 8 percent contributed in 1980. In the 1996 campaign, 8.6 percent contributed. American National Election Studies Cumulative File, 1948–1996.
4. The Federal Election Campaign Act of 1971 limited the amount that individuals may contribute to candidates for federal office, political party organizations, and political action committees. The act authorized PACs to collect campaign contributions and channel them to candidates for Congress. It continued the earlier restrictions on contributions to candidates for federal office made by labor unions and corporations. Contributions covered by those restrictions are referred to as "hard" money. Contributions not covered by those restrictions are referred to as "soft" money. They can be used for party-building activities but not to promote an individual candidate. In the 1990s, there was an enormous increase in the amounts of soft money flowing to congressional party organizations and other party organizations at the national level, as well as those at the state level. See, for example, Paul S. Herrnson, "Parties and Interest Groups in Postreform Congressional Elections," in *Interest Group Politics,* 5th ed., ed. Allan J. Cigler and Burdett A. Loomis (Washington, D.C.: CQ Press, 1998), 145–167; M. Margaret Conway and Joanne Connor Green, "Political Action Committees and Campaign Finance," in Cigler and Loomis, *Interest Group Politics,* 193–214; M. Margaret Conway, "Republican Party Nationalization, Campaign Activities, and Their Implications for the Political Party System,"*Publius* 13 (1983): 1–17; Frank J. Sorauf, *Money in American Elections* (Glenview, IL.: Scott, Foresman, 1988), chap. 3; and Robert Biersack, Paul S. Herrnson, and Clyde Wilcox, eds., *Risky Business?* (Armonk, N.Y.: M. E. Sharpe, 1994). See also the discussion of campaign finance in Chapter 5.
5. Among them were the Republican and Democratic National Committees, the congressional campaign committees of the Democratic and Republican Parties, and the League of Women Voters. For a discussion of political mobilization efforts in the 1996 and 1998 campaigns, see M. Margaret Conway, "Political Mobilization in America," in *The State of Democracy in America,* ed. William M.

Crotty (Washington, D.C.: Georgetown University Press, 2000). Prior to the implementation of the National Voter Registration Act on January 1, 1995, a very high proportion of those who were registered had voted. See Robert S. Erikson, "Why Do People Vote? Because They Are Registered," *American Politics Quarterly* 9 (1981): 259–276. However, between 1980 and 1984, turnout among those who registered appears to have declined by approximately 3 percent; see Committee for the Study of the American Electorate, *Non-Voter Study 84–85.* (Washington, D.C., January 7, 1985), 2. Between 1984 and 1988, the proportion of the electorate registered to vote declined by 1.7 percent, whereas turnout by those registered to vote declined by 2.7 percent. "Voting and Registration in the Election of November 1986," Bureau of the Census, *Current Population Reports,* ser. P-20, no. 414 (Washington, D.C.: Government Printing Office, September 1987), Table A and Table B; and "Voting and Registration in the Election of November 1988" (advance report), Bureau of the Census, *Current Population Reports,* ser. P-20, no. 435 (Washington, D.C.: Government Printing Office, February 1989), Table A. The decline in turnout among registered voters continued through 1996. Turnout was lower among those who registered at the motor vehicle bureaus and state social service agencies. See Lynn M. Casper and Loretta E. Bass, "Voting and Registration in the Election of November 1996," Bureau of the Census, *Current Population Reports,* ser. P20, no. 504 (Washington, D.C.: Government Printing Office, July 1998), Tables 1 and 2; and David B. Hill, "The Path to Participation? The Aggregate and Individual Level Effects of the National Voter Registration Act," Ph. D. Diss., University of Florida, 1999.

6. Alexis de Tocqueville, *Democracy in America,* ed. Phillips Bradley (New York: Vintage, 1957), 1: 259–260; 2: 114–116, 123–125.

7. Sidney Verba, Norman H. Nie, and Jae-on Kim, *Participation and Political Equality* (Cambridge: Cambridge University Press, 1978), chap. 5.

8. Sidney Verba and Norman H. Nie, *Participation in America* (New York: Harper and Row, 1972), 186–187; Norman H. Nie et al., "Participation in America: Continuity and Change" (paper delivered at the annual meeting of the Midwest Political Science Association, Chicago, April 14–16, 1989); Sidney Verba, Kay Lehman Schlozman, and Henry E. Brady, *Voice and Equality* (Cambridge: Harvard University Press, 1995), chap. 12.

9. Alan R. Gitelson, M. Margaret Conway, and Frank B. Feigert, *American Political Parties: Stability and Change* (Boston: Houghton Mifflin, 1984), chaps. 2, 3, 4.

10. Gitelson, Conway, and Feigert, *American Political Parties,* 26. Table 2-2. See also Jahnige, "Critical Elections."

11. For discussions of electoral party systems in American political history, see James Sundquist, *The Dynamics of the Party System,* rev. ed. (Washington, D.C.: Brookings Institution Press, 1983); Walter Dean Burnham, *Critical Elections and the Mainsprings of American Politics* (New York: Norton, 1970); and Jerome Clubb, William H. Flanigan, and Nancy Zingale, *Partisan Realignment: Voters, Parties, and Government in American History* (Beverly Hills, Calif.: Sage, 1980). For different perspectives on American political history, see Byron E. Shafer, "The Notion of an Electoral Order: The Structure of Electoral Politics at the Accession of George Bush," in *The End of Realignment?,* ed. Byron E. Shafer (Madison: University of Wisconsin Press, 1991); Stephen Skowronek, *The Politics Presidents Make* (Cambridge: Belknap Press, Harvard University Press, 1993); Thomas Ferguson, *Golden Rule: The Investment Theory of Party Competition and the Logic of Money-driven Political Systems* (Chicago: University of Chicago Press, 1995).

12. Sundquist, *Dynamics of the Party System,* chap. 3; Clubb, Flanigan, and Zingale, *Partisan Realignment,* chap. 1; and Gitelson, Conway, and Feigert, *American Political Parties,* 35–36.

13. John Petrocik, "Issues and Agendas: Electoral Coalitions in the 1988 Election"; and Helmut Norpoth and Michael Kagay, "Another Eight Years of Republican Rule and Still No Partisan Realignment?" (two papers delivered at the annual meeting of the American Political Science Association, Atlanta, August 31–Sep-

tember 3, 1989). Another view is that secular realignments can best be described as issue evolutions: Issues develop that alter the political environment, and as a consequence, new patterns of voter support emerge. Proponents of this view argue that the concept of issue evolution allows for more gradations of change in the political environment than does the concept of political realignment. See Edward G. Carmines and James A. Stimson, *Issue Evolution* (Princeton: Princeton University Press, 1989).

14. Kristi Andersen, *The Creation of a Democratic Majority, 1928–1936* (Chicago: University of Chicago Press, 1979).

15. See Sundquist, *Dynamics of the Party System,* chap. 5.

16. See ibid., chapter 10, with reference to the role of conversion in the political realignment of the 1930s.

17. Norpoth and Kagay, "Another Eight Years of Republican Rule"; and Petrocik, "Issues and Agendas." For the exposition of a general theory of realignment through generational replacement, see Paul Allen Beck, "A Socialization Theory of Partisan Realignment," in *The Politics of Future Citizens,* ed. Richard G. Niemi and associates (San Francisco: Jossey-Bass, 1974), 199–219.

18. Calculated using data in the American National Election Studies Cumulative File, 1948–1996, and the 1998 American National Election Study.

19. Charles E. Johnson Jr., "Nonvoting Americans," Bureau of the Census, *Current Population Reports,* ser. P-23, no. 102 (Washington, D.C.: Government Printing Office, April 1980), 2, Table A.

20. Kleppner, *Who Voted?,* chap. 3; and Marc V. Levine, "Standing Political Decisions and Critical Realignments: The Pattern of Maryland Politics, 1872–1938," *Journal of Politics* 38 (1976): 292–325.

21. See Philip E. Converse, "Change in the American Electorate," in *The Human Meaning of Social Change,* ed. Angus Campbell and Philip E. Converse (New York: Russell Sage, 1972), chap. 8; Walter Dean Burnham, "Theory and Voting Research: Some Reflections on Converse's 'Change in the American Electorate,'" *American Political Science Review* 68 (1974): 1002–1023; and Philip E. Converse, "Comment on Burnham's 'Theory and Voting Research,'" *American Political Science Review* 68 (1976): 1024–1027.

22. Johnson, "Nonvoting Americans," 2, Table A; and 3, Fig. 1.

23. Burnham, *Critical Elections,* chap. 2.

24. See Richard P. Claude, *The Supreme Court and the Electoral Process* (Baltimore: Johns Hopkins University Press, 1970); and V. O. Key Jr., *Southern Politics* (New York: Vintage, 1949), chaps. 25–30.

25. Kleppner, *Who Voted?,* chap. 4.

26. Walter Dean Burnham, "The Changing Shape of the American Political Universe," *American Political Science Review* 59 (1965): 7–28.

27. Andersen, *Democratic Majority,* 70–71.

28. Robert S. Erikson and Kent L. Tedin, "The 1928–1936 Partisan Realignment: The Case for the Conversion Hypothesis," *American Political Science Review* 75 (1981): 951–962.

29. Johnson, "Nonvoting Americans," 5, Table B; and 6, Fig. 3.

30. John Petrocik argues that the realignment of the 1980s had not by 1988 produced a Republican majority. His research suggests that the realignment was a consequence of shifts in support by many groups, the most prominent among them being white southerners, Catholics, blacks, and the households of northern union members. In contrast, Martin Wattenberg argues that the partisan realignment of the 1980s is a "hollow" realignment, for citizens based their judgments and allegiance decisions more on individual candidates than on perceived differences in the parties' issue stands and competence to govern. Helmut Norpoth and Michael Kagay conclude that generational replacement contributed to a secular realignment; the Republican Party had gained an increasing proportion of partisan identifiers by 1988, but it still lagged behind the Democratic Party in terms of the proportion of the electorate declaring a party affiliation. See Petrocik, "Issues and

Agendas"; Norpoth and Kagay, "Another Eight Years of Republican Rule"; and Martin Wattenberg, "The Hollow Realignment Continues: Partisan Change in 1988" (paper delivered at the annual meeting of the American Political Science Association, Atlanta, August 31–September 3, 1989). Harold Stanley and Richard G. Niemi argue that the New Deal coalition has eroded to such an extent that it no longer exists. See "The Demise of the New Deal Coalition: Partisanship and Group Support, 1952–92," *Democracy's Feast: Elections in America, 1992,* ed. Herbert F. Weisberg (Chatham, N.J.: Chatham House, 1995), 220–240.

31. Warren E. Miller and J. Merrill Shanks, *The New American Voter* (Cambridge: Harvard University Press, 1996), chaps. 3, 4, and 5.

32. Harold D. Lasswell and Abraham Kaplan, *Power and Society: A Framework for Political Inquiry* (New Haven: Yale University Press, 1950), 241–242. For alternative perspectives on political and social movements, see Anne N. Costain and Andrew S. McFarland, eds., *Social Movements and American Political Institutions* (Lanham, Md.: Rowman and Littlefield, 1998); and Doug McAdam, John D. McCarthy, and Mayer N. Zald, eds., *Comparative Perspectives on Social Movements* (Cambridge: Cambridge University Press, 1996).

33. Allan J. Cigler and John Mark Hansen, "Group Formation through Protest: The American Agricultural Movement," in *Interest Group Politics,* ed. Allan J. Cigler and Burdett A. Loomis (Washington, D.C.: CQ Press, 1983), 86–88.

34. See Sundquist, *Dynamics of the Party System,* chap. 5; Daniel A. Mazmanian, *Third Parties in Presidential Elections* (Washington, D.C.: Brookings Institution Press, 1974); Paul S. Herrnson and John C. Green, eds., *Multiparty Politics in America* (London: Rowman and Littlefield, 1997); and Steven J. Rosenstone, Roy L. Behr, and Edward H. Lazarus, *Third Party Politics in America,* 2d ed. (Princeton: Princeton University Press, 1994).

35. For a discussion of the Weathermen, public reaction to their activities, and subsequent changes in their strategies, see Robert Brent Toplin, *Unchallenged Violence* (Westport, Conn.: Greenwood Press, 1975), 18–120.

36. Marjorie Random Hershey and Darrell M. West, "Single Issue Politics: Prolife Groups and the 1980 Senate Campaigns," in Cigler and Loomis, *Interest Group Politics,* 44–46; and Marjorie Random Hershey, *Running for Office* (Chatham, N.J.: Chatham House, 1984), chaps. 6 and 7.

37. Hershey and West, "Single Issue Politics"; and Hershey, *Running for Office,* chaps. 6 and 7. The anti-abortion movement has also used more unconventional forms of political action, including the picketing of abortion clinics and even some acts of violence. Unconventional forms of political participation are in chapters 6 and 7.

38. See Thomas B. Edsall and Haynes Johnson, "High Tech, Impersonal Computer Net Is Snaring Prospective Republicans," *Washington Post,* April 22, 1984.

39. Bruce E. Cain and Ken McCue, "The Efficacy of Registration Drives," *Journal of Politics* 47 (1985): 1221–1230. For an examination of community-based efforts to mobilize African Americans to vote, see Katherine Tate, "Black Political Participation in the 1984 and 1988 Presidential Elections," *American Political Science Review* 85 (1991): 1159–1176. Political parties' mobilization efforts and their effectiveness in the 1998 midterm elections are analyzed in Conway, "Political Mobilization in America."

40. Cain and McCue, "Efficacy of Registration Drives," 1226.

41. Gerald Kramer, "The Effects of Precinct Level Canvassing on Voter Behavior," *Public Opinion Quarterly* 34 (1970): 560–572; William M. Crotty, "The Party Organization and Its Activities," in *Approaches to the Study of Party Organizations,* ed. William M. Crotty (Boston: Allyn and Bacon, 1968), 268–306; Raymond E. Wolfinger, "The Influence of Precinct Work on Voting Behavior," *Public Opinion Quarterly* 27 (1963): 387–398; Daniel Katz and Samuel Eldersveld, "The Impact of Local Party Activity upon the Electorate," *Public Opinion Quarterly* 25 (1961): 1–24; Phillips Cutright, "Measuring the Impact of Local Party Activity on the General Election Vote," *Public Opinion Quarterly* 27 (1963):

372–386; Phillips Cutright and Peter Rossi, "Party Organization in Primary Elections," *American Journal of Sociology* 64 (1958): 262–269; and John Frendries, James L. Gibson, and Laura Vertz, "The Electoral Relevance of Local Party Organizations," *American Political Science Review* 84 (1990): 225–235. One study found that contacts did not increase voter turnout; see John C. Blydenburgh, "A Controlled Experiment to Measure the Effects of Personal Campaigning," *Midwest Journal of Political Science* 15 (1971): 365–381.

42. Nathaniel Sheppard Jr., "Black-Oriented Radio Key in Chicago's Election," *New York Times*, March 15, 1983, D24.

43. Parent and Shrum, "Critical Electoral Success," 659–703.

44. But there have been some exceptions. In the presidential elections of 1964, 1984, and 1996, turnout was higher among those who thought the election would not be close. Calculated from data in the American National Election Studies Cumulative File, 1948–1996.

45. Kenneth D. Wald, "The Closeness-Turnout Hypothesis: A Reconsideration," *American Politics Quarterly* 13 (1985): 643–651.

46. Gregory A. Caldeira and Samuel C. Patterson, "Contextual Influences on Participation in U.S. State Legislative Elections," *Legislative Studies Quarterly* 7 (1982), 376, Table 2.

47. Gregory A. Caldeira and Samuel C. Patterson, "Getting Out the Vote: Participation in Gubernatorial Elections," *American Political Science Review* 77 (1983): 684–685.

48. Ibid., 675–689.

49. Robert A. Jackson, "Voter Mobilization in the 1986 Midterm Election," *Journal of Politics* 55 (1993): 1081–1099; and Robert A. Jackson, "A Reassessment of Voter Mobilization," *Political Research Quarterly* 49 (1996): 331–349.

50. Caldeira and Patterson, "Contextual Influences," 369–378.

51. Ibid., 376–377.

52. Lee Sigelman and Malcolm E. Jewell, "From Core to Periphery: A Note on the Imagery of Concentric Circles," *Journal of Politics* 48 (1986): 440–449.

53. Kim Quaile Hill and Jan E. Leighley, "Mobilizing Institutions and Class Representation in U.S. State Electorates," *Political Research Quarterly* 47 (1994): 137–150.

54. V. O. Key Jr., *Parties, Politics, and Pressure Groups* (New York: Crowell, 1958), chap. 14; Patrick J. Kenney and Tom W. Rice "The Effects of Primary Divisiveness in Gubernatorial and Senatorial Elections, *Journal of Politics* 46 (1984): 905–915; Patrick J. Kenney and Tom W. Rice, "The Relationship between Divisive Primaries and General Election Outcomes," *American Journal of Political Science* 31 (1987): 31–44; Donald B. Johnson and James L. Gibson, "The Divisive Primary Revised: Activists in Iowa," *American Political Science Review* 68 (1974): 67–77; Patricia L. Southwell, "The Politics of Disgruntlement: Nonvoting and Defection among Supporters of Nomination Losers," *Political Behavior* 8 (1986): 81–95; and Walter J. Stone, "Prenomination Candidate Choice and General Election Behavior," *American Journal of Political Science* 28 (1984): 372–389.

55. Walter J. Stone, Lonna Rae Atkeson, and Ronald B. Rapoport, "Turning On or Turning Off: Mobilization and Demobilization Effects of Participation in Presidential Nomination Campaigns," *American Political Science Review* 36 (1992): 665–695; and James E. McCann et al., "Presidential Nomination Campaigns and Party Mobilization: An Assessment of Spillover Effects," *Journal of Politics* 40 (1996): 756–767.

56. Gitelson, Conway, and Feigert, *American Political Parties*, 239, Table 10.1.

57. Graber found that local television news broadcasts give limited coverage to state and local government. Doris A. Graber, *Mass Media and American Politics*, 5th ed. (Washington, D.C.: CQ Press, 1997), 320.

58. Ibid., 102–108.

59. Ibid., chap. 5.

60. Ibid., 381–382; and Austin Ranney, *Channels of Power* (New York: Basic Books, 1984), chap. 3.

61. This is the proportion responding "always" or "most of the time" to the question, "How much of the time do you think you can trust the government in Washington to do what is right?" American National Election Studies Cumulative File, 1948–1996.

62. Seymour Martin Lipset and William Schneider, *The Confidence Gap* (New York: Free Press, 1983), 48–49, Table 2-1.

63. http://www.gallup.com/poll/indicators/indconfidence.ASP. October 27, 1999.

64. Michael J. Robinson, "American Political Legitimacy in an Era of Electronic Journalism: Reflections on the Evening News," in *Television as a Social Force*, ed. Douglass Cater and Richard Adler (New York: Praeger, 1975), 97–139. For extensive discussions of the patterns, causes, and consequences of political trust in the United States, see Stephen C. Craig, *The Malevolent Leaders*, (Boulder, Colo.: Westview Press, 1993); Joseph S. Nye Jr., Philip D. Zelikow, and David C. King, eds., *Why People Don't Trust Government* (Cambridge: Harvard University Press, 1997); and *Deconstructing Trust* (Washington, D.C.: Pew Research Center for the People and the Press, n.d.).

65. Michael J. Robinson, "Public Affairs Television and the Growth of Political Malaise," *American Political Science Review* 74 (1976): 425. For experimental studies that demonstrate the detrimental effects of negative advertising in political campaigns, see Stephen Ansolabehere and Shanto Iyengar, *Going Negative: How Attack Ads Shrink and Polarize the Electorate* (New York: Free Press, 1995).

66. Arthur H. Miller, Edie Goldenberg, and Lutz Ebring, "Type-Set Politics: Impact of Newspapers on Public Confidence," *American Political Science Review* 73 (1979): 67–84.

67. Shanto Iyengar and Donald R. Kinder, *News That Matters: Television and Public Opinion* (Chicago: University of Chicago Press, 1987).

68. See C. Anthony Broh, "Presidential Preference Polls and Network News," in *Television Coverage of the 1980 Presidential Campaign*, ed. William Adams (Norwood, N.J.: Ablex, 1983), 29–48.

69. Timothy Crouse, *The Boys on the Bus* (New York: Random House, 1973), 140.

70. Thomas E. Patterson, *The Mass Media Election* (New York: Praeger, 1980), chap. 5. See also John H. Aldrich, *Before the Convention* (Chicago: University of Chicago Press, 1980), 176–192.

71. For discussions of campaigns' effects, see Dan Nimmo, *The Political Persuaders* (Englewood Cliffs, N.J.: Prentice-Hall, 1970), 164–172; George Comstock et al., *Television and Human Behavior* (New York: Columbia University Press, 1978), 339–341; and Thomas M. Holbrook, *Do Campaigns Matter?* (Thousand Oaks, Calif.: Sage, 1996). For an analysis of hypotheses about the effects of news coverage of campaigns and the effects of voters' beliefs on their choice of candidate, see Stephen Ansolabehere and Shanto Iyengar, "Winning through Advertising: It's All in the Contest," in *Campaigns and Elections*, ed. James A. Thurber and Candice J. Nelson (Boulder, Colo.: Westview Press, 1995), 101–111. See also Graber, *Mass Media and American Politics*, chap. 6; Ranney, *Channels of Power*, 80–86; Patterson, *Mass Media Election*; and Ansolabehere and Iyengar, *Going Negative*.

72. Thomas E. Patterson and Robert McClure, *The Unseeing Eye* (New York: Putnam, 1976), 16–120.

73. Michael J. Robinson, "The Media in 1980: Was the Message the Message?," in *The American Elections of 1980*, ed. Austin Ranney (Washington, D.C.: American Enterprise Institute, 1981), 177–211.

74. Calculated from data in the 1994 American National Election Study.

75. M. Margaret Conway, "Mass Media Use, Candidate Contacts, and Political Participation in Congressional Elections" (paper delivered at the annual meeting of the Southern Political Science Association, November 6–8, 1980).

76. C. Anthony Broh, "Horse Race Journalism: Reporting the Polls in the 1976 Cam-

paign," *Public Opinion Quarterly* 44 (1980): 514–529; and Patterson, *Mass Media Election,* chap. 3. A study of newspaper coverage of presidential candidates during the 1976 campaign concluded that articles focused most frequently on their personal qualities; only 22 percent included discussion of the candidates' competence to govern. See Graber, *Mass Media and American Politics,* 258, Table 8.5.

77. Norman Frohlich and Joe A. Oppenheimer, *Modern Political Economy* (Englewood Cliffs, N.J.: Prentice-Hall, 1978), chap. 5; and Gregory Brunk, "The Impact of Rational Attitudes Models on Voting Participation," *Public Choice* 35 (1980): 549–564.

78. Kurt Lang and Gladys Engel Lang, *Voting and Non-voting* (Waltham, Mass.: Blaisdell, 1968); Harold Mendelsohn and Irving Crespi, *Polls, Television, and the New Politics* (Scranton, Pa.: Chandler, 1970), chap. 4; and Douglas A. Fuchs, "Election Day Radio-Television and Western Voting," *Public Opinion Quarterly* 30 (1966): 226–236.

79. Sam Tuchman and Thomas E. Coffin, "The Influence of Election-Night Television Broadcasts in a Close Election," *Public Opinion Quarterly* 35 (1971): 315–326.

80. Raymond E. Wolfinger and Peter Linquiti, "Tuning In and Turning Out," *Public Opinion* 4 (1981): 57–58.

81. John E. Jackson, "Election-Night Reporting and Voter Turnout," *American Journal of Political Science* 27 (1983): 615–635.

82. Ibid., 620–621.

83. Michael X. Delli Carpini, "Scooping the Voters? The Consequences of the Networks' Early Call of the 1980 Presidential Race," *Journal of Politics* 46 (1984): 866–885.

84. See J. Ronald Milavsky et al., "Early Calls on Election Results and Exit Polls: Pros, Cons, and Constitutional Considerations," *Public Opinion Quarterly* 49 (1985): 1–18; Seymour Sudman, "Do Exit Polls Influence Voting Behavior?," *Public Opinion Quarterly* 50 (1986): 331–339; Ronald J. Busch and Joel A. Lieske, "Does Time of Voting Affect Exit Poll Results?," *Public Opinion Quarterly* 49 (1985): 94–104. Other studies of the effects of election forecasts on voter turnout and election results include Paul Wilson, "Election Night 1980 and the Controversy over Early Projections," in *Television Coverage of the 1980 Presidential Campaign,* ed. William C. Adams (Norwood, N.J.: Ablex, 1983); Percy H. Tannenbaum and Leslie J. Kosrtich, *Turned-On TV, Turned-Off Voters: Policy Options for Election Projections* (Beverly Hills, Calif.: Sage, 1983), Paul J. Lavrakas and Jack K. Holley, eds. *Polling and Presidential Election Coverage* (Newbury Park, Calif.: Sage, 1991); and Paul J. Lavrakas, Michael Traugott, and Peter V. Miller, *Presidential Polls and the News Media* (Boulder, Colo.: Westview Press, 1995).

85. Mary Ellen Leary, "California 1974: The Browning of Campaign Coverage," *Columbia Journalism Review* 15 (1976): 18–21.

86. James B. Lemert et al., "Journalists and Mobilizing Information," *Journalism Quarterly* 54 (1977): 721–726.

87. Verba, Schlozman, and Brady, *Voice and Equality,* chap. 13.

88. Jan E. Leighley, "Group Membership and the Mobilization of Political Participation," *Journal of Politics* 58 (1996): 447–463; and Robert Huckfeldt and John Sprague, "Political Parties and Electoral Mobilization: Political Structure, Social Structure, and the Party Canvass," *American Political Science Review* 56 (1992): 70–86.

89. Calculated using data in the 1996 American National Election Study.

Chapter 5

The Legal Structure and
Political Participation

In this chapter we examine, first, the struggle for the right to vote, including the efforts to extend the suffrage to all white males, then to women and to minorities. Second, we analyze the ways in which the rules determining eligibility to vote and the laws and procedures governing the conduct of elections affect electoral participation. Third, we consider the influence of numerous interest groups and how local, state, and national governments—with their legislative, executive, and judicial systems, and their bureaucracies—both encourage and inhibit the various forms of political participation.

The Struggle for the Right to Vote

In the United States, ordinary citizens gained the right to participate in elections only after a long struggle. The motto of the American Revolution, "No taxation without representation," expressed the deep commitment of the nation's founders to preserve what they considered to be a natural right. The United States was the first nation to have universal suffrage and competitive free elections,[1] although in recent years the right to vote has been exercised by only about half of the eligible citizens in elections for national offices (see Table 1-1). In state and local elections, the figure is usually less than half.

The Founding Fathers set out to create not a pure democracy but a republic, in which sovereign power would reside in a restricted electorate and be exercised by the electorate's representatives. Many of the nation's early leaders believed that ordinary citizens lacked the knowledge and wisdom necessary to participate in governing. But some framers of the Constitution thought otherwise, and the question of who should have the right to vote generated such disagreement in the Constitutional Convention in 1787 that the decision was left to the states.[2] The Constitution simply declared (Article 1, Section 2) that any person who was eligible to vote in elections to the most numerous branch of a state's legislature was also eligible to vote in elections to the federal House of Representatives. However, Article 1, Section 4, gave Congress the power to enact laws concerning the "times" and "manner" of holding elections for its members; the state legislatures could only prescribe.

Before the Revolution, only those who owned property could vote in the colonial elections, and the newly formed states continued to impose this restriction. The colonies had been formed as business corporations, and an individual was not considered to be a member unless he owned property in the corporation. As the colonies evolved into political entities, some of them imposed additional restrictions on suffrage, including criteria relative to race, age, sex, color, and religion. For example, Catholics, Jews, and free nonwhites were forbidden to vote in several colonies. In some colonies, mainly in New England a potential voter had to prove that he met standards of "good character." After the colonies joined together to form the United States of America, some of these restrictions on eligibility to vote were continued.[3]

Property restrictions were usually stated in terms of either the value of the property or the number of acres owned.[4] In some states, a minimum level of wealth remained a condition for eligibility for more than fifty years after the ratification of the Constitution, although the requirement was later more likely to be stated in terms of the amount of taxes paid than of the amount of property owned.[5]

Even after property ownership and taxpaying conditions were eased or eliminated, voter turnout rates remained low. In the 1828 presidential election, only about one-fifth of the nation's adult population voted, but, of course, women and nonwhite males did not have the right to vote at that time. In the presidential election of 1844, the first one in which no state had a property or taxpaying requirement for voting, slightly less than 31 percent of the adult population voted. Before 1920, the highest turnout was in the election of 1876, when 37.1 percent of the adult population cast votes; that election focused on economic issues and the end of Reconstruction in the South.[6] Voter turnout as a proportion of the eligible voters was higher during the latter part of the nineteenth century than at any other time in American history. The proportion began to decline after the political realignment of 1896 and has never returned to that high level.

Women's Suffrage

Women did not have the right to vote in colonial America. In 1787, Abigail Adams, the wife of John Adams, wrote to him asking that he "remember the ladies" and support women's right to vote.[7] Her plea was ignored. Actually, the struggle for women's suffrage had begun even earlier. Margaret Brent, a wealthy resident of Maryland, had petitioned the Maryland Council in 1647 for the right to vote. She was the agent and legal representative of Lord Baltimore, the proprietor of the Maryland colony, and the executrix of the estate of Leonard Calvert, the deceased brother of Lord Baltimore. Appearing before the colonial council, she demanded that it grant her not one but two votes, one for herself and one as the executrix of Calvert's estate and Lord Baltimore's representative. She argued that if she was not granted two votes, she would demand that all proceedings of the council be declared invalid. Not persuaded by her arguments, the council denied her request.[8]

Women were not excluded by law from voting at this time, because it did not occur to most men that women would want to vote or attempt to vote. However, in a few local communities some women of prominent families did participate in elections, and it became such a common occurrence that some states enacted laws late in the eighteenth century to prohibit it. In New Jersey, no law excluding women from the suffrage was enacted until 1807, when it appeared that women's votes might influence the outcomes of elections in a direction opposed by those holding political power in the state.[9]

In the nineteenth century, women began an organized campaign to obtain the right to vote. Through their participation in the abolitionist movement, women learned to organize, speak in public on political issues, and conduct campaigns to gain support for a policy. Furthermore, many women employed in the factories and textile mills actively protested the wretched conditions in which they worked. Although their protests were unsuccessful, they, too, learned how to organize, petition, and lobby.[10]

The antislavery movement also helped generate the leadership of the women's movement. In 1840, a world antislavery convention was held in London, attended by both male and female delegates from the United States. The convention's majority ruled, over the protests of the U.S. delegates, that women could not be delegates to the convention and would have to take seats in the spectators' galleries.[11] Among the American women attending the convention were Lucretia Mott and Elizabeth Cady Stanton, and their experience prompted them to discuss the condition of women in the United States and throughout the world. Some of the fundamental ideas of the women's movement took form then, and Mott and Stanton became its first leaders. Later, Stanton moved with her family to the small town of Seneca Falls, New York. Burdened by housework and child care, without servants to help her, and frequently alone because her husband was traveling on business, she came to resent her situation and realized that many other women shared her circumstances. She and several other women expressed their resentment in a small advertisement placed in the *Seneca County Courier*, calling for a Woman's Rights Convention to be held in the Wesleyan Chapel on July 19 and 20, 1848. The convention issued a "Declaration of Principles" and drafted a set of resolutions to implement it. The declaration and accompanying resolutions are recognized as the beginning of the women's rights movement in the United States; they state the issues that were the focus of the movement and that set the public policy agenda for women in the nation.[12]

As they continued their struggle, women made gains after the Civil War in areas such as free public elementary and secondary education, and a few colleges admitted a limited number of women. The strategy that evolved was one of emphasizing the acquisition of the right to vote, for it was considered to be the key to success in obtaining other rights.[13] Widows with school-age children had been granted the right to vote in Kentucky's school elections in 1838, but the next state to enfranchise women in school elections, Kansas, did not do so until 1861. Voting in school elections was regarded as a natural extension of women's role as mothers, and twenty-six states had granted women suffrage to that extent by 1920. However, support for full suffrage for women (the right to vote in all elections) does not appear to have been closely related to granting them the right to vote in school elections.[14]

Women first obtained full suffrage in the territory of Wyoming in 1871, and this provision was retained when Wyoming became a state in 1890. As the leaders of the women's movement had predicted, other rights came with the right to vote. The women of Wyoming also gained the right to serve on juries, to exercise control over their own property, and not to be discriminated against in employment as teachers. By 1918, full women's suffrage had been granted in fourteen other states (all but one of them, New York, were western states), and by the end of 1919, eleven more states had followed suit.[15] The women's suffrage amendment to the Constitution was proposed in Congress in 1919 and was certified as having been ratified by the requisite thirty-six states on August 26, 1920—culminating a struggle that had begun in 1848.

What explains women's success in finally gaining adoption of the Nineteenth Amendment? First, twenty-six states already permitted women to vote by 1920. Second, women's rights leaders, such as Carrie Chapman Catt, emphasized the strategy of presenting the issue as one of equity, not of role change. Third, women had played active roles in World War I; they joined the war relief effort and worked in nontraditional occupations as replacements for men who had entered military service. Fourth, Catt had obtained the active support of President Woodrow Wilson by supporting his policies both during and after the war. Women's rights leaders also sought his advice on the strategy and tactics to use in their campaign. Fifth, women's suffrage became a component of the Progressive-Era reform movement, which had middle-class support.[16]

The opposition to women's suffrage at the turn of the century had come from several groups. They included southern political leaders, who were inheritors both of a patriarchal culture and of memories of northern women's strong support for the antislavery movement, and conservative church leaders, primarily those of the Catholic Church and fundamentalist Protestant sects. Some business interests feared that women voters would support child labor laws and the legal recognition of unions. Many political bosses believed that women would support reforms that would weaken the power of their political machines. The liquor and brewery interests thought that women would support a constitutional amendment to forbid the manufacture and sale of alcoholic beverages. But by 1919, child labor regulations, political reforms, and the Eighteenth (Prohibition) Amendment had already been enacted, without the benefit of women's votes, so some of the opposition to women's suffrage weakened.[17]

Although women had obtained the right to vote, many of them did not immediately exercise it. Voting is an acquired habit that must be learned over time and through experience. Those intimidated by past cultural norms were slow to learn the value of the vote. Although the Nineteenth Amendment had been in force since August 1920, several states did not reopen their voter registration rolls to allow women to register to vote in that year's presidential election. Many women had difficulty getting to voter registration offices because of their household and child care responsibilities and the limited means of transportation. Some had to travel to register at a county courthouse, township office, or city hall that was open only during working hours on weekdays. Gradually, however, women began to participate in elections in larger numbers. Women's voter turnout rates have equaled or exceeded those of men in presidential elections since 1980 and have approximated those of men in midterm elections since 1986.[18]

Minority Group Suffrage

Members of minority groups have also been denied their political rights. Although the Fifteenth Amendment to the Constitution formally ended racial barriers to voting in March 1870, effective enfranchisement of most black citizens living in the South and of minority citizens living in other areas did not come until passage of the Voting Rights Act in 1965. The Fifteenth Amendment specified that "the right of citizens of the United States to vote shall not be denied or abridged by the United States or by any State on account of race, color, or previous condition of servitude." The second section of the amendment gave Congress the power to enact legislation to enforce it. However, several laws enacted by Congress in the 1870s, which sought to put an end to acts of violence and intimidation aimed at preventing black citizens from voting, were narrowly interpreted by the Supreme Court and proved to be ineffective.[19]

A number of methods were used in the southern states to prevent minority citizens from voting. The poll tax, for example, had to be paid before a citizen could register to vote. Though often a seemingly nominal sum, the tax was nevertheless a burden to those of very low income, and in effect it made voting a luxury not only for poor blacks but for poor whites as well. The tax often had to be paid many months before an election, so it disenfranchised newcomers to the district and absent-minded citizens who forgot to pay it.[20]

Another device was the literacy test, which required that citizens demonstrate their ability to read and interpret a specific document, such as the state constitution or the federal Constitution. Considering the problems that judges often have in agreeing how a constitutional provision should be interpreted, this requirement, even if administered fairly, could be difficult to meet—and voting registrars in many southern states failed to administer it fairly. In addition, some states attempted to exempt white citizens from the literacy requirement altogether by specifying that men who had been eligible to vote before a specified date, as well as their sons and grandsons, could continue to vote. The Supreme Court eventually struck down this so-called grandfather clause.[21]

A device used to prevent black citizens in the South from voting was the white primary. After the end of Reconstruction in 1877, the Democratic Party became the dominant party in most of the South. Thus, the decisive point in the election process was the Democratic Party's nominating convention or primary election. In 1923, Texas enacted a law stating that only white citizens could vote in the Democratic primary. This law was overturned by the Supreme Court in 1927.[22] The Texas legislature then passed a law giving the Democratic Party the right to specify who was eligible for party membership and participation in party activities. The Supreme Court struck down this law in 1932.[23] Other southern states adopted similar measures. However, in 1941 the Supreme Court ruled that primary elections are subject to federal control if they are an integral part of the election process and if they effectively determine the choices available to voters in the general election, and in 1944 the white primary was held to be a violation of the Fifteenth Amendment.[24]

Violence was also used in an attempt to deny voting rights to black southerners. During Reconstruction, a secret society—the Ku Klux Klan—was organized in the South, and among its principal activities were threats or acts of violence and economic coercion aimed at intimidating black citizens so they would refrain from exercising their right to vote and other civil rights.[25] These practices continued well into the twentieth century—indeed, in some areas of the South, even after the passage of the 1965 Voting Rights Act.[26] This act made it a federal crime to threaten, intimidate, or coerce or to attempt to threaten, intimidate, or coerce people to prevent them from exercising their right to vote.[27] Unfortunately, however, a general climate of intimidation, and especially the threat of economic retaliation, is both difficult to overcome and difficult to prove in court.

Southern political leaders whose own political interests were served by the exclusion of blacks from effective political participation tried to prevent federal protection of the rights of black citizens. One way was to use the tradition of unlimited debate (the filibuster) in the Senate to kill proposed civil rights legislation. After the Democrats gained a majority in Congress in the election of 1932, southern Democrats used their positions of leadership in congressional committees to block such legislation. Furthermore, the Democratic Party's requirement, which was in effect until 1936, that a presidential candidate must receive two-thirds of the votes in the convention in order to win the nomination, gave the South an effective veto in the Democratic Party's presidential nominating process.[28]

The systematic denial of minorities' basic political rights came under increasing attack during the 1950s and 1960s. Four federal laws, a constitutional amendment, extensive litigation, and vigorous federal enforcement were all parts of a broad effort to guarantee the right to vote to all citizens. The first civil rights law enacted in the postwar era was the Civil Rights Act of 1957, which authorized the United States attorney general to seek court injunctions on behalf of specific individuals whose right to vote had been interfered with on the basis of race. If, for example, a black citizen tried to register to vote in a southern county and was subsequently fired from his job, the attorney general could apply for an injunction to have the citizen returned to his job. But such suits had to be filed in the federal district court in whose jurisdiction the intimidation took place, and some southern federal district judges were slow to act on these cases. Furthermore, the victims of the discriminatory acts were hesitant to become involved in legal proceedings. The 1957 act also established the Civil Rights Commission and the Civil Rights Division of the Department of Justice and extended the jurisdiction of the federal district courts in civil cases. Nevertheless, it did not prove to be effective in securing voting rights for all Americans.

Consequently, another civil rights statute was enacted in 1960, giving the U.S. attorney general the right to file suits against states as well as against specific individuals, such as local registrars of voters.[29] This expansion of federal authority was deemed necessary because in some states registrars had resigned and had not been replaced, leaving no one who could be sued in an attempt to end discriminatory practices. The 1960 act also authorized the federal courts to appoint voting referees, who could register voters in a particular county if the court found a pattern or practice of discrimination there.[30] The problem, however, was that these remedies had to be applied on a case-by-case basis. The proceedings were often very slow, and some southern federal district court judges were reluctant to find a pattern of discrimination. Thus, the 1960 law did not bring an end to racial discrimination in determining access to the ballot box.

In the Civil Rights Act of 1964, Congress attempted to ensure that literacy tests, when used, would be administered fairly. The law required each state to establish a uniform set of standards, procedures, and practices for the administration of elections. Alleged (undocumented) completion of a sixth-grade education was to be considered sufficient proof of literacy for eligibility to vote in a federal election. When literacy tests were used, they had to be individually administered in writing, with a copy of the test and its results made available within twenty-five days to the individual who had taken it and a copy retained by the registrar of voters as part of the official records.

These provisions, however, still did not end the abuse of literacy tests and the use of other discriminatory tactics. Therefore, the Voting Rights Act of 1965 suspended the use of literacy tests in all states or counties where less than 50 percent of the voting-age population of the state or county was registered to vote as of November 1, 1964. The act authorized the appointment of federal examiners to evaluate the qualifications of persons seeking to register to vote in those areas. Eligible persons would be registered, and lists of those registered were to be provided to state election officials. Initially, the act was to be in effect for a period of five years, but in 1970 it was extended for another five years, in 1975 for eight years, and in 1982 for twenty-five years.[31] The act and its extensions have been highly effective in the

TABLE 5-1
Voter Registration by Race in Eleven Southern States, 1960–1996

	Percent of Voting-Age Population Registered	
Year	White	Black
1960	61.1	29.1
1970	56.0	43.5
1980	71.9	65.8
1988	67.0	63.7
1996	68.3	64.9

SOURCES: Bureau of the Census, *Statistical Abstract of the United States 1982–1983* (Washington, D.C.: Government Printing Office, 1984), 488, Table 799. The 1988 data were calculated from "Voting and Registration in the Election of November 1988" (advance report), Bureau of the Census, *Current Population Reports,* ser. P-20, no. 435 (Washington, D.C.: Government Printing Office, February 1989), Table C. The 1996 data were calculated from Lynn M. Casper and Loretta E. Bass, "Voting and Registration in the Election of November 1996," Bureau of the Census, *Current Population Reports,* ser. P-20, no. 504 (Washington, D.C.: Government Printing Office, July 1998), Detailed Tables 2, 3, Table 4.

fight against the discriminatory administration of election laws. Racial differences in the proportion of the voting-age population that is registered to vote have greatly declined since 1960, but they have not been entirely eliminated (see Table 5-1).

Registration and Election Laws and Procedures

Even fairly administered election laws and procedures may constitute obstacles to voting. The extent to which they do is a function of both the nature of the laws and procedures and certain characteristics of the electorate.

Comparisons of voter turnout rates among states within the United States and between the United States and other developed democracies reveal that obstacles to voting created by election administration laws and procedures do have a depressing effect on turnout. Furthermore, in states or countries where the costs of voting are higher in terms of time and effort (expended in part for information gathering), individuals with fewer of those resources are less likely to vote, unless the lack of resources is offset by the political mobilization effects of group membership and group activity.[32] In effect, then, the election procedures common in the United States prior to 1995 contributed to class differences in voter registration and turnout. Middle- and upper-class citizens are more likely to vote than are lower-class citizens.[33] Educational attainment is an important determinant of who votes, and one reason is that those with more education are usually more able to cope with the bureaucratic hurdles created by the registration and election administration procedures.[34]

Voter turnout rates in the United States lag substantially behind those found in other developed democracies. In his study of voter turnout, G. Bingham Powell Jr. reports that in the period 1972–1980, an average of 80 percent of the eligible voters in twenty developed democracies actually voted; during the same years the average voter turnout in the United States was 54 percent.[35] Compared with other developed democracies, however, the United States has a political culture that is more supportive of political participation. Americans are more likely to consider themselves a member of a political party, to have a sense of internal political efficacy, and to express at least some interest in politics, although they are less likely to express trust in government. Americans are also more likely to discuss politics with others, to try to convince others how to vote in an election, and to work for a candidate or political party. Demographic characteristics associated with higher voter trunout rates (such as higher level of education and white-collar employment) are also more prevalent in the United States.[36] Why, then, are Americans much less likely to vote than the citizens of other democratic countries?

Political scientists generally agree that the voter registration and election administration laws, as well as certain characteristics of the political party system and the governmental system structure, contribute to lower voter turnout rates in the United States. They disagree, however, concerning the extent to which the low voter turnout rates can be explained by institutional structure rather than by political culture. Powell concludes that between 1971 and 1980, the absence of nationally competitive election districts and the weakness of links between various societal groups and the political parties, together with the large number of younger voters, contributed significantly to lower turnout in the United States. Also significant in the preceding decade (1961–1970) was the absence of either automatic registration procedures or government-conducted voter registration. The previously mentioned aspects of American political culture (an interest in politics and a sense of internal political efficacy), as well as a relatively well educated electorate, increased voter turnout in the United States by about 5 percent over that of other developed democracies. However, Powell estimates that the necessity for American citizens to take the initiative to register to vote decreased voter turnout by 16 percent during the 1970s. Moreover, the weak link between American political parties and groups in the society decreased voter turnout by an estimated 3 percent, and the low level of competitiveness among political parties in some electoral constituencies reduced turnout by 3 percent.[37]

Other scholars have argued that the party system and the institutional structure, not aspects of political culture such as interest in politics and sense of internal political efficacy, help to explain low voter turnout. Robert W. Jackman, for example, examined the same developed democracies as Powell, with the exception of Spain, and used data from the same decades. Jackman reports that five institutional factors contribute to *increased* voter turnout: (1) mandatory voting, (2) a unicameral legislature, (3) a two-party system rather than a multiparty system, (4) nationally competitive election districts, and (5) fewer disproportionalities in translating votes cast into seats won in the lower house of the national legislature. Although multiparty systems offer the voters more choices, Jackman argues that institutional arrangements that allow the electorate a more direct role in the formation of the government, as a two-party system does, are more likely to stimulate turnout.[38]

Voter Registration and Turnout

Voter registration systems were established to ensure that only those who are legally entitled to vote do so and that each voter casts only one ballot in each election. Most countries limit eligibility to vote to their own citizens who have reached a minimum age. In the United States, citizens must also be legal residents of the state in which they vote in order to be eligible.[39] But the registration process frequently constitutes a major barrier to voting. Those who do not register cannot vote, but those who do register are likely to vote. Surveys conducted by the Census Bureau show that in 1968, 72.3 percent of the voting-age population was registered to vote, and 93.8 percent of those registered voted in the 1968 presidential election.[40] In 1996, only 65.9 percent of the voting-age population was registered to vote and only 82.2 percent of those registered voted in the 1996 presidential election. Almost one-third of the voting-age population was not registered in 1996.[41] Thus, voting turnout in the United States has declined both because a smaller percentage of those eligible have registered and because fewer of those registered are voting than have voted in the past.[42] The large majority of nonvoters are individuals who have not registered.

Early voter registration laws authorized local officials to prepare registration lists on the basis of existing lists and their own knowledge of community residents. A citizen did not have to apply personally in order to be registered.[43] The problem with this system was that it permitted errors of both omission and commission. Some eligible voters were missed, and local officials could list as eligible those who had died, who lived in some other district, or who simply did not exist. These defects led to the establishment of registration systems in which an individual had to make personal application to register, usually at some centrally located office.

Voter registration systems were established in the colonies and in some of the original thirteen states but were soon abolished in most jurisdictions because of annoyed citizens' objections to the inconvenience. Their reestablishment began largely in the 1860s—first in states with large cities, where voting fraud was more prevalent, and then in rural areas and small towns, when it became clear that voting fraud could occur there as well. Registration requirements were instituted first in the North and East, then spread to the West and South.[44] In his study of voter registration, Joseph P. Harris observed: "The historical trend of registration laws has been constantly to extend the application, and, as voting frauds occur, to make the system more and more stringent. The result is that registration in many states has become expensive, cumbersome, inconvenient to the voter, and not yet particularly effective in preventing frauds."[45]

In the past, most registration laws required lengthy residence in the state, proof of residence, and registration only at a central office (such as a county courthouse or city hall), and the registration books had to be closed long before the election. Once registered, an individual had only to vote at least once every few years (usually four or five) in order to remain registered, a system known as permanent registration.

Some states used a periodic registration system, in which voters had to register periodically, whether they had voted or not. It is in part because of these requirements that the voter turnout rate in the United States has been and remains one of the lowest among the developed democracies.[46]

Voter registration systems are designed to prevent voting fraud. However, putting the burden of registration on the citizen means that for many citizens, the costs imposed by such a system (in terms of the inconvenience of having to go to a central registration office that may be open only during working hours) exceed the perceived value derived from voting. These are the citizens who do not register and do not vote.[47]

During the 1960s and 1970s, many registration procedures were changed to make it easier for citizens to vote. Some of these changes were imposed by the courts because some state election administration laws violated the Constitution. For example, the Supreme Court has ruled that, except in rare circumstances, registration books should close no earlier than thirty days before an election.[48] Other changes were made by state legislatures seeking to encourage voting participation. The length of residency required was shortened in many states.[49] Several states moved the closing date for registration nearer to the day of the election or established procedures so that citizens could register on the day of the election. Some states made absentee ballots easier to obtain, or permitted individuals to register at motor vehicle bureaus, social service agencies, or by mail, although the latter might require the signature of a witness or notarization of the citizen's signature by a notary public. The state of Washington experimented with conducting primary elections by mail-in ballots in some counties; Oregon adopted voting-by-mail procedures.

Were these changes successful in increasing registration and turnout? One study concluded that the states that had higher rates of turnout were those that facilitated registration by keeping voter registration offices open for consistent times and for evening and weekend registration, set the closing date for registration closer to the date of the election, and allowed nonvoters to remain on the voter registration rolls for a longer period before being purged.[50] Another study indicated that each day added to the closing date for registration reduced turnout by one-tenth of 1 percent.[51] Voter registration was found to increase in states that permitted citizens to register at motor vehicle bureaus.[52]

Analysis of voter registration patterns in the 1972 presidential election suggests that just a few changes would have increased voting turnout by more than 9 percent. The change that would have produced the largest increase would be to eliminate the closing date for registration. Turnout would also be increased by keeping registration offices open during the forty-hour work week, in the evenings, and on Saturdays, and by permitting absentee registration for the sick, the disabled, and those away from the district on election day.[53]

Use of same day registration effectively increased turnout in Minnesota, Maine, and Wisconsin, all of which adopted this procedure in the mid-1970s. Between 1976 and 1992, the average increase in turnout in those three states was 3.04 percent; states not using same day registration had a 1.69 percent decrease in turnout.[54] The states vary significantly in the conditions governing use of the absentee ballot. Some states permit anyone to request an absentee ballot, whereas others—fearing voter fraud—make voting by absentee ballot more difficult. States that are more lenient have higher rates of voter turnout.[55] States that permit citizens to vote by mail (as do Washington and Oregon) have substantially increased voter turnout.[56] Some research suggests that allowing citizens to register by mail does not significantly increase turnout, however.[57]

The National Voter Registration Act and Turnout

Concern with the barriers to voting created by the voter registration process in many states led to a campaign to enact federal laws regulating the registration process. That campaign resulted in the National Voter Registration Act of 1993 (NVRA), also known as the "motor voter" law. It required the states to make several changes in their voter registration laws by January 1, 1995. All states that did not have same day registration (allowing citizens to register to vote on election day) were required to implement an active "motor voter" program. Persons being served in a state's motor vehicle bureau are supposed to be asked if they want to register to vote and to be registered if they respond positively. States are also required to offer voter registration opportunities, inquiring whether clients want to register to vote, in their social service agencies. In agency-based registration, it is to be made clear to clients that they need not register in order to be eligible for agency services. States also have to offer their residents the opportunity to register to vote by mail, with no verification by notarization or the signature of a witness required. Before the names of persons on the voter registration rolls can be purged for failure to vote, a letter of notification must be sent.[58]

Several states initially refused to implement the law and sued to have it declared unconstitutional. The objections included the alleged federal government's usurpation of the power granted to the states in Article I, Section 4 of the Constitution to regulate the times, places, and manner of holding elections for United States senators and representatives. However, that section of Article I also states that Congress "may at any time by law make or alter such regulations, except as to the places of chosing Senators." The states suing to have the law declared unconstitutional lost, but the suits did delay implementation of the NVRA in those states. Another major concern of many states was the possibility of fraud—that is, some persons might register who were not citizens or might register more than once. States also opposed the law's notification requirement concerning removal of non-voters' names from the voter registration rolls. Some objections also came from Republican governors and attorneys general, who feared that agency-based registration would be used largely by persons who would be more likely to support Democratic Party candidates.

What have been the consequences of the National Voter Registration Act? Research by the Federal Election Commission suggests that it has been effective in increasing voter registration; 71.77 percent of the eligible voters registered in 1996.[59] The effects on voter turnout were limited, however. One estimate is that the law did increase voter turnout in those states that had to make the most major changes in their voter registration laws. The impact of the NVRA between 1995 and 1996 was greater in those states that were more willing to implement its requirements; mean voter turnout declined by 1.5 percent less in those states unwilling to do so. (Turnout declined in all states between 1992 and 1996.)[60] The NVRA certainly makes it easier to register to vote, but the citizens who actually vote are those who are politically involved. If they are not, registration of this type will not automatically increase voter turnout.

Political Mobilization and Voter Registration

Citizens who are registered can be mobilized to vote. Mobilization processes can be cognitive, in which individuals acquire and process political information, have the requisite attitudes and beliefs to perceive political participation as being in their interest and to know which choices of candidate best serve their interests, and are sufficiently stimulated to participate in politics and to vote. Political mobilization can also be spurred by external forces, either informally by friends and acquaintances or more formally through targeted drives carried out by candidates, political party organizations, and interest groups. The 1998 elections provide many examples of effective political mobilization drives focusing on specific states, congressional districts, or segments of the electorate. For example, in 1998 supporters of a casino gambling proposition on the California ballot targeted all of the state's registered Latino voters to mobilize them to vote in favor of the ballot proposition. African American leaders in South Carolina targeted all of the state's registered African Americans, urging them to support the Democratic candidates for governor and United States senator. Emily's List, a political action committee that supports pro-choice Democratic women candidates, targeted 3.4 million women to mobilize them in support of Democratic women candidates for the U.S. House and Senate.[61] Thus, the NVRA can contribute to increased voter turnout when issues or candidates stimulate political involvement or when candidates or political organizations conduct effective voter turnout drives to mobilize a targeted subset of those who have registered.

As of 1998, one state (North Dakota) did not require its citizens to register to vote and six states had adopted election day registration.[62] In one of these six states (Maine), citizens must register at a central office in the local jurisdiction before going to the polling place, but in the other five, they may register at the polling place itself. In Wisconsin, citizens may register at the polling place if they have identification or can be identified by a witness. The two states that were using election day registration at the time of the 1976 election (Wisconsin and Minnesota) had an increase in voter turnout, but turnout declined that year in most other areas of the country.[63]

Election day registration does present certain problems. If a large number of people attempt to register on election day, there may be considerable delay at the polling places. This occurred in Minnesota in 1976, when almost 23 percent of those voting registered at a polling place on election day.[64] Another problem is the danger of fraudulent registration; vigilant and vigorous enforcement of the law is more difficult when large numbers of people attempt to register on election day. One way of limiting registration fraud is to mail, after the election, a nonforwardable verification to the address of each election day registrant. Although that technique may curb repeat performances by those who registered illegally on election day, the outcome of the election in which they have already voted is, unfortunately, not affected.

An evaluation of election day registration in Wisconsin after the 1976 election found such problems as long lines of voters angered by the delays, confusion caused by the process, voters who registered in the wrong districts, multiple registrations by some individuals, acceptance of inadequate proof of residence, and substantial additional costs of administration. Some of the same problems were encountered in Minnesota in 1976, but as noted, voter turnout did increase in both states, and there were substantial increases in some of the larger cities.[65]

Alternative Methods of Voter Registration

A major difficulty with voter registration procedures in the United States is that citizens who have recently moved must either re-register if they have moved to a different jurisdiction, or file a change of address form if they have moved within the same city or county. Approximately 17 percent of the electorate moved at least once within a two-year period (1995–1996); almost one-third of the eligible voters between the ages of twenty and twenty-nine moved within that two-year period.[66] The combination of such registration procedures and the high mobility rate of the U.S. population depresses voter turnout. The effects of moving on voting registration are greatest among those with less education, who moved more recently, or who have relatively little political interest.[67]

In most other democratic countries, the burden of voter registration is assumed by the government rather than by the individual. The government crates a register of eligible voters by taking names from lists maintained for other purposes, or verifying eligibility of voters by mail or by door-to-door inquiry, or some combination of these procedures. One study of twenty-four democratic countries found that only five required citizens to apply for inclusion on the voter registration list. In the other nineteen, either citizens were automatically registered because they were on some other government list, such as a residency list or a list of taxpayers, or the government actively sought to register citizens by systematically sending representatives to every household.[68] Canada used an enumeration system. Two enumerators were appointed in each election district—one person from each of the two parties winning the largest proportion of the votes cast in that district in the preceding election. They went door to door within the constituency, listing the names of every eligible voter in each household. If, after making several calls at a household, they found no one at home, the enumerators left a notice informing the residents of their efforts to reach them, and included a telephone number so that the residents could call and register themselves. A new list of registered voters was compiled before each election.[69] In 1997 Canada changed its voter registration system. Elections Canada—the government agency now in charge of administering federal elections—creates a National Register of Electors, a computerized, permanent data base of persons eligible to vote in such elections. Citizens may elect not to have their name on the list, but then they must register before each federal election in their voting district with the supervisor of the election for that district. The National Register of Electors is updated with information from various other government agencies at the local, provincial, and national levels, and about 20 percent of the information in the register changes each year. The process makes possible continuous updating of the list of eligible voters and enables Elections Canada to provide each federal district election supervisor with a current eligible voter list before an election.[70]

Scheduling of Elections and Voter Turnout

Elections for government offices are held more frequently in the Untied States than in most other democracies. In his analysis of six states, Richard W. Boyd found that an average of eleven elections were held during a four-year period, 1972–1976.[71] Political leaders in most states prefer not to have state elections held in presidential election years, because they assume that national politics will influence state election outcomes.[72] Therefore, some states elect their governors and members of state legislatures at a time when no federal-level officials (president, senator, or representative) are being elected. The increased use of primaries to nominate candidates for state and local offices and to select delegates to national nominating conventions adds to the number of elections. Boyd's study indicated that the average registered voter for whom records could be checked voted more than four times between 1972 and 1976.[73]

The use of runoff primaries in some states, designed to ensure that the party's nominees for office are selected by a majority rather than a plurality, may reduce voter turnout by increasing the total number of elections in which citizens are called upon to vote. Runoff primaries are held primarily in the South and date from the time when the southern states traditionally elected only Democrats to public office. Turnout declined between the initial primary and the runoff primary in three-fourths of all Democratic primaries that preceded gubernatorial, senatorial, and congressional runoff elections held from 1956 to 1984. One explanation for this is the increasing presence of Republican opposition in the general-election contests; as Republican candidates' possibility of success in the general election increased, turnout in the Democratic Party's runoff primaries decreased. Other explanations for the decreased turnout in runoff elections are the closed primary and a longer period between the initial primary and the runoff primary.[74]

Although voter turnout in some states has been decreasing at the same time that the number of elections held in them has been increasing, it has also decreased in states that do not hold more elections now than they did in the past.[75] Studies comparing voter turnout among states over time, using state election data and voting-age population estimates, suggest that although the large number of elections held in the United States (as compared with other democracies) may decrease turnout in the nation as a whole, the differences in turnout among the states cannot be accounted for by differences in the number of elections they hold.

The use of survey data permits controlling for the effects of personal characteristics—both sociodemographic and attitudinal—while testing for the effects on voter turnout of the simultaneous holding of contests for various types of offices. Using survey data collected in 1976, 1980, and 1984, Boyd "Effects" concluded that residents of states that held gubernatorial elections at the same time as presidential elections were slightly more likely to vote. Holding senatorial elections concurrently with presidential elections had no effect on the turnout of those surveyed, but presidential primaries had the effect of depressing voter turnout in the general election.[76]

Many countries hold elections on a rest day, rather than on a workday as in the United States. Of twenty-seven democracies studied by Ivor Crewe in 1980, thirteen scheduled elections on a rest day and five scheduled them for a two-day period that included a workday and a rest day.[77] The number of hours the polls remain open, which may also affect turnout, varies in the United States from fifteen in New York to "at least four" in New Hampshire.[78] Other variables, such as the number of voting machines and the length of time a citizen must wait to vote, can affect the turnout rate.

Changing voter registration procedures would facilitate voting and would probably increase voter turnout. One change might be to have the U.S. Postal Service supply voter registration offices with change-of-address forms, thus allowing those who have recently moved to register or register in order to maintain their eligibility to vote in elections for federal offices. Administrative procedures would have to be changed in some states, but there would probably be a substantial increase in turnout by persons who have recently moved.[79] Making less restrictive the rules for voting by mail could also increase turnout. A number of democracies make it easier than the United States does for citizens to vote by mail. Several countries also establish polling places in such institutions as hospitals and homes for the aged.[80]

Opportunities for Other Forms of Political Participation

Citizen participation may occur not only directly (by voting; contacting public officials; contributing money to a candidate, political party, or political action committee; or running for public office), but also indirectly, through interest groups, which can have a significant impact on public policy at each stage of the policy process.

The making of policy can be viewed as having five stages: (1) enacting the law; (2) writing the regulations to put into effect the intent of the law; (3) developing the implementation procedures for carrying out the law and its accompanying regulations; (4) developing and putting into effect enforcement mechanisms to make sure that the policy is carried out and the relevant laws and regulations are enforced; and (5) creating and using evaluation procedures to determine whether the law is having the desired effects. The potential for citizen involvement exists at each stage, but it varies with the policy area, the decision-making structure, the government agency's attitudes toward citizen participation, and the characteristics of the citizens.

Running for Public Office

The rules governing the electoral system determine not only who votes but also who runs for public office. States differ in their eligibility requirements. Some states require potential candidates to pay a filing fee, and some also require them to obtain a specified number of signatures on a petition in order to run in a nominating election. The requirement of a high filing fee or a large number of signatures might discourage some citizens from running for office, although it is unlikely that a candidate who is able to attract the support of a significant number of individuals would be discouraged by such a requirement.

To eliminate frivolous candidacies, several states require that, to be eligible to enter a primary to seek their party's nomination for a major statewide office, such as governor, potential candidates receive the support of some party organization or group of officials. Usually this is done formally, at a state party convention. (The proportion of convention delegates needed for this purpose is not high—for example, 15 percent in Connecticut, 25 percent in New York, and 30 percent in Colorado.) Endorsements may also be granted informally, by party leaders. In some states, party leaders' support is also important in winning a party nomination for state legislative office.[81]

Campaign finance laws can, in effect, limit who can run for public office. The costs of political campaigns have increased more rapidly than the consumer price index. This has been in large part a consequence of the use of more expensive methods, such as polling and television advertising, and of a professional campaign staff, which usually includes advertising and survey research experts, to do work that formerly either was not done at all or was done by volunteers. Campaign finance laws at the national level and in many states specify who may contribute and how much may be contributed. These laws work to the advantage of candidates who are able to raise large sums of money consisting of small amounts from many contributors. The Federal Election Campaign Act of 1971 (amended in 1974, 1976, and 1979) regulates campaigns for federal office. Individual contributors are not permitted to donate more than $1,000, and political action committees no more than $5,000, to any one candidate in one election contest (general election or primary). Wealthy candidates for Congress and presidential candidates who refuse federal funding may spend unlimited amounts of their own money. Thus, candidates who can raise large sums in individual contributions of $1,000 or less, who attract many PAC contributions, and who are independently wealthy and can make large contributions or loans to their own campaigns are in a more favorable position.[82] Because of the financial burden they impose on most candidates, campaign finance laws have stimulated the use of mass mail fund-raising solicitations by individual candidates, party organizations, and interest groups. However, the proportion of citizens who reported making political contributions in a presidential election was no greater in 1996 than in 1968 (see Table 1-2).

Interest Group Activity

There are many potential contact points between citizens and public officials—at the federal, state, and local levels. Slightly more than one-fourth of the respondents to a 1976 survey reported having expressed their views in writing to a government official.[83] Much of the contacting of public officials that influences public policy occurs as a result of the activity of interest groups. Many thousands of such groups continually lobby the executive and legislative branches at all levels of government. They represent the interests of their members as perceived by the group's officers and staff, and their activities are often conducted without much awareness on the part of many of the members—who nonetheless help support these activities through their membership dues. The interests of college students are represented by both the U.S. Student Association and the Coalition of Independent College and University Students. In 1982, when the Reagan administration proposed changes in the eligibility criteria as well as reductions in funding for the programs providing grants and loans to college students, the association was an active member of a coalition of educational and other interest groups that successfully lobbied to prevent such changes.[84]

Interest groups can also influence government policy through the judicial system. An interest group that believes an action by the executive or legislative branch is illegal or unconstitutional can seek to have it overturned by a court decision. The number of government programs has increased substantially since the mid-1960s, and so has the use of the courts by interest groups pursuing a litigation strategy to obtain policy outcomes they have not been able to obtain from the executive or legislative branches.[85]

Direct Citizen Contact

Since 1960, there has been an increase in both the number of regulatory agencies and the number of regulations issued. The expansion of the regulatory process, particularly at the federal level, has increased the opportunity and the necessity for citizen contacts with the government. These contacts probably occur most often through the medium of groups representing business, labor, the consumer, and the general public, as well as the interest groups just mentioned, but some individual citizen contact also occurs. For example, citizens may comment on the regulations drafted to carry out a new law or on proposed revisions of existing regulations. State laws often mandate that public hearings be held before public utility commissions can grant rate increases to electric, gas, water, and telephone companies. Participation by citizens' organizations in these hearings varies considerably among the states; in about half the states, these grass-roots organizations seem to meet with greater success when they focus on issues with very little technical complexity but the potential for substantial political impact.[86]

Individual citizens often contact the government concerning not the broad content of a policy or the policy process but their own immediate problems. A citizen may complain to a local official or agency about such things as inadequate bus service, potholes in the streets, insufficient street lighting, or the lack of an adequate science education program in the local high school. These contacts reflect not only the need and the demand for a service but the awareness of a governmental unit's ability and responsibility to deliver it.[87] Some research suggests that the demand for services is a function of socioeconomic status; citizens of higher socioeconomic status are more likely to contact government agencies with demands for services than are citizens of lower socioeconomic status who have similar levels of service needs and awareness of governmental responsibility.[88] Other research indicates that older citizens who have more positive evaluations of service-provision agencies are more likely to contact public agencies for services or information and to file complaints with them. Income level appears not to be a consideration.[89] The extent to which citizens contact government agencies may vary with governmental structure: those of lower socioeconomic status are more likely to request service delivery in cities or counties where agencies have a centralized complaint bureau.[90]

Citizen participation is sometimes required by the law that establishes a government program. Funding for many public works projects cannot be approved unless evidence is provided that the environmental impact of the project has been studied, an environmental impact statement prepared, and a public hearing held to obtain citizens' reactions to the project. If citizens residing in an area through which a new road is to be built decide that the laws governing the determination of the route of a new road were not followed, they can, individually or as an organized group, petition their state's transportation department to have the route changed, or they can file suit in court to try to block the construction. Citizens and citizen organizations have made increasing use of lawsuits, both to overturn laws and decisions and to compel the responsible government agency to require strict enforcement of the laws.

Many government programs also require the establishment of citizen advisory boards, which can be a forum for input by ordinary citizens. Sometimes, however, these boards are composed largely of the representatives of specific interests associated with the program—companies or business associations that either receive the program's services or are involved in delivering them. Citizen participation in the advisory process may lend increased legitimacy to a policy and its implementation, but if the resulting policy or its implementation is not in accord with the preferences of the citizen advisers, negative attitudes toward the agency and its policies are a likely consequence.[91]

Summary

Patterns of political participation can be significantly influenced by a government's structure and by its laws and regulations. In the United States, the federal system of government and the division into three separate branches at the federal level create many access points at which citizens can make their views known to government officials—to influence government policy or to seek specific benefits under existing government programs. One outgrowth of the federal system is the multiplicity and frequency of elections, offering more opportunities for electoral participation than are available in most other democratic nations. Because the Constitution reserves most aspects of election regulation and administration to the states, there is considerable variation in electoral laws. In the past many citizens had to surmount problems to gain access to the ballot, but recent constitutional amendments, as well as laws and court decisions at both state and federal levels, have eliminated most of them.

Registration procedures, however, are still an electoral obstacle in many states. In the United States, citizens are required to register themselves in order to vote. In most other democratic nations, government agents carry out voter registration; no citizen initiative is required. That fact has a significant effect on who participates in elections in the United States. Even in states that allow voter registration by mail, the citizen must obtain the appropriate form, fill it out, and mail it, a procedure that requires a degree of initiative and effort. The use of an absentee ballot (which tends to reduce voter turnout) also varies widely among the states.

The National Voter Registration Act of 1993, which became effective in 1995, requires state motor vehicle bureaus to ask clients if they want to register. State social service agencies also provide opportunities to register to vote, but both the states and their agencies vary significantly in the vigor with which they promote voter registration.

Patterns of campaign participation are influenced by the government laws and regulations that govern eligibility to be a candidate for office and that govern campaign finance. In most states, the laws and regulations that concern political parties have tended to limit their role in nominating candidates and in managing and funding campaigns, and to increase the activity of the candidates' own organizations, such as Nixon's Committee for the Re-election of the President (CREEP).

Americans have traditionally organized formal groups for the purpose of influencing the making, administering, and enforcement of government policy. Since the 1960s, the increased activity of government in many areas has led to a substantial increase in the number of interest groups represented in Washington. Organized activity seeking to influence government policy has also expanded at the state and local levels. In part, this can be attributed to laws that require the views of citizens to be obtained during the decision-making process; local government units often must hold public hearings before making final decisions on budgets, capital improvements, or the issuance of regulations.

Comparative studies of patterns of political participation have reached different conclusions about the relative importance of political systems and governmental institutions and of social and political culture, but research provides evidence that both contribute to the patterns found in developed democracies. A different institutional structure and cultural differences would undoubtedly produce different patterns and levels of political participation in the United States.

Notes

1. Today, only one-fourth of the world's nations have competitive free elections in which the people decide who shall govern. See David Butler, Howard R. Penniman, and Austin Ranney, "Introduction: Democratic and Non-Democratic Elections," in *Democracy at the Polls,* ed. David Butler, Howard R. Penniman, and Austin Ranney (Washington, D.C.: American Enterprise Institute, 1981), 1–6; G. Bingham Powell Jr., *Contemporary Democracies: Participation, Stability, and Violence* (Cambridge: Harvard University Press, 1982); Lawrence LeDuc, Richard G. Niemi, and Pippa Norris, "Introduction: The Present and Future of Democracies," chap. 1 in *Comparing Democracies,* ed. Lawrence LeDuc, Richard G. Niemi, and Pippa Norris (Thousand Oaks, Calif.: Sage, 1996).
2. The arguments on this subject at the Constitutional Convention are presented in Madison's "Notes on the Constitution"; see Max Farrand, ed., *The Records of the Federal Convention of 1787,* 3 vols. (New Haven: Yale University Press, 1911).
3. See Kirk Harold Porter, *A History of Suffrage in the United States* (New York: AMS Press, 1971), chap. 1; and Dudley O. McGovney, *The American Suffrage Medley* (Chicago: University of Chicago Press, 1949), chap. 2.

4. The amount of property required varied with the nature of the state's agrarian economy. In New England, few farms were as large as 50 acres, whereas in the South most farms were at least that large. See Porter, *History of Suffrage,* 7–14.
5. Ibid., chaps. 2, 3, and 4.
6. Charles E. Johnson Jr., *"Nonvoting Americans,"* Bureau of the Census, *Current Population Reports,* ser. P-23, no. 102 (Washington, D.C.: Government Printing Office, April 1980), 2, Table A.
7. Eleanor Flexner, *Century of Struggle* (Cambridge: Harvard University Press, 1959), 15.
8. Ibid.
9. Ibid., 164.
10. Ibid., chap. 3.
11. Ibid., chap. 5.
12. Ibid., 74–77.
13. Barbara Sinclair Deckard, *The Women's Movement,* 3d ed. (New York: Harper and Row, 1983), 255–264; and Nancy McGlen and Karen O'Connor, *Women, Politics, and American Society,* 2d ed. (Upper Saddle River, N.J.: Prentice Hall, 1998), 20–40; M. Margaret Conway, Gertrude A. Steuernagel, and David W. Ahern, *Women and Political Participation* (Washington, D.C.: CQ Press, 1997) 7–14.
14. John J. Stucker, "Women as Voters: Their Maturation as Political Persons in American Society," in *A Portrait of Marginality,* ed. Marianne Githens and J. L. Prestage (New York: McKay, 1977), 268.
15. Ibid., 269–270.
16. Deckard, *Women's Movement,* 281; Flexner, *Century of Struggle,* chap. 17; and McGlen and O'Connor, *Women, Politics, and American Society,* 27–37.
17. Flexner, *Century of Struggle,* chap. 22.
18. Conway, Steuernagel, and Ahern, *Women and Political Participation,* 79–80, Tables 5.1 and 5.2.
19. Richard P. Claude, *The Supreme Court and the Electoral Process* (Baltimore: Johns Hopkins University Press, 1970), 53–63.
20. For a discussion of the use of the poll tax to exclude black voters in the South, see V. O. Key Jr., *Southern Politics* (New York: Vintage, 1949), chap. 27.
21. *Guinn v. United States,* 238 U.S. 347 (1915); and *Lane v. Wilson,* 307 U.S. 263 (1939). For a discussion of these cases, see Claude, *Supreme Court,* 74. On the origins and use of the grandfather clause, see Key, *Southern Politics,* 535–539.
22. *Nixon v. Herndon,* 273 U.S. 536 (1927).
23. *Nixon v. Condon,* 286 U.S. 73 (1932).
24. *US. v. Classic,* 313 U.S. 299 (1941); and *Smith v. Allwright,* 321 U.S. 659 (1944).
25. David M. Chalmers, *Hooded Americanism: The First Century of the Ku Klux Klan, 1865–1965,* 2d ed. (New York: Franklin Watts, 1981); Arnold S. Rice, *The Ku Klux Klan in American Politics,* Southern Literature and History Series, no. 65 (Brooklyn: MSG Haskell House, 1972); and William Gillette, *Retreat from Reconstruction, 1869–1879* (Baton Rouge: Louisiana State University Press, 1979), 25–28, 52–55.
26. See Commission on Civil Rights, *Political Participation* (Washington, D.C.: Government Printing Office, 1968), part 111, chap. 7.
27. Sections 3 and 11b, *Voting Rights Act of 1965,* 79 Stat. 437, 42 U.S.C. 1973.
28. For an analysis of the rule and its repeal, see Austin Ranney, *Curing the Mischiefs of Faction* (Berkeley: University of California Press, 1975), 71, 75–76.
29. The text of the 1960 act and the Civil Rights Act of 1957 can be found in House Committee on the Judiciary, *Civil Rights Acts of 1957, 1960, 1964, 1968 (As Amended through the 93d Congress, First Session),* 93d Cong., 1st sess., 1974.
30. The 1960 act also required that election records, voter registration documents, and poll tax records be kept for twenty-two months, and upon request be provided to the U.S. attorney general.
31. For a brief history of the extensions, see "Voting Rights Act Extension Cleared

for President Reagan," *Congressional Quarterly Weekly Report,* June 26, 1982, 1503.

32. Sidney Verba, Norman H. Nie, and Jae-on Kim, *Participation and Political Equality* (Cambridge: Cambridge University Press, 1978).

33. M. Margaret Conway, "Political Participation in Midterm Congressional Elections: Attitudinal and Social Characteristics during the 1970s," *American Politics Quarterly* 9 (1981): 229–232; Jan E. Leighley and Jonathan Nagler, "Socioeconomic Class Bias in Turnout, 1964–1988: The Voters Remain the Same," *American Political Science Review* 86 (1992): 725–736; Jonathan Nagler, "The Effects of Registration Laws and Education on U.S. Voter Turnout," *American Political Science Review* 85 (1991): 1393–1465; Howard L. Reiter, "Why Is Turnout Down?," *Public Opinion Quarterly* 43 (1979): 297–311; Stephen D. Shaffer, "A Multivariate Explanation of Decreasing Turnout in Presidential Elections, 1960–1976," *American Journal of Political Science* 25 (1981): 68–95; Ruy A. Teixeira, *The Disappearing American Voter* (Washington, D.C.: Brookings Institution Press, 1992), chaps. 3 and 4; and Richard J. Timpone, "Structure, Behavior, and Voter Turnout in the United States," *American Political Science Review* 92 (1998): 145–158.

34. Raymond E. Wolfinger and Steven J. Rosenstone, *Who Votes?* (New Haven: Yale University Press, 1980), 18. See also Gabriel A. Almond and Sidney Verba, *The Civic Culture: Political Attitudes and Democracy in Five Nations* (Princeton: Princeton University Press, 1963), 379–384; and Robert E. Lane, *Political Life* (Glencoe, Ill.: Free Press, 1959), chap. 16.

35. G. Bingham Powell Jr., "American Voting Behavior in Comparative Perspective," *American Political Science Review* 80 (March 1986): 23.

36. Ibid., 19, Table 1.

37. Ibid., 33–37.

38. Robert W. Jackman, "Political Institutions and Voter Turnout in the Industrial Democracies," *American Political Science Review* 81 (June 1987): 405–423.

39. For a discussion of the origins and aims of voter registration systems, see Joseph P. Harris, *Registration of Voters in the United States* (Washington, D.C.: Brookings Institution, 1929).

40. Bureau of the Census, *Statistical Abstract of the United States 1998* (Washington, D.C.: Government Printing Office, October 1998), 297, Table 485.

41. Lynn M. Casper and Loretta E. Bass, "Voting and Registration in the Election of November 1996," Bureau of the Census, *Current Population Reports,* ser. P-20, no. 504 (Washington, D.C.: Government Printing Office, July 1998).

42. Ibid.

43. Harris, *Registration of Voters,* 67.

44. Ibid., 72–89.

45. Ibid., 89.

46. Ivor Crewe, "Electoral Participation," in Butler, Penniman, and Ranney, *Democracy at the Polls,* 232–239.

47. Francis Fox Piven and Richard A. Cloward, "Government Statistics and Conflicting Explanations of Nonvoting," *PS: Political Science & Politics* 22 (September 1989): 580–588.

48. See *Oregon v. Mitchell, Texas v. Mitchell, United States v. Idaho, United States v. Arizona,* 400 U.S. 112 (1970); *Dunn v. Blumstein,* 405 U.S. 330 (1972); *Marston v. Lewis,* 410 U.S. 679 (1973); and *Burns v. Forston,* 410 U.S. 686 (1973).

49. In 1950, the requirement for residency in the state was six months in eleven states, one year or twelve months in thirty-four, and two years in five. Council of State Governments, *The Book of the States 1950–1951* (Chicago: Council of State Governments, 1950).

50. Teixeira, *Disappearing American Voter,* chap. 4.

51. Staci Rhine, "Registration Reform and Turnout Change in the American States," *American Politics Quarterly* 23 (1995): 409–426.

52. Stephen Knack, "Does Motor Voter Work? Evidence from State-Level Data," *Journal of Politics* 57 (1995): 796–811; Rhine, "Registration Reform," 409–426.
53. Wolfinger and Rosenstone, *Who Votes?*, 72–78.
54. Mark J. Fenster, "The Impact of Allowing Day of Registration Voting on Turnout in U.S. Elections from 1960 to 1992," *American Politics Quarterly* 22 (1994): 74–87.
55. J. Eric Oliver, "The Effects of Eligibility Restrictions and Party Activity on Absentee Voting and Overall Turnout," *American Journal of Political Science* 40 (1996): 498–513.
56. David Foster, "States Get Creative to Raise Voter Turnout," *Nation's Cities Weekly*, October 31, 1994, 10; Paul E. Parker and James T. Przybylski, "It's in the Mail–Present Use and Future Prospects of Mail Elections," *State and Local Government Review* 25 (1993): 97–106.
57. Rhine, "Registration Reform"; and Teixeira, *Disappearing American Voter*, chap. 4.
58. *National Voter Registration Act of 1993*, Public Law 103–31. http://thomas. loc.gov.cgi-bin/bdquery/z?d103:HR00002:Tom:/bss/d103query.html.|
59. Federal Election Commission, *Executive Summary of the Federal Election Commission's report to the Congress on the Impact of the National Voter Registration Act of 1993 on the Administration of Federal Elections*, June 1997. Http://www. fec.gov/votregis/nvrasum.htm.
60. Michael D.Martinez and David B. Hill, "Did Motor Voter Work?," *American Politics Quarterly* 27 (1999): 296–315.
61. M. Margaret Conway, "Political Mobilization in America," in *The State of Democracy in America*, ed. William M. Crotty (Washington, D.C.: Georgetown University Press, 2000).
62. Council of State Governments, *The Book of the States 1998–1999* (Lexington, Ky.: Council of State Governments, 1998), 164, Table 5.6.
63. Richard Smolka, *Election Day Registration* (Washington, D.C.: American Enterprise Institute, 1977), 45.
64. Ibid., 26.
65. Ibid., 23–26, 40–45.
66. Bureau of the Census, *Statistical Abstract of the United States 1998* (Washington, D.C.: Government Printing Office, October 1998), 32, Table 32.
67. Peverill Squire, Raymond E. Wolfinger, and David P. Glass, "Residential Mobility and Voter Turnout," *American Political Science Review* 81 (March 1987): 45–65.
68. Interparliamentary Union, *Parliaments of the World* (New York: Macmillan, 1976). See also Crewe, "Electoral Participation," 240–250.
69. William M. Crotty, *Political Reform and the American Experiment* (New York: Crowell, 1977), 76–78.
70. Elections Canada On-line—National Register of Electors. http://ww.elections.ca. register/national_e.html.
71. Richard W. Boyd, "Decline of U.S. Voter Turnout: Structural Explanations," *American Politics Quarterly* 9 (1981): 145. Only eleven states have gubernatorial elections scheduled in 2000. Council of State Governments, *Book of the States 1998–1999*, 151–154, Table 5.1.
72. Boyd, "Decline of U.S. Voter Turnout," 140.
73. Ibid., 147.
74. Stephen G. Wright, "Voter Turnout in Runoff Elections," *Journal of Politics* 51 (May 1989): 385–397.
75. Richard W. Boyd, "Election Calendars and Voter Turnout," *American Politics Quarterly* 14 (January–April 1986): 89–104; Jeffrey Cohen, "Change in Election Calendars and Turnout Decline," *American Politics Quarterly* 10 (1982): 246–254.
76. Richard W. Boyd, "The Effects of Primaries and Statewide Races on Turnout," *Journal of Politics* 51 (1989): 730–739.
77. Crewe, "Electoral Participation," 242–247, Table 10-4.

78. Council of State Governments, *Book of the States 1998–1999*, 163, Table 5.5.
79. See Squire, Wolfinger, and Glass, "Residential Mobility," 57–58.
80. Crewe, "Electoral Participation," 242–247, Table 10-4. An objection to the use of absentee ballots is that they may contribute to problems of fraud and voter intimidation. For example, during the 1960s, in one small county in a midwestern state, more persons appeared to have voted than actually lived in the county according to the 1960 census data, and many of the votes had been cast by means of absentee ballots. Potential voters may feel obligated to vote for a particular set of candidates if political leaders have obtained absentee ballots for them (which in itself may be illegal).
81. Council of State Governments, *Book of the States 1998–1999*, 159, Table 5.3; Malcolm E. Jewell and David M. Olson, *American State Political Parties and Elections*, rev. ed. (Homewood, Ill.: Dorsey, 1982), 111–120.
82. M. Margaret Conway and Joanne Connor Green, "Political Action Committees and Campaign Finance," in *Interest Group Politics*, 5th ed., ed. Allan J. Cigler and Burdett A. Loomis (Washington, D.C.: CQ Press, 1998), 193–214.
83. Calculated from data in the American National Election Studies Cumulative File, 1948–1996.
84. Patterns of interest group politics are examined in Allan J. Cigler and Burdett A. Loomis, "Introduction: The Changing Nature of Interest Group Politics," in *Interest Group Politics*, 2d ed., ed. Allan J. Cigler and Burdett A. Loomis (Washington, D.C.: CQ Press, 1986), 1–27.
85. For a discussion of the litigation strategies of interest groups, see Stephen L. Wasby, "Interest Groups in Court: Race Relations Litigation," in Cigler and Loomis, *Interest Group Politics*, 251–270; Karen O'Connor, *Women's Organizations' Use of the Courts* (Lexington, Mass.: Lexington Books, 1970); and Karen O'Connor and Lee Epstein, "The Rise of Conservative Interest Group Litigation," *Journal of Politics* 45 (1983): 479–489.
86. William T. Gormley Jr., "Policy, Politics, and Public Utility Regulation," *American Journal of Political Science* 27 (1983): 86–105.
87. Bryan D. Jones et al., "Bureaucratic Response to Citizen-Initiated Contacts: Environmental Enforcement in Detroit," *American Political Science Review* 71 (1977): 148–165.
88. Elaine B. Sharp, "Citizen-Initiated Contacting of Government Officials and Socioeconomic Status: Determining the Relationship and Accounting for It," *American Political Science Review* 76 (1982): 109–115; and Elaine B. Sharp, "Citizen Demand in the Urban Context," *American Journal of Political Science* 28 (1984): 654–670.
89. Rodney E. Hero, "Explaining Citizen-Initiated Contacting of Government Officials: Socioeconomic Status, Perceived Need, or Something Else?," *Social Science Quarterly* 67 (1986): 626–635.
90. Arnold Vedlitz, James A. Dyer, and Roger Durand, "Citizen Contacts with Local Governments: A Comparative View," *American Journal of Political Science* 24 (1980): 50–67.
91. J. Vincent Buck, "The Impact of Citizen Participation Programs and Policy Decisions on Participants' Opinions," *Western Political Quarterly* 37 (1984): 468–482; and Daniel A. Mazmanian and Jeanne Nienaber, *Can Organizations Change? Environmental Protection, Citizen Participation, and the Army Corps of Engineers* (Washington, D.C.: Brookings Institution Press, 1979).

Chapter 6

The Rationality of Political Participation

In Chapters 1–5 we examined several explanations for and influences on political participation: the social characteristics of individuals, their attitudes, beliefs, and values; and the political environment, including the legal structure, the administration of elections, and the organizational structure of government. In this chapter we turn to an alternative explanation, which emphasizes the competition to obtain political outcomes based in part on the analogy of competition in free market economic systems. We consider whether participation in different types of political activity is rational, as that term is defined in rational choice theory. We also examine alternative explanations for the formation and maintenance of groups, usually referred to in this context as interest groups, from the perspective of rational choice theory.

The question has often been raised as to whether a rational person participates in politics at all. A rational person may be defined as one "who moves toward his goals in a way which, to the best of his knowledge, uses the least possible input of scarce resources per unit of valued output."[1] To be rational, then, is to be efficient in the allocation and use of scarce resources to obtain one's goals.[2] A rational person considers all alternatives, arrives at a "transitive preference ordering" among them, and chooses the one most preferred.[3] (*Transitive preference ordering* means that if *A* is preferred to *B*, and *B* is preferred to *C*, then *A* is preferred to *C*.) In rational choice theory, an approach to the study of human behavior developed first in economics, the classic definition of a rational person is one who "maximizes expected utility."[4]

According to a somewhat elaborate and restrictive conception of rational choice, "(1) the individual evaluates alternatives in his environment on basis of his preferences among them; (2) his preference

ordering is consistent and transitive; (3) he always chooses the preferred alternative." This conception is subject to three restrictions.
First, the individual evaluates alternatives in terms of expected values
and does not give direct consideration to changes in the happiness of
others caused by his actions—that is, "does not value the utility of
others as an end in itself." Second, the individual acts in conformity
with a particular set of roles. The actions associated with one specified role are more important than the actions associated with any
other role, and "the sources of the benefits and costs which accrue to
the individual from the specified role are differentiated from [inde-
pendent of] other aspects of the environment." Third, the individual
has access to a substantial amount of information when evaluating alternatives but makes predictions about the behavior of others with
some degree of uncertainty.[5]

It is explicit in this conception (and implicit in other conceptions)
that rational individuals do not give direct consideration to changes in
the happiness of others as a consequence of their choices, but it can be
argued that rationality does not preclude individuals from being motivated by altruistic values.[6] Several scholars have incorporated various forms of motivation other than narrow self-interest in their formulation of the calculus of rational choice. For example, in their
analysis of voting participation, William H. Riker and Peter C. Ordeshook include such considerations as the "social" satisfactions gained
from affirming allegiance to the political system, expressing a party
preference in deciding how to vote, and complying with democratic
norms, which include voting as a civic duty.[7] In his formulation of
vote choice, Anthony Downs refers to "long-run participation value"
—the value contributed to the survival of the political system as a result of citizens' participation in key political processes such as voting.[8]
It can be argued, however, that long-run participation value has "ex-
tra-rational" connotations, that is, it violates the basic assumptions of
rational choice theory.

If to be rational is to be efficient in the allocation and use of scarce
resources in seeking to obtain one's goals, then we may ask whether
political participation is an efficient use of resources. What can an individual try to obtain through political participation? The answer to
this question can be divided into two parts, political outcomes and
personal outcomes. Political outcomes include the victory of a preferred candidate or party in an election, the appointment of a partic-

ular person to public office, the passage or defeat of a referendum measure or an initiative, the defeat or enactment of a particular law, and the enforcement of a law or policy as a result of the implementation of particular regulations. Personal outcomes are frequently ignored, but they can be important. Individuals may enjoy participating politics for its own sake, in the same way that they enjoy sailing or playing softball or tennis. They may participate for the social contacts or for the sense of possibly contributing to the future success of a cause in which they believe.

Voting as Rational Behavior

If the rationality of the decision to vote were based on the probability that one person's vote would determine the outcome of the election, most citizens would conclude that this probability is so small that voting would not be an efficient use of resources unless it was costless. But a majority or near-majority of the electorate does vote in presidential elections, so for most citizens, the benefits of voting appear to outweigh its costs in terms of time, effort, and money spent gathering the information necessary to make a choice, registering to vote (which may involve merely filling out a postcard and putting it in the mail or the more costly act of traveling to the county or city courthouse, motor vehicle bureau, or social service agency), and going to the polls (which may require taking time off from work or may involve inconvenience costs, such as getting to the polls early before going to work or finding and paying a baby-sitter).

Downs has set forth five propositions with regard to voting:

1. When voting is costless, every citizen who is indifferent abstains, and every citizen who has any preference whatsoever votes.

2. If voting is costly, it is rational for some indifferent citizens to vote and for some citizens with preferences to abstain.

3. When voting costs exist, small changes in their size may radically alter the distribution of political power.

4. The costs of voting act to disenfranchise low-income citizens relative to high-income citizens.

5. It is sometimes rational for citizens to vote even when their short-run costs exceed their short-run returns, because social responsibility produces a long-run return.[9]

Riker and Ordeshook have stated the evaluative decision of whether to vote as an equation,

$$R = PB - C + D,$$

where R is the expected utility an individual derives from voting minus the expected utility of abstaining; P is the probability that the individual's vote will make a difference in the outcome of the election; B is the benefit an individual receives if his or her preferred candidate or party wins the election; C is the cost of voting; and D is the previously mentioned social satisfactions derived from voting, which include the long-run participation value, compliance with the democratic norm that the good citizen always votes, affirmation of allegiance to the political system, thus contributing to its maintenance and survival, expression of party preference, and, generally, involvement in the political process.[10]

Since the value of P is generally very small—say, 1/10,000—it is apparent that D, the social satisfactions derived from voting, must be very large if citizens are to be motivated to vote.[11] It would also help if C were kept as small as possible. That can be achieved individually by using easily recognizable cues for how to vote, such as party identification or the virtues of an already known candidate, and collectively by instituting procedures to facilitate registration (possibly having it done by the government rather than relying on citizen initiative), allowing time off from work to vote or holding the election on a Sunday or on a national holiday, and providing easily accessible polling places (see Chapter 5).

Other interpretations have been offered for the D term in the preceding equation. "Minimax regret," for example, is based on the assumption that voters seek to minimize their maximum level of regret at what the outcome would be if they did not vote. Suppose an individual had a favorite candidate but did not vote and did not encourage friends to vote, and the candidate lost in a very close election; that individual would have a maximum level of regret. Voters vote and encourage their friends to vote in order to avoid that experience.[12]

It has also been argued that citizens vote because of an ethical imperative, a belief that they have a moral obligation to vote. This belief is more widely held than acted upon, however; far more citizens state in surveys of public opinion that a good citizen should vote than actually turn out to vote in elections.[13] Another explanation is that, in deciding whether to vote, citizens take into account not merely the impact of their one vote but also the impact of the votes of people who have certain characteristics in common with them or who think as they do.[14] For example, rather than thinking only about the effect of one vote in electing people to office who will be vigilant in protecting the environment, a citizen may consider what the effect will be if many other people who care about environmental quality cast their votes on the basis of the candidates' past records on environmental issues and their promises for future action. The group impact could be considerable if voters make known that they care about an issue and that their vote choice (whether to vote and for whom to vote) will be significantly influenced by a particular policy or set of policy concerns.

One reason that people care about an issue and the policies associated with it is that they perceive how the issue affects them. The expected benefit from a policy that a candidate promises to maintain, or to work to put into place, can stimulate citizens' political interest and is one of the motivations to be active politically. This type of benefit, derived from political activity, is an investment benefit. A distinction can be made between *investment benefits,* which are dependent on the election outcome, and *consumption benefits,* which are derived from participation in a particular activity, such as the pleasure individuals derive from voting against candidates they dislike or the approval they get from politically interested friends because they have voted for a certain candidate.

If the leaders of a group can promise increased voter turnout among their members, they can use it as a bargaining tool. Anticipating an increase in either the probability of victory or the margin of victory, a candidate may thus be persuaded to adopt policies more favorable to the group or to maintain already favorable policies, if elected or reelected. (The probability that a candidate will negotiate for additional group support can be expected to decrease with the size of the expected victory margin.) Then the group leaders will have policy benefits that can either be distributed as rewards to members or used in part to reward themselves—for example, with new positions administering the programs that may result. The rewards may also be altruistic, as when those who advocate programs to improve environmental quality know that they have contributed to the attainment of that goal.[15]

A common approach to rationality in voting is to examine the fit between a citizen's issue positions and the perceived issue positions of the candidates seeking office. If one candidate's position is close to the citizen's issue preferences and the other candidate's position is quite far from them, the citizen will have a clear issue-difference basis for voting. Assuming that this issue is important to the citizen, he or she will be more likely to vote in the election. However, if the issue positions of both candidates are perceived as equally close to those of the citizen, there will be no stimulus for a decision to vote based on issue differences. Alternatively, the issue positions of the two candidates may be perceived as being equally distant from those of the citizen; this perceived distance could result in nonvoting among citizens who care about issue differences among candidates. John F. Zipp tested these assumptions about the voting-decision process, using data collected during the 1968, 1972, 1976, and 1980 presidential elections. Lack of difference between candidates' issue positions was important in accounting for nonvoting in 1972, 1976, and 1980, although the significant issues differed among elections. Alienation from the candidates on the basis of the distance of their issue positions from those of the citizen reduced voter turnout in 1968, 1972, and 1976, but again the significant issues differed.[16]

John H. Aldrich has argued that voter turnout is not a good example of a collective-action problem because many citizens perceive voting as a low-cost, low-benefit activity. Moreover, many characteristics of American elections and the electoral system violate the assumptions on which rational choice models are based—one of which is that there is only one contest, when in fact there are many, at different levels of government and also for different offices at the same level of government. He argues that voting decisions are not costly for most citizens, for information is readily available, its dissemination subsidized by candidates (as well as by political parties and interest groups) and facilitated by the news media. In contests for most offices he views citizens' other decision costs as minimal; most voters are guided by political party identification, interest group endorsements, and the experience and personality of the candidates.[17]

Having argued that voting is largely perceived as a low-cost, low-benefit activity, Aldrich draws several conclusions: (1) many variables are related to voter turnout at a weak or moderate level; (2) we cannot fundamentally explain why some citizens vote and others do not; (3) citizens make many errors (violations of rationality) in deciding whether to vote and if so for whom; (4) because the methodology of researching voter turnout is error-laden, estimations based on models of voter turnout will be subject to error. Aldrich also concludes that voter turnout is an "atypical" example of the types of collective-action problems that rational choice theory seeks to explain. Usually these problems concern high-cost and high-benefit activities. Aldrich in effect argues for a mobilization theory of voter turnout, in which politicians mobilize voters strategically in close elections.[18] He points out that rational choice models are election-specific, and therefore they are not the optimal means to explain long-term trends such as the decline in voter turnout that began in 1960. Aldrich argues for a more expansive definition of the *D* term in Riker and Ordeshook's equation, which would result in giving more weight to the consumption benefits of voting than to its investment benefits.[19]

The Substitutability of Other Forms of Political Participation

Experimental studies have shown that individuals who become aware of the low probability that their vote will make a difference in an election's outcome become more negative toward voting.[20] If that is the case, then citizens may choose to participate in politics in other ways, either in addition to or as a substitute for voting. They may view other forms of participation as more cost-effective. For example, writing a letter to an elected official urging support for a particular policy, such as keeping a neighborhood elementary school open, may be perceived as a more efficient way of obtaining the desired outcome —if the citizens can assume that the elected official is both attentive and responsive to their preferences. Or citizens might resort to more aggressive forms of participation, such as rent strikes, protest marches and other public demonstrations, occupation of buildings, or even acts of violence, in the belief that they are more likely to be effective.

The 1976 American National Election Study, conducted by the Center for Political Studies of the University of Michigan, includes data that can be used to examine the extent to which individuals who do not vote engage in other forms of political activity. The individuals

TABLE 6-1
Participation in Political Activities in the Preceding
Two or Three Years by Voters and Nonvoters, 1976

	Voters	Nonvoters
Nationally oriented activities		
Wrote letter to editor	4.7	2.0
Worked with others	11.0	3.9
Wrote to representative or other national leader	21.6	13.1
Signed petition	13.0	7.3
Participated in sit-in or other demonstration or protest	1.7	1.3
Locally oriented activities		
Attended school board or city council meeting	25.2	15.7
Wrote letter to editor	6.3	3.2
Worked with others	26.0	18.0
Spoke to or wrote to official	23.9	14.5
Signed petition	25.3	18.1
Participated in sit-in or other demonstration or protest	3.2	0.9
N	(1,087)	(689)

SOURCE: 1976 American National Election Study.

surveyed in 1976 were asked whether they had voted that year and whether in the preceding two or three years they had engaged in a number of other activities oriented toward (1) national problems and issues and (2) local government and politics. Patterns of political participation can also be examined in the light of the respondents' reported frequency of voting in past presidential elections in which they were eligible to vote.

Tables 6-1 and 6-2 indicate that of those interviewed in 1976, voters were more likely than nonvoters to have engaged in all forms of national and local political activity, regardless of whether it consisted of contacting the media or elected officials, community work, or protest demonstration. Political participation in 1976 may have been constrained by the unusual context of the election, which followed the Watergate scandal and the prior resignations from office of both the president and the vice-president elected in 1972. Examining participation in national and local political activities by reported frequency of voting in past presidential elections, and not just the 1976 election, is one way to remove some of the effects of the unusual context. Table 6-2 indicates that habitual voters are more likely to engage in all forms of national and local political activity than are those who

TABLE 6-2

Participation in Political Activities in the Preceding
Two or Three Years by Frequency of Voting in
Past Presidential Elections, 1976

	Frequency of voting in past presidential elections			
	Every election	Most elections	Some elections	No elections
Nationally oriented activities				
Wrote letter to editor	6.4	1.5	1.4	0.0
Worked with others	13.5	6.2	5.7	0.5
Wrote to representative or other national leader	27.6	13.6	8.9	6.8
Signed petition	16.1	9.4	3.2	4.8
Participated in sit-in or other demonstration or protest	2.6	0.5	1.1	0.0
Locally oriented activities				
Attended school board or city council meeting	28.8	20.6	9.6	13.0
Wrote letter to editor	8.1	4.0	2.8	1.0
Worked with others	29.8	23.8	11.0	13.5
Spoke to or wrote to official	27.8	18.9	14.5	8.2
Signed petition	31.7	19.6	6.0	17.9
Participated in sit-in or other demonstration or protest	3.2	1.5	1.1	1.0
N	(862)	(403)	(282)	(207)

SOURCE: 1976 American National Election Study.

report having voted infrequently (or not at all) in past presidential elections. However, those who in the 1976 survey claimed never to have voted in a presidential election did report having engaged in some forms of political activity more frequently than did those who voted infrequently. The participation gap was larger with regard to locally oriented activities than nationally oriented activities.

Other questions included in the American National Election Study asked if respondents had ever been involved in several types of campaign activity. Voters' and nonvoters' frequency of participation in these activities from 1964 to 1996 is compared in Table 6-3. If a substitution effect is occurring, we would expect nonvoters to participate in campaign activities relatively frequently. Table 6-3 shows that, as would be expected, voters were more likely to have engaged in various forms of campaign activity than nonvoters. However, almost 20

TABLE 6-3

Participation in Various Campaign Activities by Voters and Nonvoters, 1964–1996

Campaign activity	1964		1976		1988		1992		1996	
	Voters	Nonvoters	Voters	Nonvoters	Voters	Nonvoters	Voters	Nonvoters	Voters	Nonvoters
Tried to persuade others how to vote	35.5	17.3	43.6	19.6	35.8	13.2	43.3	19.3	33.8	11.9
Attended political meetings or rallies	10.6	2.4	8.3	3.0	9.4	2.0	10.2	1.4	7.2	1.1
Worked for a party or candidate	6.4	0.9	6.0	0.6	4.5	0.4	4.2	0.9	3.5	0.3
Wore campaign button or displayed campaign sign or bumper sticker	18.4	9.9	9.8	2.2	11.3	2.8	13.6	3.9	12.1	4.3
Gave money to party or candidate	12.8	3.1	19.6	7.9	11.9	1.0	9.2	1.3	10.7	2.2

SOURCE: American National Election Studies Cumulative File, 1948–1996.

percent of the nonvoters did claim to have attempted to persuade someone how to vote in the 1976 election. But why should people who do not vote themselves try to persuade others how to vote? One explanation relates to the time frame of the question. Respondents were asked about their activities "during the campaign," and it is not clear how they interpreted that phrase. They may have tried to persuade others how to vote during the nominating process, that is, in the primary or caucus; then, if their preferred candidate did not get the nomination, they did not vote in the general election. Another possibility is that nonvoters tried to persuade others not to vote. Persuasive efforts may also have been in part a function of the perceived closeness of the contest or some other contextual variable.

Nonvoters' reported participation in various forms of campaign activity was much less frequent than that reported by voters. Nonvoters were also less likely to report having been approached by others in persuasion efforts than were voters.

Two summary indexes can be constructed from the 1976 response data: participation in locally oriented political activities in 1976 and the preceding two or three years, and participation in nationally oriented political activities during that period. Slightly less than half the respondents whose voting participation could be checked reported engaging in at least one type of locally oriented political activity in 1976 and the preceding two or three years (see Table 6-4). Nonvoters scored lower than voters on both indexes, but when nonvoters did participate in politics, it was more likely to be in locally oriented activities than in nationally oriented activities.

This analysis of the relative frequencies of participation in campaigns and in nationally and locally oriented political activities suggests that although nonvoters are not entirely nonparticipants in politics, they tend to engage in these forms of political activity less often than do voters. Nonvoters' reported participation in campaign activities generally decreased between 1976 and 1988 (see Table 6-5). It is true that some nonvoters report that they frequently engaged in political activities other than voting, but they represent a very small proportion of nonvoters. It appears that, for the most part, citizens do not perceive other forms of political activity as an appropriate substitute for voting—though that does not in itself refute the rationality of engaging in such activity.

TABLE 6-4
Indexes of Political Activity by Voters and Nonvoters, 1976 and the Preceding Two or Three Years

Number of activities	All respondents	Voters	Nonvoters
Locally oriented activities			
0	52.6	47.7	60.5
1	21.9	22.8	20.5
2	11.8	12.4	10.9
3	8.1	10.0	5.1
4	3.3	4.0	2.3
5	2.2	3.1	0.7
Nationally oriented activities			
0	73.9	69.1	81.4
1	15.0	17.2	11.6
2	7.4	8.7	5.4
3	2.2	2.9	1.2
4	1.2	1.7	0.4
5	0.2	0.4	0.0
N	(1,776)	(1,087)	(689)

SOURCE: 1976 American National Election Study.
NOTE: 0 = participated in none of the political activities listed in Table 6-1 (nationally or locally oriented activities) or Table 6-3 (various campaign activities).

The Rationality of Interest Group Formation and Maintenance

The Nature of Collective Goods

An inquiry into the rationality of political activity should consider why people join together to seek to obtain what economists call "collective goods." A collective good is distinguished by two characteristics: indivisibility of benefit, and jointness of supply. *Indivisibility of benefit* means that the good is available for use by all citizens, even if they have not contributed to its provision. A public highway is one example: Anyone can use it, whether or not they paid a share of the taxes with which it was constructed. *Jointness of supply* means that one person's use of the good does not reduce the amount available to others. A frequently cited good in joint supply is air; examples of goods in joint supply that are provided by the government are fire protection and police protection.[21] Collective goods are subject to "crowding," if so many people try to use them that the enjoyment of them is limited. For example, a city highway may become so clogged

TABLE 6-5
Number of Campaign Activities Participated in by Voters and Nonvoters, 1964–1996

Number of activities	1964		1976		1988		1992		1996	
	Voters	Nonvoters	Voters	Nonvoters	Voters	Nonvoters	Voters	Nonvoters	Voters	Nonvoters
0	52	75	46	75	54	84	48	78	57	83
1	28	18	34	21	29	13	34	19	29	15
2	10	5	12	4	9	2	10	2	9	2
3	5	2	5	0.9	4	0.6	4	0.2	3	0.0
4	3	0.3	2	0.0	2	0.2	2	0.2	2	0.5
5	2	0.0	1	0.1	0.7	0.0	1	0.4	1	0.0

SOURCE: American National Election Studies Cumulative File, 1948–1996.

by traffic during rush hours that the vehicles move very slowly, or so many people may go to a public park on a pleasant summer weekend that most of them enjoy it less than they would if it were less crowded. Collective goods may also be optional; that is, people can exclude themselves from the use of the good. For example, publicly funded education through grade twelve is a collective good in the United States, but individuals may withdraw from school before completing the twelfth grade if they have reached the age designated by state law beyond which school attendance is no longer mandatory. Furthermore, some public education facilities are exclusionary; institutions of higher education generally have admissions requirements, such as a minimum grade-point average or entrance examination score. The government may also supply collective goods through its regulation of private actions, as in the case of the Federal Aviation Administration's supervision of the air traffic control system.

If individuals are expected to be utility maximizers, and if each is concerned with maximizing only his or her interests and not the interests of others, as rational choice theory generally assumes, then why would any individual contribute to obtaining a collective good? It would be rational to do so only if the benefit to be derived exceeded the cost involved and if the individual's contribution was crucial for obtaining it. But why should an individual contribute to the construction of, say, a new public park, when other citizens will give sufficient money for its construction and it will be open to all whether or not they have contributed?

Some scholars argue that, indeed, citizens will not contribute to the provision of a collective good unless they are coerced. One form of such coercion is the mandatory payment of taxes, with the tax revenues being used to provide such collective goods as fire and police protection, schools, hospitals, and streets and highways. Alternatively, individuals may be induced to contribute to the provision of a collective good by an offer of goods or services only to those who do contribute—that is, a selective incentive. Many groups that lobby the government to obtain collective goods beneficial to their members also use selective incentives such as low-cost insurance, reduced rates for travel, and free publications as inducements for people to become and remain group members. These members contribute either directly (through their activities) or indirectly (by belonging to, and hence adding to the numerical strength of, the group) to efforts to persuade the government to provide the desired collective good, which could be a special tax deduction or reduced government regulation of their businesses.[22]

The Free Rider Problem

In his theory of collective action, Mancur Olson Jr. emphasizes the impossibility of excluding individuals who have not contributed to the supply of a collective good from the enjoyment of its use. This is usually referred to as the "free rider" problem. Olson hypothesizes that a contribution to collective action will occur if the benefits accruing to an individual as a result of the collective action exceed the individual's costs. If benefits exceed costs for a number of individuals, Olson argues, a group will form; his term for this group is "privileged." If benefits do not exceed costs, the group is "latent." Unless incentives are offered to stimulate individual contributions to the provision of the collective good, collective action will not occur. Olson also posits a relationship between group size and privilege or latency and asserts that large groups may fail to supply a collective good whereas small groups may succeed. The larger the group, the less benefit any one member receives from the increment in the collective good provided through his or her contribution; the implication is that, in a large group, the benefit derived by the individual will be less than the cost of the increment.[23] But Russell Hardin points out that there is not necessarily a relationship between group size and group latency. Rather, what is crucial is the size of any *subgroup* that will benefit from the provision of the collective good, this size being a function of the cost of the good and its benefit to the members of the subgroup.[24] When a subgroup has formed, it may act on behalf of the entire group.

Evidence from both experimental and field studies demonstrates that Olson's theory does not adequately account for collective behavior. Experimental studies, including some that allowed for discussion among participants and some that did not, show patterns of contribution to collective action that are contrary to what would be predicted by the theory.[25] Outside the experimental laboratory, it is apparent that many citizens contribute to collective action without coercion or incentives. Indeed, it appears that since 1960 there has been a considerable increase in the number, activity, and impact of interest groups—some of them quite large—seeking to influence the public agenda or policy outcomes.[26] These groups seek not only the provision of collective goods but also the elimination of "collective bads."[27] How are these phenomena to be explained?

Explanations for Voluntary Collective Action

Five explanations have been suggested for voluntary collective action. The first emphasizes the role of "entrepreneurs" in organizing and maintaining interest groups. A second, related explanation is that individuals are by nature group oriented; narrow self-interest is a learned behavior and individuals vary in the types of activities in which narrow self-interest guides their behavior. Third, "implicit contract by coordination" is the major mechanism by which organizations aimed at obtaining collective goods are formed. Mutual agreement is reached on a strategy that satisfactorily rewards all participants in an activity. This agreement can be achieved in two ways: (1) all participants may realize, through reasoning processes, that a particular strategy is the best for each to pursue, or (2) participants may have a series of reward-and-punishment experiences from which they learn which strategy maximizes their own utility.[28] Fourth, individuals have not one but two utility functions—the satisfaction of self-interest and the satisfaction of group interest—and they distribute their resources between the two. Fifth, individuals derive utility from the very act of seeking collective goods; in other words, the supposed cost should actually be treated as a benefit.

In the first of these suggested explanations, political leaders are viewed as entrepreneurs who stimulate the organization of groups by promising to provide group members either with desired values, such as services, which could function as incentives, or with collective goods.[29] The entrepreneur recruits members, structures the group to provide them with benefits, and manages the group's internal operations as well as its external relations with rival organizations, cooperating organizations, and political and administrative decision makers. The entrepreneur must ensure that costs and benefits are such that both the members and the entrepreneur experience a net gain as a result of the group's activities.[30] Communication with members through both direct and indirect contacts can be an incentive (in addition to explicitly selective incentives) as well as an organizational tool. More important, the entrepreneur can promote group membership by emphasizing the roles of the members and the entrepreneur in the creation and continued availability of collective goods. The entrepreneur's activities with regard to the administration of collective goods and representation of group interests can be an incentive to join in organized activity and to contribute to obtaining the collective good.[31]

Much of the research on interest group formation and activity assumes that narrow economic self-interest is the basis on which cost-benefit calculations and decisions whether to contribute to group activity are made. Such an assumption simplifies the decision process, but it does not reflect the realities of interest group formation and activity. Contributions to group activity may be motivated by many different kinds of incentives, both tangible and intangible.[32] The pursuit of collective goods by some of the single-issue groups that have been formed since the 1960s appears to be based on their members' fervent belief in a cause. There are two types of payoffs from contributions to an effort to obtain noneconomic collective goods, such as clean air or legalization of abortion: the enactment and enforcement of the policy; and the benefit the citizen derives from the activity of trying to obtain the collective good—that is, from the political participation itself. The entrepreneur's management of group activities and communications can foster these payoffs to group members.

Individuals can use three strategies to cope with the realization that the return from their contributions to collective action may be quite small. As previously mentioned, they can assess their activity in terms of the interest group's efforts, reasoning that their efforts will have had an impact if the group has an impact. A second strategy is to reduce the cognitive dissonance created by the perceived discrepancy between their effort and the potential impact of their contribution by "credit claiming"—that is, either by taking disproportionate credit for the effects of the group's activities or by ignoring the relative size of their contribution to the group's activities. A third strategy is to emphasize the outcomes of interactions within the group rather than the effects of group activities.[33]

A formulation of the rational actor theory of voting that also focuses on the role of entrepreneurs suggests that group leaders, through manipulation of the stimuli presented to members, can enhance their normative sense of group identity and their awareness of the importance of a particular political outcome to them. Group leaders bargain with politicians to augment group benefits. The closer the politicians' issue positions are to those preferred by group members, the greater will be the members' support for those politicians, expressed through political participation. The implications are that individuals participate in collective action in part because of their normative commitments to the group, and that collective action is stimulated by group leaders through effective bargaining with political leaders. (Group leaders may, for example, promise members' votes or turnout in return for policy adjustment.) The individual group members gain through both policy benefits (which may be small) and consumption (participation) benefits. This formulation has been summarized as follows. "Group elites . . . provide their memberships [or identifiers] with incentives to vote in order to capture a collective benefit for the group through shifts in candidate position. . . . Leaders jockey for position in turnout space as candidates move in policy space; the leaders' payoffs consist of policies, while the candidates' payoffs consist of votes." The individual voters' payoffs consist of a small policy term and a large consumption benefit.[34]

There is a fundamental distinction here between an *interest group,* which is organized to make demands on government, and a *reference group,* with which an individual identifies and whose perceived norms guide the individual's behavior. Leaders stimulate reference group identification, and when the reference group becomes an interest group, leaders endorse those politicians who support the group's demands and also direct communications to group members urging their support.

Group leaders rely on both psychological and material incentives. Members are motivated to engage in collective action by their sense of reference group membership and their commitment to the group. The commitment is group-specific and subject to manipulation by group leaders to increase expenditure of individual resources (such as time, money, effort, talent, and votes) to obtain benefits for the reference group (votes in Congress against an immigration bill or in support of an import quota, or a commitment from the president or a legislator to support a constitutional amendment authorizing school prayer).

Research has demonstrated that reference group identification does have a significant impact on voter turnout.[35]

Strategic Decision Making

The question of whether to contribute to the attainment of a collective good can be considered as a problem in strategic decision making in which individuals must analyze the effects of the alternative choices that they could make when the outcome depends both on their choice and on the choices that others make. Game theory is a method of assessing these effects that was developed in the late 1930s and early 1940s by mathematicians; it has been elaborated since then by social scientists for the analysis of strategic decision-making problems.[36] Assume that two men are arrested by the police and charged with a serious crime. If either prisoner is incriminated by the other, he faces a ten-year sentence; if neither incriminates the other; the police will have less evidence but the two can be convicted on a less serious charge, leading to a sentence of only three years. The prosecutor has promised each prisoner a one-year reduction of either sentence if he does testify against the other. The various sentencing possibilities are shown in the following table (a "payoff matrix"), where the first number in each pair represents the sentence for prisoner *A* and the second number represents the sentence for prisoner *B*:

		Prisoner *A*	
		Be silent	Testify
Prisoner *B*	Be silent	3,3	2,10
	Testify	10,2	9,9

Each prisoner is best off if he testifies against the other while the other remains silent, but each is worst off if he remains silent while the other testifies against him. If both remain silent or both testify, the outcomes are indeterminate. Since the police do not allow the two to talk to each other, neither knows what the other is going to do, and so it is intrinsically difficult for them to know which decision on their part would be in their own best interest. This kind of situation has been called the "prisoner's dilemma."

As another example of such a situation, suppose the people in a neighborhood want to build a swimming pool for their use, and they form an association for that purpose. The pool will cost $100,000, so if all 500 households join the association, the cost will be $200 each. If only half of them join, the cost will be $400 for each of them—but for the other half, the pool will be free. If only one-quarter of them join, the cost will be $800 each, and faced with that kind of cost, they may decide not to join and the pool will not be built. Should a family decide to join, on the assumption that others will join and share the cost, or should it not join, let others bear the cost, and run the risk of not having the pool at all?

To take a real-life example on a larger scale, consider the case of Chesapeake Bay, which is home to many varieties of fish, shellfish, and waterfowl. Pollution of the bay's waters by inadequately treated waste from city and county sewage treatment plants is destroying the animal and plant life on which the fish and fowl depend. Should a city spend money to build a new treatment plant? If only one city does, the pollution will not be reduced very much, and the voters in that city might feel that their money has been wasted. If all the cities that contribute to the pollution build new treatment plants, they will all benefit from the improved conditions in the bay—but none of them can be sure that all the others will build plants. Faced with such a situation, environmentalists might form or join organizations such as the Sierra Club or the Chesapeake Bay Foundation to lobby for government programs that would induce or force local governments— and perhaps also corporations, farmers, and others—to take measures to reduce the pollution.

Collective-action problems can be treated as an iterated prisoner's dilemma game in which "coordination by convention" develops. (*Iterated* means that the same players make similar strategic choices over and over again, as when certain members of Congress vote the same way on several energy policy issues in a number of congressional sessions.) A convention to cooperate in obtaining the collective good develops only if there are incentives to cooperate, the participants know each others' preferences and perceptions of the situation, and the same situations are repeated.[37] Hardin argues that the overlapping nature of much group activity increases the possibility that coordination by convention will occur and also facilitates the enforcement of such conventions. Conventions are honored because participants in the interaction learn that it is in their interest to adhere to them.[38]

Robert Axelrod presents a case for coordination in collective-action situations based on reward-and-punishment processes. Using computer simulation methods and testing a number of solutions to a prisoner's dilemma game against each other, Axelrod has found that the best decision rule, dubbed "TIT FOR TAT," is a reward-and-punishment strategy that enables the player pursuing it to attain as favorable an outcome as he might expect by following any other strategy. The TIT-FOR-TAT strategy is to cooperate on the first play, then respond to the other player's previous move on each subsequent play. Although a participant pursuing this strategy does not do substantially better than other players, he does not do any worse.[39] Axelrod describes the TAT-FOR-TAT strategy as being nice, forgiving, retaliatory, and clear.

Piotr Swistak argues that strategies that are fair and unexploitable are superior for tournaments of iterated games. TIT FOR TAT is appropriate only for tournaments of iterated games with two kinds of players—natives and invaders—in which sophisticated players determine their strategies before the tournament, do not change strategies in the course of the tournament, do not know the strategies their opponents will use, and seek to maximize their scores throughout the tournament rather than to win any one play. Swistak demonstrates that strategies that are fair and unexploitable are superior to TIT FOR TAT, which is more limited. Such strategies thus provide for greater flexibility, in that a player may choose to defect at any time and restore cooperation at any time. Swistak provides a proof for the following theorem:

If [a player using] TIT FOR TAT plays in a tournament with fair and unexploitable strategies, and if the length of the tournament is such that every player has a chance to retaliate against its opponent's defection, then TIT FOR TAT wins the tournament.[40]

For asymmetric games with more than two kinds of populations, Swistak argues that the best strategies are nice, unexploitable, and envious.[41]

Cooperation can be promoted by increasing the costs of noncooperation (what Axelrod refers to as "enlarging the shadow of the future"), making the payoffs for cooperation greater, and teaching participants the values, facts, and skills that underlie cooperation.[42] This assumes that participation in collective action on the basis of self-interest is a learned behavior. An alternative view is that cooperative behavior is innate, and that it is egoistic behavior, based on narrow self-interest, that is learned.[43]

The usual choice in prisoner's dilemma games is only between cooperation and defection, but a third choice is also possible: exit, or refusal to play the game altogether. Certainly that option exists in real-world situations; for example, people who dislike the policies of a city, county, or state may move elsewhere.[44] One set of experimental studies reports that when this option is available, exit rates are lower in groups where discussion is permitted; participants whose initial choice was noncooperation have higher exit rates than those who at first cooperated.[45] Other experimental studies have demonstrated the role of a sense of justice or fairness in determining collective-action strategies.[46]

Howard Margolis presents a quite different solution to the problem of explaining why individuals contribute to collective action, which he labels the "fair share" model. This model also assumes rationality, but Margolis defines it as "consistency of choice" in individual behavior.[47] It is further assumed that individuals see utility both in pursuing their self-interest and in contributing to the welfare of others. The latter is based on two kinds of motivation: "goods altruism" and "participation altruism." Goods altruism means that the individual "gains utility from an increase in the goods available to others: his utility function incorporates a taste for having other people better off."[48] Participation altruism is the utility gained from the act of giving resources away for the benefit of others.

The concepts of goods altruism and participation altruism are important in the fair share model in accounting for the individual's distribution of resources between self-interest and group interest. Individuals vary in the weight given to self-interest; one who has given less to the group in the past is motivated to give more in the future, up to the point where an equilibrium occurs between self-interest and group interest. The equilibrium point varies with the individual's valuation of group interest, needs at a given time, and available resources.[49] Margolis describes the individual's decision to allocate resources between himself and the group as follows: "The larger the share of my resources I have spent unselfishly, the more weight I give to my selfish interests in allocating marginal resources. On the other hand, the larger the benefit I can confer on the group compared with the benefit from spending marginal resources on myself, the more I will tend to act unselfishly."[50] According to this allocation rule, spending on the group is a superior good, and those who have higher incomes allocate a greater share of their resources to group interests.

Axelrod describes three types of group interest: (1) based on kinship or family; (2) reciprocal, such as that growing out of the patterns of cooperative interaction; and (3) "group-focused altruism," in which individuals are not motivated by any benefit to themselves. Group-focused altruism can be strengthened by increasing the importance of future considerations in current decision making, increasing the payoffs to those who allocate resources to the group, and deliberately inculcating values, skills, and facts that promote cooperative behavior.[51] Margolis points out that for most individuals, the resources allocated to group interest are quite small compared with the resources allocated to self-interest; therefore, most decisions about both the quantity of resources to allocate to group interest and their distribution among various instruments of group interest are probably based on a minimal information search. To develop decisions on the basis of full information would be an inefficient use of the resources allocated to group interest.[52] In his model, the ordinary citizen is represented as *Smith* and the resources devoted to group interests are *G*. Margolis observes:

In a large society, both Smith's spending and the benefits from that spending will be microscopically small from a social point of view. It will often be hard, therefore, for Smith to "see" the ratio of benefit to cost directly in terms of his own act. However, it may be quite easy to estimate this ratio (in particular to compare this ratio across alternative ways of using *G* resources) in terms of a judgment about the ratio of aggregate benefits and costs of everyone in Smith's position behaving in a certain way.[53]

In Margolis's view, *G* resources do not personally benefit the individual providing the resources.

Economist Amartya K. Sen has also been critical of the view that individuals are rational egoists. He argues that their choices may be influenced by sympathy (concern for others that directly affects an individual's own sense of welfare and is therefore egoistic) or by commitment (concern about situations that directly affect others but do not make the individual feel personally worse off). Sen's concept of commitment is similar to Margolis's group-focused altruism, in that it assumes that individuals may choose outcomes that do not serve their own narrowly defined self-interest.[54]

The economic model of collective action assumes that individual preferences that reflect human needs are fixed. Logically, however, collective-choice decisions can vary with changes in individual preference orderings. Such a notion is not unknown in either philosophy or economics,[55] but it greatly complicates both the theorizing and the research that use a political economy approach to the analysis of political decisions. Harry G. Frankfurt argues that individuals can have several different preference orderings simultaneously and use different ones as the basis for decision making at different times. He sees individuals as having not only first-order desires, which are ascertainable from the choices they make (a standard assumption in rational choice theory), but also second-order desires, which may not coincide with their first-order preferences. Individual choices frequently involve determining which set of preference orderings should be operational in a particular situation.

Another explanation of the formation and maintenance of groups that seek collective goods without reliance on selective incentives requires a reconsideration of costs and benefits. It has already been noted that some individuals derive enjoyment from—in effect, benefit from—the act of participating in politics. These "political junkies" form groups and seek to achieve group goals in part for the enjoyment gained from such activity. The enjoyment may be either socially or purposively (goal-attainment) oriented.[56] Several studies of participation in political party activity report the importance of both types of incentives.[57]

Albert O. Hirschman argues that in the pursuit of public action to remedy problems or address needs, both the actions aimed at obtaining the desired collective good and the collective good itself have positive value. In other words, what rational choice theory considers to be costs are for many citizens who are engaging in collective action, part of the benefit.[58] Perhaps, however, this does not apply equally to all actions to obtain collective goods, but primarily to actions directed at goods that affect the quality of life of certain individuals and others, as they perceive the situation. Thus, the quality of the water in Chesapeake Bay is, to many of those concerned about it, not an economic matter; but to those who earn their living from fishing in the bay, it is very much an economic concern. Similarly, most people active in groups seeking action to combat acid rain do not depend on forestry in the Appalachian Mountains, New England, or Canada for their living; rather, they are concerned that the general quality of life for themselves and for future citizens will be diminished by the degradation of the lakes, streams, and forests of the affected areas.

Efforts to expand the theory of collective action in the ways that have been discussed here have met with at least two objections. First, they focus on the behavior of individuals rather than the behavior of groups, thus changing the nature of the problem being studied. But this is specious reasoning, for individual motivations in making contributions to group action are basic to collective-action theory and to an analysis of interest group formation and maintenance. Second, adding variables to the theory does not increase its explanatory power, for the behavior of individuals in group settings can be adequately explained using calculations of individual costs and benefits, narrowly defined.[59]

Scholars have suggested several different solutions to the Olson free rider problem. The role of entrepreneurs in the establishment and maintenance of organizations seeking collective goods has been examined in several studies based on samples of national organizations or of their members.[60] A number of experimental studies have examined the incidence of, and in some cases the evolution of, cooperation by convention, but field research has been limited to a few analyses of coalition formation to effect change in the national policy arena. The degree to which generalization is possible on the basis of computer simulations and laboratory experiments can be questioned,[61] but the evidence from many of these studies does suggest that purely egoistic behavior occurs less frequently than Olson's theory implies.

Summary

Is political participation rational? Obviously, the answer to this question depends on how the term *rational* is defined. If rationality is taken to mean consistency in choices, then rationality (or irrationality) is easy to observe in patterns of political participation. If to be rational means to be a utility maximizer, and if utility is narrowly defined as immediate personal benefit exceeding the cost of participating, then many types of political participation are not rational.

Is voting rational? If voting is considered to be rational only if the vote of any one individual makes a significant difference in the outcome of an election, then voting usually is not rational. However, citizens may take other impacts of their vote into account by evaluating the utility of voting. These include the psychic rewards obtained from the act of participating, from conforming to a democratic norm that calls for participation, and from the sense of contributing to the survival of the political system (the long-run participation value). Individuals can also derive satisfaction from joining with others to vote for or against candidates on the basis of a particular issue about which the members of the group feel very strongly and concerning which they believe their vote will have an effect.

Scholars do not agree on how to explain the formation and maintenance of interest groups that seek collective goods, but it is obvious that such groups do form. Debate continues as to the types of incentives that motivate individuals to contribute to the attainment of a collective good, either individually or as members of a group, or through their efforts to have the government distribute the cost of providing the collective good to all members of society.

Critics of rational choice theory have attacked its basic assumptions, including the assumption that individual decision making is rational and motivated by self-interest, and assumptions about the decisions that risk-adverse individuals make. They have also faulted research methodology used by rational choice theorists. These criticisms have stimulated lively debates between and among the advocates and critics of rational choice theory.[62]

Notes

1. Anthony Downs, *An Economic Theory of Democracy* (New York: Harper and Row, 1957), 5.
2. Russell Hardin, *Collective Action* (Baltimore: Johns Hopkins University Press, 1982), 10.
3. Terry M. Moe, *The Organization of Interests* (Chicago: University of Chicago Press, 1980), 3.

4. William H. Riker and Peter C. Ordeshook, *An Introduction to Positive Political Theory* (Englewood Cliffs, N.J.: Prentice-Hall, 1973), 20.
5. Norman Frohlich, Joe A. Oppenheimer, and Oran Young, *Political Leadership and Collective Goods* (Princeton: Princeton University Press, 1971), 26–29.
6. Moe, *Organization of Interests*, 14.
7. Riker and Ordeshook, *Positive Political Theory*, 63.
8. Downs, *Economic Theory of Democracy*, 266–271.
9. Ibid., 260–261.
10. Riker and Ordeshook, *Positive Political Theory*, 62–63.
11. Paul Meehl, "The Selfish Voter Paradox and the Thrown Away Vote Argument," *American Political Science Review* 71 (1977): 11–30.
12. John Ferejohn and Morris Fiorina, "The Paradox of Not Voting," *American Political Science Review* 68 (1974): 525–536.
13. Robert E. Goodin and K. W. S. Roberts, "The Ethical Voter," *American Political Science Review* 69 (1975): 925–928.
14. Carole Jean Uhlaner, "Political Participation, Rational Actors, and Rationality: A New Approach," *Political Psychology* 7 (1986): 551–557.
15. Carole Jean Uhlaner, "Rational Turnout: The Neglected Role of Groups," *American Journal of Political Science* 33, no. 1 (1989): 390–422; Carole Jean Uhlaner, "'Relational Goods' and Participation: Incorporating Sociability into a Theory of Rational Action," *Public Choice* 62 (3) (1988): 253–285.
16. John F. Zipp, "Perceived Representativeness and Voting: An Assessment of the Impact of 'Choices' vs. 'Echoes'," *American Political Science Review* 79 (1985): 50–61.
17. John H. Aldrich, "Rational Choice and Turnout," *American Journal of Political Science* 37 (1993): 261–263.
18. Ibid., 264–270.
19. See also Robert W. Jackman, "Rationality and Political Participation," *American Journal of Political Science* 37 (1993): 279–290.
20. Gregory Brunk, "The Impact of Rational Participation Models on Voting Attitudes," *Public Choice* 35 (1980): 549–564.
21. For discussions of the nature of collective goods, see Mancur Olson Jr., *The Logic of Collective Action* (Cambridge: Harvard University Press, 1971), 14–16; and Hardin, *Collective Action*, 16–20.
22. Olson, *Logic of Collective Action*, 2.
23. Ibid., 20–36.
24. Assuming a fixed number of participants N and the cost of the total good C, which has a value V to individual i, the subset k that would be large enough to benefit from providing the good would be "the smallest integer larger than C/V." Hardin, *Collective Action*, 42–49.
25. See, for example, Gerald Marvell and Ruth E. Ames, "Experiments on the Provision of Public Goods: 1. Resources, Interest, Group Size, and the Free Rider Problem," *American Journal of Sociology* 84 (1979): 1335–1360; Gerald Marvell and Ruth E. Ames, "Experiments on the Provision of Public Goods: 2. Provision Points, Experiences, and the Free Rider Problem," *American Journal of Sociology* 85 (1980): 927–937; and Norman Frohlich and Joe A. Oppenheimer, "Beyond Economic Man: Altruism, Egalitarianism, and Difference Maximizing," *Journal of Conflict Resolution* 28 (1984): 3–24. Results of survey research examining the effect of public goods, altruistic motives, and social as well as private incentives in stimulating participation in collective action are presented in Edward N. Muller and Karl-Dieter Opp, "Rational Choice and Rebellious Collective Action: Public Goods, Psychological Gratification, and Socialist Class Consciousness," *American Political Science Review* 80 (1986): 471–489; and Karl-Dieter Opp, "Soft Incentives and Collective Action: Participation in the Nuclear Freeze Movement," *British Journal of Political Science* 16 (1986): 87–112.
26. See Jack Walker, "The Origins and Maintenance of Interest Groups in America," *American Political Science Review* 77 (1983): 983, Fig. 1. The increase in the

number of groups appears to have been stimulated by outside resources (such as foundations, government agencies, and wealthy individuals), as well as by member resources.

27. Jeffrey M. Berry, *The Interest Group Society* (Boston: Little, Brown, 1984); Jeffrey M. Berry, *Lobbying for the People* (Princeton: Princeton University Press, 1977); M. Margaret Conway and Joanne Connor Green, "Political Action Committees and Campaign Finance," in *Interest Group Politics*, 5th ed., ed. Allan J. Cigler and Burdett A. Loomis (Washington, D.C.: CQ Press, 1998), 193–214; and Robert C. Mitchell, "National Environmental Lobbies and the Apparent Illogic of Collective Action," in *Collective Decision Making*, ed. Clifford S. Russell (Baltimore: Johns Hopkins University Press, 1979), 87–121.

28. Hardin, *Collective Action*, 155–156 and chap. 10; and Robert Axelrod, *The Evolution of Cooperation* (New York: Basic Books, 1984), 12–19.

29. Norman Frohlich and Joe A. Oppenheimer, "I Get By with a Little Help from My Friends," *World Politics* 23 (1970): 104–120; Moe, *Organization of Interests*, 37–39; Frohlich, Oppenheimer, and Young, *Political Leadership*; Robert H. Salisbury, "An Exchange Theory of Interest Groups," *Midwest Journal of Political Science* 13 (1969): 1–32; and Richard Wagner, "Pressure Groups and Political Entrepreneurs: A Review Article," in *Papers on Nonmarket Decision Making*, ed. Gordon Tullock (Charlottesville: University of Virginia Press, 1966), 161–170.

30. Moe, *Organization of Interests*, chap. 3.

31. Ibid., 57.

32. Uhlaner, "Rational Turnout"; Uhlaner, "'Relational Goods' and Participation"; Moe, *Organization of Interests*, 114; Brian Barry, *Sociologists, Economists, and Democracy* (Chicago: University of Chicago Press, 1977), 33.

33. Karl-Dieter Opp, "Economics, Sociology, and Political Protest," in *Theoretical Models and Empirical Analyses: Contributions to the Explanation of Individual Actions and Collective Phenomena*, ed. Weruer Raub (Groningen, Netherlands: Utrecht, 1982), 166–185.

34. Uhlaner, "Rational Turnout," 395–396.

35. Arthur H. Miller et al., "Group Consciousness and Political Participation," *American Journal of Political Science* 25 (1981): 495–511; and M. Margaret Conway, "Group Identification, Perceived Group Interest, and Patterns of Political Participation" (paper delivered at the annual meeting of the Western Political Science Association, Denver, March 26–28, 1981).

36. Game theory was originally developed largely by John von Neumann and Oskar Morgenstern; see their *Theory of Games and Economic Behavior* (Princeton: Princeton University Press, 1944). Anatol Rapoport played a major role in the evolution of its use in psychology and other social sciences; see his *Two-Person Game Theory* (Ann Arbor: University of Michigan Press, 1966); and *N-Person Game Theory* (Ann Arbor: University of Michigan Press, 1970). Another early exposition of the ideas underlying the social science applications of game theory is found in R. Duncan Luce and Howard Raiffa, *Games and Decisions* (New York: Wiley, 1957).

37. Hardin, *Collective Action*, 72.

38. Ibid., 175. See also Robert Axelrod, *The Evolution of Cooperation* (New York: Basic Books, 1984), chap. 6; and David Lewis, *Convention* (Cambridge: Harvard University Press, 1982).

39. Axelrod, *Evolution of Cooperation*, 31–32.

40. Piotr Swistak, "A Theory of Tournaments of Iterated Prisoner's Dilemma Game" (working paper, Department of Government and Politics, University of Maryland, College Park, November 1989); Piotr Swistak, "Stability and Invasion in Tournaments of Iterated Prisoner's Dilemma Game" (working paper, Department of Government and Politics, University of Maryland, College Park, January 1990).

41. Piotr Swistak, personal communication, March 12, 1990.

42. Axelrod, *Evolution of Cooperation*, chap. 7.

43. Uhlaner, "Political Participation," 566–567. See also Carol Gilligan, *In a Different Voice* (Cambridge: Harvard University Press, 1982).

44. Albert O. Hirschman, *Exit, Voice, and Loyalty* (Cambridge: Harvard University Press, 1970).

45. John M. Orbell, Peregrine Schwartz-Shea, and Randy T. Simmons, "Do Cooperators Exit More Readily than Defectors?," *American Political Science Review* 78 (1984): 147–162.

46. Frohlich and Oppenheimer, "Beyond Economic Man," 9–16.

47. Howard Margolis, *Selfishness, Altruism, and Rationality* (Cambridge: Cambridge University Press, 1984), 6, 14.

48. Ibid., 21.

49. Ibid., 29.

50. Ibid., 36.

51. Axelrod, *Evolution of Cooperation*, chap. 7.

52. Margolis, *Selfishness, Altruism, and Rationality*, 49–50.

53. Ibid., 51.

54. Amartya K. Sen, "Rational Fools: A Critique of the Behavioral Foundations of Economic Theory," *Philosophy and Public Affairs* 6 (1977): 326–329.

55. Harry G. Frankfurt, "Freedom of the Will and the Concept of a Person," *Journal of Philosophy* 58 (1971): 5–20; and Sen, "Rational Fools."

56. James Q. Wilson, *Political Organizations* (New York: Basic Books, 1973).

57. Samuel Eldersveld, *Political Parties: A Behavioral Analysis* (Chicago: Rand McNally, 1964); M. Margaret Conway and Frank B. Feigert, "Motivation, Incentive Systems, and the Political Party Organization," *American Political Science Review* 62 (1968): 1159–1173; and Peter Gluck, "Research Note: Incentives and the Maintenance of Political Styles in Different Locales," *Western Political Quarterly* 25 (1972): 753–760.

58. Albert O. Hirschman, *Shifting Involvements* (Princeton: Princeton University Press, 1982), 85–86 and 126.

59. Hardin, *Collective Action*, 14.

60. Barry, *Sociologists, Economists, and Democracy;* Mitchell, "National Environmental Lobbies"; and Thomas L. Gais, Mark A. Peterson, and Jack L. Walker, "Interest Groups, Iron Triangles, and Representative Institutions in American National Government," *British Journal of Political Science* 14 (1984): 161–185.

61. When an experiment defines the choice regarding cooperation as being between personal interest and group interest, social pressure on respondents may produce a biased distribution of results. See, for example, Hardin, *Collective Action*, 114. Research designs usually attempt to control such factors, but may not always be possible, and the designs may not capture reality sufficiently accurately to permit valid generalizations to real-world choice situations. See also Robert E. Goodin, "Itinerants, Iterations, and Something In-Between," *British Journal of Political Science* 14 (1984): 129–132.

62. See Jane J. Mansbridge, ed., *Beyond Self-Interest* (Chicago: University of Chicago Press, 1990); Donald P. Green and Ian Shapiro, *Pathologies of Rational Choice Theory* (New Haven: Yale University Press, 1994); Jeffrey Friedman, ed., *The Rational Choice Controversy* (New Haven: Yale University Press, 1996); and Robin M. Hogarth and Melvin W. Reder, eds., *Rational Choice: The Contrast between Economics and Psychology* (Chicago: University of Chicago Press, 1987).

Chapter 7

Explanations of Patterns of Political Participation

The discussion in the preceding chapters has centered on five types of variables that contribute to an understanding of who participates in politics and in what ways and to what extent they do so. Patterns of political participation are influenced by the life circumstances of citizens, their psychological orientations with regard to politics, their political and legal environments, the laws and governmental regulations that affect political participation (especially voting), and the choices citizens make about their participation. In this chapter we examine the effect of some of these explanatory variables on trends in voter turnout, the relative weight of the variables, and the emphasis given to them in alternative explanations of participation.

Unfortunately, the data necessary for a comprehensive analysis of patterns of political participation are not available. Survey results that provide a full set of valid and reliable measures of all five types of explanatory variables do not exist, and measures of some kinds of participation are not included in all the survey results that do exist. Moreover, not all studies use the same measures of important explanatory variables.[1] Measures of voter turnout have been included in national surveys of the electorate since 1952; measures of other forms of participation have been included less frequently.

Trends in Voter Turnout

Trends in voter turnout in the eleven states generally referred to as the South (the states that were part of the Confederate States of America during the Civil War) differ from trends in the rest of the United States. African Americans in the South were denied the right to vote and other civil rights until the enactment and enforcement of the Voting Rights Act of 1965. Voter registration and turnout in the southern states increased in 1968 and have declined only slightly since then. Voter registration and turnout were considerably higher in the rest of the United States in the early 1960s, but since 1968 they have declined more in nonsouthern states than they have in the South.

A number of measures of political engagement (psychological involvement in politics) were discussed in Chapter 3. They include party identification, sense of external political efficacy, caring about who wins the election, and level of political trust. The effects of these psychological involvement variables on voter turnout patterns may be altered by changes in the distribution of citizens with the regard to the variables. For example, the proportion of the electorate that calls itself Independent has increased at the expense of the proportion identifying with one of the two major political parties. Among those living outside the South, Independents are generally less likely to vote in presidential elections than party identifiers; since 1960 the decline in turnout has been greater among Independents than among party identifiers (see Table 7-1). Another pattern has persisted since 1960: those who identify weakly with the Democratic Party have been less likely to vote than weak identifiers with the Republican Party.

Voters who have a high level of external political efficacy have regularly been 20 to 30 percent more likely to vote than those who have a low level, but since the 1970s a smaller proportion of the electorate has had high levels of external political efficacy (see Chapter 3). Caring about who wins the election—another measure of political engagement—is also related to turnout. Over time, the turnout rates of those who say they care who wins the presidential election have remained relatively stable, but voting participation has declined among those who say they "don't care or don't know" who wins (see Table 7-2).

We would expect that those who follow the presidential election campaign in the mass media would be more likely to vote and to participate politically in other ways. The media exposure index is a sum of the number of different types of media that individuals report using as a source of political news to follow the campaign. Those who do not follow the campaign in any of the media are scored 0, and those who rely on all four types of media—newspapers, television, ra-

TABLE 7-1

Reported Voter Turnout outside the South in Presidential Elections by Party Identification, 1960–1996

	1960	1964	1968	1972	1976	1980	1984	1988	1992	1996
Strong Democrat	83	85	86	82	82	85	90	87	90	90
Weak Democrat	81	79	74	75	70	67	71	71	78	72
Independent Democrat	74	77	74	76	76	69	66	72	77	74
Independent	84	64	64	56	61	54	61	58	68	58
Independent Republican	88	86	85	81	75	78	80	70	75	78
Weak Republican	90	87	84	81	75	77	78	79	80	80
Strong Republican	92	94	87	91	93	90	91	93	91	96

SOURCE: American National Election Studies Cumulative File, 1948–1996.

dio, and magazines—are scored 4. As Table 7-3 indicates, those who rely on more types of media are more likely to vote in presidential elections, a trend that has been generally increasing since 1952.

Nationally the proportion of those surveyed who report following the presidential campaign in the newspapers has varied over time, but the proportion of respondents who reported regularly reading articles about the campaign in the newspapers declined from almost one-half in 1960 to one-quarter in 1980.[2] Moreover, a pattern of decreased reliance on newspapers has been evident since 1986. In contrast, beginning in 1956 and continuing until 1992, more than 85 percent of re-

TABLE 7-2

Reported Voter Turnout outside the South in Presidential Elections, by Selected Variables, 1960–1996

	1960	1964	1968	1972	1976	1980	1984	1988	1992	1996
Strength of party identification										
Independent	74	62	65	53	57	54	60	50	60	54
Leaning toward	78	76	76	74	73	72	70	64	73	72
Weak	80	77	75	74	70	70	72	68	75	73
Strong	85	84	84	83	85	85	86	84	86	89
Concern with outcome										
Don't care or don't know	65	66	66	60	61	61	62	53	51	54
Care who wins	87	84	80	81	80	79	80	80	83	82
Level of external political efficacy										
Low	60	77	64	64	63	57	57	65	70	75
Medium	78	79	80	77	73	74	59	80	83	82
High	90	86	87	85	85	85	73	87	88	86

SOURCE: American National Election Studies Cumulative File, 1948–1996.

TABLE 7-3

Voting in Presidential Elections, by Media Exposure Index Score and Level of General Interest in Government and Politics, 1952–1996

	1952	1956	1960	1964	1968	1972	1976	1980	1984	1988	1992	1996
Media exposure index score												
Low	31	39	31	48	40	44	26	34	33	—	38	48
2	52	52	62	59	56	60	53	54	52	—	66	66
3	71	76	79	75	74	73	66	67	73	—	78	80
4	83	85	90	83	84	83	80	80	82	—	91	90
High	91	92	82	90	89	88	86	92	90	—	93	95
Level of general interest in government and politics												
Low	—	—	—	50	52	40	38	46	47	35	41	45
2	—	—	—	70	70	57	54	64	65	62	67	66
3	—	—	—	83	81	74	77	76	80	80	80	82
High	—	—	—	85	86	88	86	87	88	86	90	92

SOURCE: American National Election Studies Cumulative File, 1948–1996.

spondents reported following the campaign on television. In 1996, that proportion decreased to 75 percent. Reliance on television as a major source of political news has increased substantially since 1960, yet a television news program can present only a limited amount of information; the script for a half-hour news broadcast can be printed on one page of a newspaper.

Several socioeconomic variables are related to political participation, including voter turnout. Among them are age, education, and income. The relation between these three variables and voter turnout outside the South between 1960 and 1996 is shown in Table 7-4. Turnout is higher among those who are older; the increase in turnout continues until these citizens reach their mid-70s. At that point, turnout among older citizens generally decreases from previous levels. The table shows a pronounced decrease (13 percent) in voter turnout among those with a high school education or less. However, the effect of this decrease is moderated by the increase in the educational level of the electorate since 1960, which means that there are fewer people in the lower educational attainment categories. As was discussed in Chapter 3, education serves as a sorting mechanism; those who have higher levels of educational attainment are more likely to acquire both the resources that facilitate political participation and what researchers refer to as democratic enlightenment.[3] Table 7-4 also shows

TABLE 7-4

Reported Voter Turnout outside the South in Presidential Elections, by Age, Education, and Income, 1960–1996

	1960	1964	1968	1972	1976	1980	1984	1988	1992	1996
Age										
17–24	57	58	56	61	56	51	51	43	52	53
25–34	74	71	72	71	66	65	70	61	71	66
35–44	79	83	78	79	79	77	79	74	77	76
45–54	87	82	85	80	82	79	81	78	81	82
55–64	80	82	79	77	78	79	83	77	83	82
65–74	86	78	76	73	76	83	84	81	83	83
75–99+	63	77	65	60	64	68	68	70	77	81
Education										
Less than high school	76	76	66	64	61	55	60	62	56	63
High school	89	85	86	78	72	72	72	68	77	76
Some college	89	90	81	87	85	77	83	81	85	84
College degree	93	89	92	90	87	92	91	92	93	89
Income percentile										
0–16	65	64	60	60	54	56	53	47	52	61
17–33	71	73	66	63	65	68	69	59	68	64
34–67	81	79	79	70	71	72	74	71	77	75
68–95	85	86	87	86	80	81	84	82	88	88
96–100	94	88	92	90	91	87	91	96	90	96

SOURCE: American National Election Studies Cumulative File, 1948–1996.

the disparities in voter turnout by income, which of course is appreciably affected by level of educational attainment.

Accounting for Voter Turnout

A number of scholars have attempted to assess the relative impact of the five types of variables that might explain patterns of voter turnout, especially its decline. Some have focused on a limited set of variables,[4] whereas others have attempted to be more inclusive.[5] The research designs and the methods of analysis have varied significantly. When studies of different elections use different models and analytical methods but reach similar conclusions, the inferences drawn have greater reliability.

The evidence is quite strong that two aspects of psychological involvement in politics—sense of external political efficacy and party identification—have played a significant role in the decline in voting participation since 1960. One set of analyses concludes that approximately three-fourths of the decline can be attributed to the weakening of party identification and sense of external political efficacy.[6] But the changing age distribution of the electorate has also been important. The post–New Deal generation has become a larger proportion of the electorate since the mid-1980s, and these citizens are much less likely to vote than members of the New Deal and pre–New Deal generations.[7] Turnout is also very low among the youngest generation of citizens. However, the improvements in educational attainment level, income, and occupational status have had a generally positive effect on voter turnout.[8]

The political and legal environments in which elections are held have changed dramatically since 1965. The barriers to voting created by the systems of voter registration that existed before the enactment and implementation of the National Voter Registration Act of 1993 were most troublesome for those who were more mobile (such as younger citizens), those who were less psychologically involved in politics, and those for whom political participation was a "luxury" item.[9] The NVRA has greatly facilitated voter registration in the United States (see Chapter 5). Changes in the political environment include the decline in party identification, which has been accompanied by an increasing emphasis on the personal characteristics of the candidates[10] and on incumbents' ability to provide services to constituents.[11]

The role of changes in political trust in accounting for a decline in voter turnout is in dispute. One view is that the increase in political distrust reflects a decline in support for political institutions, especially by citizens with relatively extreme preferences concerning major policy issues. The distrustful appear to be polarized into two groups —those on the left, who support policies promoting social change, and those on the right, who prefer a less activist government and a reversal of many welfare state policies. Members of both groups are more likely than other citizens to feel alienated from the system. The dissatisfaction applies to both Republican and Democratic administrations, but it is more prevalent among citizens whose party does not control the government.[12]

A different interpretation is that the political trust scale used in studies of the electorate measures not citizens' support for political institutions but their evaluations of those who currently hold public of-

TABLE 7-5

Reported Voter Turnout outside the South in Presidential Elections, by Level of Political Trust, 1964–1996

	1964	1968	1972	1976	1980	1984	1988	1992	1996
Low	83	54	56	53	60	61	44	75	50
2	76	72	71	71	71	72	67	78	73
3	78	79	71	74	73	77	70	77	78
4	82	77	76	71	75	74	73	70	80
5	78	77	77	74	69	74	76	71	78
High	72	71	58	60	60	67	52	43	35

SOURCE: American National Election Studies Cumulative File, 1948–1996.

fice.[13] If the scale measured decline in the support for institutions, those who are less trusting would be less likely to vote and more likely to engage in protest activities.[14] However, the evidence does not support these conclusions. Although disagreement with current government policies may lead to feelings of political distrust, it does not necessarily result in a decline in support for political institutions, a decline in voter turnout (see Table 7-5), or an increase in the use of unconventional forms of political participation.

Political trust has also been viewed as a function of citizens' perceptions of public officials' "intentions, capabilities, and values"— that is, of their trustworthiness and their competence.[15] If citizens vote instrumentally, they weigh the perceived differences among the candidates on policies of interest to them against the perceived trustworthiness and competence of the candidates. If a candidate cannot be counted on to attempt to implement promised policies, or if the candidate is perceived as being not competent to do so, the costs of voting will be seen as outweighing the returns. According to this point of view, political trust is related both to voter turnout and to the choices among candidates. Citizens who perceive one candidate as more trustworthy and more competent than another are more likely to vote in the election and to vote for this candidate, if the candidate's policy commitments are also preferred.[16]

Some of these variables appear to have affected turnout in all three midterm elections of the 1970s, whereas others affected turnout in some midterm elections but not in others.[17] The inconsistency of the effects is perhaps not surprising, since different stimuli are present during any one election, with its myriad of candidates and offices to be filled. In addition, the issue bases of political conflict vary across congressional districts and states. Individuals also react differently to the stimuli that are present. Persons with a higher level of educational attainment and older persons (those born in 1942 and earlier) were more likely to vote in all of the midterm elections in the 1970s and 1980s. The turnout rates of those with high school and college educations increased in 1982 but declined in 1986. Voters with high levels of educational attainment were more likely to vote in 1970 and 1978, but the turnout rate of voters in all educational attainment categories except the lowest dropped in 1974. The political environment in 1974 included recovery from a severe recession and the Watergate scandal, which had culminated in that year with President Nixon's resignation and his pardon by President Ford. Evidence of the impact of the recession is that individuals' concern with their future economic well-being affected turnout in the 1974 election but not in the 1970 and 1978 elections, which were not held in the aftermath of a recession.

Individuals who earn more are more likely to vote; in the 1970s, 60 percent of those in the highest third in the income distribution voted, whereas 54 percent or less of those in the lowest third voted. In 1982, turnout increased among three of the five income groups—perhaps reflecting a reaction among the unemployed to the economic consequences of the recession that occurred during the preelection period—but in 1986 turnout declined among all income groups. It declined further in 1990 and did not rebound until 1994.

Certain political environment variables did not have the impact in the midterm elections of the 1970s that might be expected. The fact that an election for governor was being held at the same time in some states did not increase the turnout rate. The degree of competition (that is, the number of candidates) in the gubernatorial contest, the perceived closeness of the contest, and the estimated impact of the alternative outcomes of the election are probably more important in stimulating turnout than the fact that such a contest was (or was not) held. Higher levels of spending by Democratic congressional candidates were associated with higher turnout in their districts in the midterm elections, but higher levels of spending by their Republican opponents were not. That probably reflects the usually lower turnout rate of Democratic voters; there was more room for spending by Democratic candidates to have an effect on their partisans. Another political environment variable related to turnout is region of the country: citizens residing in the South have been less likely to vote than nonsoutherners.

One legal environment variable, the states' minimum residence requirements, had an impact on turnout in the 1970 midterm elections but not in later elections. By 1974, court decisions and changes in state laws had effectively removed lengthy residence requirements.

Strength of party identification did not influence turnout in the 1974 midterm elections when the effects of other variables are taken into account—although it did increase turnout in 1970 and 1978. Similarly, when the effects of other variables are taken into account, sense of external political efficacy stimulated turnout in 1974 and 1978 but not in 1970. In contrast, caring about the outcome of the election appeared to influence turnout in all three midterm elections even when other variables are controlled.

Among the comprehensive models that attempt to explain the decline in voter turnout over time is one developed by Ruy A. Teixeira. He had assumed, as have many other scholars, that increased levels of educational attainment and higher levels of income would lead us to expect an increase in voter turnout since 1960 rather than a decline.[18] But the decrease in psychological involvement in politics, as evidenced by the decline in party identification, reliance on the mass media (particularly newspapers) for political news, the belief that government is responsive to citizens, knowledge about candidates and political parties, general interest in politics, the desire to follow what is going on in politics, and interest in the campaign—all have contributed to a decline in voter turnout.[19] Teixeira concludes that the decline in the influence of party-related variables and in political involvement—which he characterizes as a general withdrawal from the political world— account for 99 percent of the explained decline in voter turnout. However, his model actually explains three-fourths of the decline in voter turnout since 1960, leaving one-fourth to be explained.[20] In sum, Teixeira views three trends as significant in helping to explain changes in voter turnout over time: (1) socioeconomic improvement, which would increase turnout, has been counterbalanced by (2) a substantial decline in social connectedness and (3) a general psychological disengagement from the political world.[21]

Teixeira suggests several explanations for the unexplained portion of turnout decline, some of which have been explored by others seeking to solve the "puzzle of political participation." He rejects as possible explanations lower turnout by African Americans and lower turnout in the South, for, as noted earlier in this chapter, turnout by African Americans in the South and by southerners in general increased after 1968 and has not declined nearly as much as has turnout by whites and by voters outside the South. Although union membership has declined substantially, there has been only a weak relationship between union membership and voter turnout. Homeowners are more likely to vote than renters, but there has been no substantial change in patterns of homeownership. Teixeira suggests that a possible explanation for the unexplained portion of the decline in voter turnout is a decline in political party moblization efforts.[22]

Certainly the style of political mobilization has changed in many areas. The personal contacts of potential voters by people known to them who were representatives of party organizations in local election districts of large cities have largely been replaced by phone banks operated by commercial firms that may be located some distance from the citizen's community. Impersonal communication through television ads, letters, and leaflets dropped on the doorstep have become the norm. Such political mobilization as occurs now is more likely to be funded by a national party committee, a candidate organization, an interest group, or a political action committee.[23] Another possible contributor to the decline in voter turnout over time is the large number and frequency of elections and the large number of offices to be filled.[24]

The political mobilization explanation for patterns of electoral politics and political participation has been thoroughly explored by, and is advocated by, Steven J. Rosenstone and John Mark Hansen. These scholars assert that those who participate in electoral politics are advantaged in terms of the resources they bring to the political arena, such as higher levels of educational attainment and income, relevant personal experiences, and psychological involvement in politics. Also important is having a stake in the outcome of the election. That stake may include psychological involvement in terms of having a party identification, caring who wins, and making a strong commitment to one candidate. Social connectedness is important in influencing participation in political activity (as Teixeira and other scholars have argued), for it serves as a major conduit through which political leaders and others attempt, either directly or indirectly, to induce citizens to vote or to engage actively in other forms of political participation.[25]

Sidney Verba, Kay Lehman Schlozman, and Henry E. Brady also emphasize political recruitment efforts in their examination of who participates in politics, why, and with what effect on representation.[26] The sophisticated model they develop to explain patterns of political participation and their consequences is the basis for their conclusion that participation in the activities of social institutions such as unions, religious organizations, and voluntary associations encourages the acquisition of skills that facilitate engagement in political activity. Their model also posits that these social institutions serve as channels for political recruitment.[27]

How well do all the explanatory variables together account for the patterns of voter turnout in the presidential elections since 1960 and the congressional elections since 1970? The methods and models used by researchers vary, but one model was able to place survey respondents correctly in the categories of voter and nonvoter approximately 70 percent of the time.[28]

Voter turnout in primary elections has received less attention. Earlier research on primaries suggested that those who voted in them were atypical of the electorate as a whole.[29] An analysis of voting in the 1980 presidential primary elections found strength of party identification to be important in explaining voter turnout among Democratic Party supporters but not among Republican Party supporters. Political context variables, such as the number of candidates in the presidential primary, the type of primary, and the perceived closeness of the national contest, were important in explaining voters' participation in Republican presidential primaries. Participation in the Democratic Party's presidential primaries was more a function of the voters' personal characteristics (those who were older, of majority race, and urban dwellers were more likely to vote), the type of primary (turnout is higher in presidential primaries that actually pick delegates than in those that merely measure voters' candidate preferences), and whether a congressional primary was held at the same time as the presidential primary (turnout is higher when the primaries are concurrent).[30]

Accounting for Other Forms of Participation

In the effort to explain patterns of participation in political activities other than voting (see the discussion of these kinds of activities in

Chapter 6), one psychological variable that may be important is the individual's values—specifically, the relative weight of material values (material well-being, including physical security) and nonmaterial values (participation in the making of important decisions, attention to aesthetic considerations such as environmental quality, and "humanitarian concerns").

Research conducted in both the United States and Europe suggests that those who emphasize nonmaterial values are more likely to engage in forms of political participation other than voting.[31] It is also possible that the more deeply people hold their values, the more likely they are to participate, whether the values are material or nonmaterial. However, no measure of the depth of commitment to particular values is available.

Only a few studies have examined participation in and support for unconventional political activity in the United States, and hardly any of them have been based on data from national samples. More research has been conducted in other countries, where unconventional participation occurs more often.[32] Explanations for this type of participation have focused on historical factors, such as the timing and rapidity of industrialization and the accompanying social mobilization, and also on the political context in which unconventional political behavior occurs. The latter explanations emphasize the importance of mediating institutions, such as political parties, interest groups, and political movements, in channeling and serving as a vehicle for discontent. Societies in which such mediating institutions are more prevalent tend to have a lower incidence of unconventional political behavior.[33] Some researchers have shown that indicators of life experiences, such as age, social class, and education—sometimes in combination with measures of attitudes and beliefs—account both for participation by the general public in unconventional political activities and for the genesis of leadership for such activities.[34]

One study of a national sample of U.S. citizens examined the relative importance of five variables in accounting for support for ten different types of protest activities, ranging from signing petitions to damaging property and engaging in personal violence. Of the five variables, age was the most important, followed by ideological conceptualization, educational level, and emphasis on material or nonmaterial values. The fifth variable, income, appeared to play no part.[35]

Other approaches to unconventional political behavior attribute it to such processes as natural selection (only the more aggressive of the species will survive) and to an innate passion for territory or space.[36] The validity and reliability of these psychobiological explanations have not yet been established.

Personality traits, such as the need for survival and security, affection, self-esteem, and self-actualization, have also been emphasized. However, need variables alone are inadequate to explain why some individuals choose to satisfy their needs through unconventional behavior while others choose conventional ways.[37] Some psychological theories focus on a particular personality type, such as the authoritarian personality. Critics of personality-based theories point to the lack of reliability and validity of the measures employed and the biased samples used in the studies.[38] Furthermore, the full range of personality traits that might account for conventional political behavior has not been examined in a comprehensive, systematic manner.

Frustration-aggression theory suggests that aggressive political behavior is a function of frustration, including an individual's sense of *relative deprivation,* which is defined as a belief that one has not received a rightful share of material goods and (or) nonmaterial goods, such as social status or a healthful environment. Theories encompassing relative deprivation may incorporate an examination of the factors that contribute to creating or increasing it.[39] Critics of frustration-aggression theory point out that it fails to explain under what conditions frustration will be expressed as unconventional political behavior and under what conditions it will be expressed in some other way. Furthermore, some research has provided evidence undermining the theory entirely.[40]

Some scholars view participation in unconventional forms of political behavior as a consequence of alienation (see Chapter 3). However, alienation, like frustration, can be expressed in many different types of behavior.

Summary

Trends in voter turnout reflect changes in the electorate's demographic characteristics, such as the increased proportion of younger voters. These trends are also related to declines in the strength of partisanship and sense of political efficacy, as well as to changes in patterns of partisanship. Although it is generally agreed that these changes have contributed to the decline in turnout, researchers do not agree on the effects of changes in political trust. It is clear that changes in the legal environment have made it easier for citizens to register and vote, and these changes, together with rising educational attainment levels, have offset some of the forces tending to lower turnout.

Other forms of political participation have received less attention from researchers than has voting—largely because of the absence of satisfactory measures of these other forms. The studies that are available, however, suggest that participation in political activities other than voting varies significantly with age, educational attainment level, and value differences. (Those for whom nonmaterial values are relatively important are more likely to participate in both conventional and unconventional political activities.) The prevalence, variety, and strength of mediating institutions also affect the extent of these nonvoting kinds of participation. The more extensive the network of mediating social institutions (such as community and civic organizations, social and sports clubs, religious organizations, unions, and political party organizations) the wider the variety of such organizations, and the greater the number of citizens who are intensely and extensively involved in them, the higher the rates of political participation are likely to be. These mediating institutions are a source of information about government activities and policies relevant to the organizations' goals and members' interests. Informal interactions among members may also lead to higher rates of political activity. Such organizations also serve as conduits for political recruitment, stimulating both voter turnout and participation in other forms of political activity, such as working on campaigns, participating in petition drives, and contacting local, state, and national officials.

Notes

1. Most studies have relied upon data obtained through surveys conducted by the Center for Political Studies of the University of Michigan. These surveys focus on attitudes and beliefs but also collect information relative to life experience indicators, and since 1952 have sought information about the political context of election contests. The surveys concentrate especially on aspects of the vote choice, including reported voter turnout and campaign activity. Some of the surveys have also included questions about unconventional political participation; the 1976 survey included measures of other forms of conventional political activity in both

the local and the national arenas. The Bureau of the Census also conducts surveys after each election to obtain information about voter registration and turnout, but only a few life experience indicators are included in its data.

Since some people claim that they have voted when they did not, "voter validation" studies have been conducted to check respondents' reported voting participation against the actual voting participation recorded in the files of the registration office or election board in those jurisdictions where such records are kept. However, these records are not available in all jurisdictions. Furthermore, voter validation studies were not conducted for a number of the surveys. Results of voter validation studies are reported in Aage Clausen, "Response Validity: Vote Report," *Public Opinion Quarterly* 32 (1968): 588–606; Michael W. Traugott and John P. Katosh, "Response Validity in Surveys of Voting Behavior," *Public Opinion Quarterly* 43 (1979): 355–377; and John P. Katosh and Michael W. Traugott, "The Consequences of Validated and Self-Reported Voting Measures," *Public Opinion Quarterly* 45 (1981): 519–535. See also Paul R. Abramson and William H. Claggett, "Race-Related Differences in Self-Reported and Validated Turnout," *Journal of Politics* 46 (1984): 719–738; Paul R. Abramson and William H. Claggett, "Race-Related Differences in Self-Reported and Validated Turnout in 1984," *Journal of Politics* 48 (May 1986): 412–422; and Paul R. Abramson and William H. Claggett, "Race-Related Differences in Self-Reported and Validated Turnout in 1986," *Journal of Politics* 51 (May 1989): 397–408.

2. Doris A. Graber, *Mass Media and American Politics*, 5th ed. (Washington, D.C.: CQ Press, 1997), 210.

3. Norman H. Nie, Jane Junn, and Keith Stehlik-Barry, *Education and Democratic Citizenship in America* (Chicago: University of Chicago Press, 1996).

4. See, for example, Paul R. Abramson and John H. Aldrich, "The Decline of Electoral Participation in America," *American Political Science Review* 76 (1982): 502–521; and Jeffrey A. Smith, *American Presidential Elections: Trust and the Rational Voter* (New York: Praeger, 1980).

5. Howard L. Reiter, "Why Is Turnout Down?," *Public Opinion Quarterly* 43 (1979): 297–311; Stephen D. Shaffer, "A Multivariate Explanation of Decreasing Turnout in Presidential Elections, 1960–1976," *American Journal of Political Science* 25 (1981): 68–95; Raymond E. Wolfinger and Steven J. Rosenstone, *Who Votes?* (New Haven: Yale University Press, 1980); M. Margaret Conway, "Political Participation in Midterm Congressional Elections: Attitudinal and Social Characteristics during the 1970s," *American Politics Quarterly* 9 (1981): 221–244; Carol A. Cassel and David B. Hill, "Explanations of Turnout Decline: A Multivariate Test," *American Politics Quarterly* 9 (1981): 181–196; Gregory A. Caldeira, Samuel C. Patterson, and Gregory Markko, "The Mobilization of Voters in Congressional Elections," *Journal of Politics* 47 (1985): 490–509; Lee Sigelman et al., "Voting and Non-voting: A Multi-election Perspective," *American Journal of Political Science* 29 (November 1985): 749–765; Ruy A. Teixeira, *The Disappearing American Voter* (Washington, D.C.: Brookings Institution Press, 1992); Steven J. Rosenstone and John Mark Hansen, *Mobilization, Participation, and Democracy in America* (New York: Macmillan, 1993); Sidney Verba, Kay Lehman Schlozman, and Henry E. Brady, *Voice and Equality* (Cambridge: Harvard University Press, 1995); Warren E. Miller and J. Merrill Shanks, *The New American Voter* (Cambridge: Harvard University Press, 1996); and Paul R. Abramson, John H. Aldrich, and David W. Rohde, *Change and Continuity in the 1996 and 1998 Elections* (Washington, D.C.: CQ Press, 1999).

6. Abramson and Aldrich, "Decline of Electoral Participation"; and Paul Kleppner, *Who Voted?* (New York: Praeger, 1982), 517. See also the references in the preceding note.

7. Shaffer, "Decreasing Turnout"; Miller and Shanks, *New American Voter*, chaps. 3, 4, and 5.

8. Ruy A. Teixeira, *Why Americans Don't Vote: Turnout Decline in the United States, 1960–1984* (Westport, Conn.: Greenwood Press, 1987).

9. Wolfinger and Rosenstone, *Who Votes?*, chaps. 3 and 5.

10. Smith, *American Presidential Elections*, 90–91 and 104–109. However, Weisberg and Grofman report research indicating that candidate-related factors have little effect on voter turnout; see Herbert F. Weisberg and Bernard Grofman, "Candidate Evaluations and Turnout," *American Politics Quarterly* 9 (1981): 197–219.

11. See, for example, Morris P. Fiorina, *Congress: Keystone of the Washington Establishment*, 2d ed. (New Haven: Yale University Press, 1989).

12. Arthur H. Miller, "Political Issues and Trust in Government: 1964–1970," *American Political Science Review* 68 (1974): 951–972.

13. Jack Citrin, "Comment: The Political Relevance of Trust in Government," *American Political Science Review* 68 (1974): 973–989.

14. Citrin, "Comment"; David O. Sears and John McConahay, *The Politics of Violence* (Boston: Houghton Mifflin, 1973); and David C. Schwartz, *Political Alienation and Political Behavior* (Chicago: Aldine, 1973).

15. Smith, *American Presidential Elections*, 148. Citizens who are more trusting are more likely to vote for incumbents in presidential elections and to vote for candidates of the party controlling the White House in midterm congressional elections. See Paul R. Abramson, *Political Attitudes in America* (San Francisco: Freeman, 1983), 199–200.

16. Abramson, *Political Attitudes*, chaps. 6 and 7. For a comprehensive examination of the trends in political trust and the implications for political behavior, see Stephen C. Craig, *The Malevolent Leaders* (Boulder, Colo.: Westview Press, 1993); and Stephen C. Craig, "The Angry Voters: Politics and Popular Discontent in the 1990s," in *Broken Contract?*, ed. Stephen C. Craig (Boulder, Colo.: Westview Press, 1996), 46–66.

17. The discussion of the three elections that follows is based in part on Conway, "Midterm Congressional Elections." See also Abramson, Aldrich, and Rohde, *Change and Continuity*, chap. 12.

18. Teixeira, *Disappearing American Voter*.

19. Ibid., 30–46.

20. Ibid., 49.

21. Ibid., 57.

22. Ibid., 50–56.

23. M. Margaret Conway, "Political Mobilization in America," in *The State of Democracy in America*, ed. William M. Crotty (Washington, D.C.: Georgetown University Press, 2000).

24. Lee Sigelman et al., "Voting and Non-voting," 749–765; Richard W. Boyd, "Decline of U.S. Voter Turnout: Structural Explanations," *American Politics Quarterly* 9 (1981): 133–160; Richard W. Boyd, "Election Calendars and Voter Turnout," *American Politics Quarterly* 14 (1986): 89–104; and Richard W. Boyd, "The Effects of Primaries and Statewide Races on Voter Turnout," *Journal of Politics* 56 (1989): 730–739.

25. Rosenstone and Hansen, *Mobilization, Participation, and Democracy*; see especially chap. 6.

26. Verba, Schlozman, and Brady, *Voice and Equality*.

27. Ibid., chap. 13.

28. See Abramson and Aldrich, "Decline of Electoral Participation." One criterion for evaluating various models is the amount of variance in the dependent variable, which is explained by the set of independent variables and summarized by the statistic R^2. The larger the proportion of variance explained, the higher is the value of R^2, with the maximum value being 1. R^2 values for several models that use the explanatory variables discussed here (and the method used to estimate those values) are as follows. Smith, in *American Presidential Elections*, $R^2 = -52$ for 1972 and 37 for 1976 (probit analysis); Conway, in "Midterm Congressional Elections," $R^2 = .24$ for 1970, .43 for 1974, and .33 for 1978 (probit analysis); Shaffer, in "Decreasing Turnout," $R^2 = .15$ for 1960, .12 for 1964, .19 for 1968, .14 for 1972, and .17 for 1976 (regression analysis). Abramson and Aldrich, in

"Decline of Electoral Participation," use a model that takes advantage of all the data from 1960 to 1980 and includes time as an independent variable. They estimate (using regression analysis) that 70 percent of the decline in turnout was due to the decline in party identification and sense of political efficacy. For a discussion of this model, see David B. Hill and Carol A. Cassel, "Comment on Abramson and Aldrich," *American Political Science Review* 77 (1983): 1011–1012; and Paul R. Abramson and John H. Aldrich, "Reply to Hill and Cassel," *American Political Science Review* 78 (1984): 792–794.

Reliance on R^2 as a criterion for evaluating models has been a subject of debate. One view is that R^2 is not a measure of the fit between the true model and the statistical model but is rather a measure of "the spread of points around the regression line." See Gary King, "How Not to Lie with Statistics: Avoiding Common Mistakes in Quantitative Political Science," *American Journal of Political Science* 30 (1986): 675. Achen argues that it is not even a good measure of that. See Christopher H. Achen, "Interpreting and Using Regression," Quantitative Applications in the Social Sciences no. 29 (Newbury Park, Calif.: Sage, 1982). For another discussion relative to the R^2 controversy, see Robert Luskin, "Abusus Non Tollit Usum: Standardized Coefficients, Correlations, and R^2s," *American Journal of Political Science* 35 (1991): 1030–1044.

29. Austin Ranney, "Turnout and Representativeness in Presidential Primary Elections," *American Political Science Review* 66 (1972): 21–47; and James L. Lengle, *Representation and Presidential Primaries: The Democratic Party in the Post-Reform Era* (Westport, Conn.: Greenwood Press, 1981).

30. Barbara Norrander, "Selective Participation: Presidential Primary Voters as a Subset of General Election Voters," *American Politics Quarterly* 14 (1986): 35–53.

31. Ronald Inglehart, "Political Action: The Impact of Values, Cognitive Level, and Social Background," in *Political Action*, ed. Samuel H. Barnes and Max Kaase (Beverly Hills, Calif.: Sage, 1979), 343–380; Ronald Inglehart, "Post-Materialism in an Environment of Insecurity," *American Political Science Review* 75 (1981): 880–900; Alan Marsh, *Protest and Political Consciousness* (Beverly Hills, Calif.: Sage, 1977); and Milton Rokeach, *The Nature of Human Values* (New York: Free Press, 1973). See also Edward N. Muller and Karl-Dieter Opp, "Rational Choice and Rebellious Collective Action: Public Goods, Psychological Gratification, and Socialist Class Consciousness," *American Political Science Review* 80 (1986): 471–487; and Edward N. Muller and Mitchell A. Seligson, "Inequality and Insurgency," *American Political Science Review* 81 (1987): 425–451.

32. For a general overview of research on unconventional forms of political participation, see Robert W. Hunt and M. L. Goel, "Unconventional Political Participation," in *Participation in Social and Political Activities*, ed. David Horton Smith et al. (San Francisco: Jossey-Bass, 1980), 133–152.

33. See, for example, Samuel P. Huntington and Joan M. Nelson, *No Easy Choice* (Cambridge: Harvard University Press, 1976); and Samuel P. Huntington, *Political Order in Developing Societies* (New Haven: Yale University Press, 1968).

34. Ted R. Gurr, *Why Men Rebel* (Princeton: Princeton University Press, 1970); Kenneth Keniston, *Young Radicals: Notes on Committed Youth* (New York: Harcourt Brace Jovanovich, 1971); Mancur Olson Jr., "Rapid Growth as a Destabilizing Force," *Journal of Economic History* 23 (1963): 529–552; I. K. Fierabend and R. L. Fierabend, "Aggressive Behaviors within Politics, 1948–1962: A Cross-National Study," *Journal of Conflict Resolution* 10 (1966): 249–275.

35. The research is described in Inglehart, "Political Action." The R^2 for the model for the United States is .27. *Ideological conceptualization* refers to the level of abstraction at which people think about politics. For example, some people think about politics in terms of "good times" or "bad times," whereas others, at a higher level of abstraction, evaluate issue positions in terms of the extent to which they are consistent with a preferred ideology, such as liberalism or conservatism. For a model of participation in illegal political activity using data collected in the former West Germany, see Edward N. Muller, *Aggressive Political Participation*

(Princeton: Princeton University Press, 1979); and Edward N. Muller, "An Explanatory Model for Differing Types of Participation," *European Journal of Political Research* 10 (1982): 1–16.

36. Konrad Lorenz, *On Aggression* (New York: Bantam, 1967); and Robert Ardrey, *The Territorial Imperative* (New York: Atheneum, 1966).

37. For research on need satisfaction and political behavior, see Jeanne N. Knutson, *The Human Basis of the Polity* (Chicago: Aldine-Atherton, 1972).

38. Theodor W. Adorno et al., *The Authoritarian Personality* (New York: Harper and Row, 1950); J. P. Kirscht and R. C. Dillehay, *Dimensions of Authoritarianism* (Lexington: University of Kentucky Press, 1963). Criticisms of *The Authoritarian Personality* can be found in Richard Christie and Marie Jahoda, eds., *Studies in the Scope and Method of "The Authoritarian Personality"* (Glencoe, Ill.: Free Press, 1954).

39. For the major formulation of frustration-aggression theory, see John Dollard et al., *Frustration and Aggression* (New Haven: Yale University Press, 1939).

40. For a criticism of the frustration-aggression theory, see Leonard Berkowitz, "The Frustration-Aggression Hypothesis Revisited: Some Implications of Laboratory Studies of Frustration and Aggression," *American Behavioral Scientist* 11 (1968): 14–19.

Chapter 8

Does Political Participation Make a Difference?

The assumption underlying any discussion of political participation is that political participation makes a difference. However, it is possible that political participation is merely symbolic, enhancing participants' patriotic sense of pride in democratic ideals, demonstrating their commitment to the political system, and conferring legitimacy on the political leaders they have elected, as well as on their actions. Alternatively, political participation may have instrumental effects, influencing those who participate, the selection of leaders, the choice of policies, and the operation of the political system. In this chapter we consider whether political participation does have instrumental effects and focus on three possible types: the effects on the individual who engages in political participation, on the representation of citizens by those engaged in the governing process, and on the products of the political system—its policy outputs and the outcomes of those policies for the citizens concerned.[1]

Effects of Participation on the Individual

In much of the recent theorizing about political participation in democracies, it is viewed as a means of controlling those who govern. That view has been summarized by Carole Pateman in what she refers to as the "contemporary theory of democracy":

Elections are crucial to the democratic method for it is primarily through elections that the majority can exercise control over their leaders. Responsiveness of leaders to non-elite demands, or "control" over leaders, is ensured primarily through the sanction of loss of office at elections; the decisions of leaders can also be influenced by active groups bringing pressure to bear during inter-election periods. "Political equality" in the theory refers to universal suffrage and to the existence of equality of opportunity of access to channels of influence over leaders. . . . "Participation," so far as the majority is concerned, is participation in the choice of decision makers. Therefore, the function of participation in the theory is solely a protective one.[2]

Critics of this view argue that participation is important because of its effects on the quality of life for the individual participant. Therefore, participation in a democracy should accomplish more than to enable citizens to exert some control over decision making by deciding "who governs."

If there is to be participatory democracy at all, the mere existence of representative institutions is not sufficient. Democracy requires participation, and participation cannot be forced, or fostered by political institutions alone. Pateman asserts that

the major function of participation in the theory of participatory democracy is . . . an educative one . . . including both the psychological aspect and the gaining of practice in democratic skills and procedures. . . . For a democratic polity to exist it is necessary for a participatory society to exist, i.e., a society where all political systems have been democratised and socialisation through participation can take place in all areas.[3]

In the participatory theory of democracy, political participation means "equal participation in the making of decisions" and political equality means equal power in determining political outcomes. The result of participation is not only a certain type of political decision and policy outcome, but also the maximum fulfillment of the human potential of all citizens. In other words, political participation is necessary to satisfy the highest need in Abraham Maslow's hierarchy of needs—the need for self-actualization.[4]

One inference to be drawn from this line of argument is that participation in other types of activity in other arenas will lead to higher levels of political participation than would otherwise be expected and that, conversely, political participation will lead to participation in decision making in a wider variety of situations than merely deciding "who governs." Another inference is that political participation should lead to an enhanced sense of political efficacy, an increased interest in public affairs, and a greater sense of involvement in and commitment to the political system. What is implied is a reciprocal relationship: increased participation in decision making involving the family, school, and place of employment leads to more involvement in and participation in politics, which in turn feeds back to greater involvement in nonpolitical decision making. More positive attitudes and beliefs about the self, others, and society would follow.

If these inferences are correct, early childhood participation in decision making in the family and school would lead to higher levels of political participation in adult life. Experiences at work and in voluntary organizations, developing a sense of control over one's life and of trust in others, would also contribute to increased political participation.

Some research does provide evidence that other forms of participation foster the attitudes and beliefs that contribute to higher levels of political participation and that political participation leads to greater confidence in one's ability to have an impact on decision making in other arenas. A study that used data collected in 1959 and 1960 in five nations—the United States, Great Britain, West Germany, Italy, and Mexico—sought to ascertain whether individuals who remembered participating in family decisions and in discussions at school and in the workplace also believed that they were competent to function effectively in the political system. The proportions that reported having had some influence in family decision making ranged from 73 percent in the United States and 69 percent in Great Britain to 57 percent in Mexico and 48 percent in Italy. The differences in perceived freedom to participate in school discussions were much greater: 40 percent of the respondents in the United States said that they had opportunities to do so and actually did, whereas the proportions making the same claim in the other countries ranged from 16 percent (Great Britain) to 11 percent (Italy).[5] Participation in both areas varied with social class, as measured by level of educational attainment, with those in higher status groups reporting higher rates of participation. Remembered participation also varied with age; those who were younger were more likely to report participating.

The proportions that reported being often or sometimes consulted about decisions in the workplace ranged from 59 percent in Mexico to 78 percent in the United States and 80 percent in Great Britain. Those in higher status occupations were more likely to have been consulted.[6]

The study found that respondents' sense of subjective competence —their confidence in their ability "to appeal to a set of regular and orderly rules in their dealings with administrative officials"—did vary to some extent with their remembered participation in family decision making and school discussions; the relationship existed primarily among those with lower levels of educational attainment and in younger age groups. No relationship was found to exist between reported participation in workplace decision making and sense of subjective competence. (This finding, however, may be a result of the questions used to measure participation in workplace decision making. The respondents were asked whether they were consulted when decisions were made on the job, the extent to which they felt free to protest if a decision they did not like was made, and the extent to which they actually did protest such a decision.) The researchers concluded that the transfer of participatory experiences in the family and school to the political system may be conditioned by a set of psychological or social factors that influence both childhood participation in decisions and discussion and participation in decision making as adults.[7]

Several studies that examined the political attitudes of factory employees who enjoyed some autonomy in job-related decisions have reported that a greater willingness to participate politically was associated with a higher-than-usual degree of democracy in the workplace and with the resulting increase in job satisfaction.[8] Other research has found that persons who have reached the need-satisfaction stage of self-actualization (see Chapter 3) are more likely to participate in politics, but the relationship was weak, and it varied with social class.[9] A study of worker-owners in a forest industry cooperative reported that they did not exhibit greater cooperative and egalitarian orientations.[10] This may reflect differences between roles of the employee and worker-owners in factory decision making.

The discussion thus far has dealt with the question of what impact participation in decision making in other areas of an individual's life has on political orientations and participation. The obverse question is whether participation in some political activities affects subsequent participation in other political activities, attitudes and beliefs about the political system, and orientations with regard to other arenas of decision making.

This question was the focus of a study of individuals who were interviewed first in 1965, when they were high school seniors, and again in 1973 and 1982.[11] Between 1965 and 1973, the Vietnam War disrupted the lives of many citizens, especially those in this age group. A significant number of the men were serving in the armed forces, and as the war became increasingly unpopular, many civilians participated in antiwar protests. One goal of the researchers was to ascertain the extent to which participation or nonparticipation in these protests affected the subjects' subsequent political attitudes, beliefs, and participation patterns.

The thesis underlying this part of their analysis was that of Karl Mannheim, who drew a distinction between a "generation as actuality" and "generation-units." A generation as actuality, he hypothesized, is created when individuals of the same age group during a period of social destabilization "participate in the characteristic social and intellectual currents of their society and period, and . . . have an active or passive experience of the interactions of forces which made up the new situation." Members of the same generation may react differently to their experiences, however, resulting in generation-units, defined as groups "within the same actual generation which work up the material of their common experience in different specific ways."[12]

The researchers controlled for the 1965 levels of subjects' political attitudes, beliefs, and participation patterns. In addition, to eliminate the effects of education, only college graduates were studied. The analysis of the data showed that protest participation between 1965 and 1973 increased the 1973 levels of political knowledge and use of the print news media, but it decreased political trust and sense of political efficacy. Protest participation also affected party identification and strength of party identification, and it altered positions on such issues as school integration and school prayer. These impacts remained even when the effects of academic major, size of the higher educational institution attended, and type of college or university attended (public versus private) were controlled. Moreover, the impacts were greater for those who had engaged in more protests. The protesters also differed from the nonprotesters in their evaluations of various groups. Thus, the Vietnam War appears to have created different generation-units; those who participated in demonstrations opposing the war revealed more significant changes in their previous attitudes, beliefs, and participation patterns and also developed different attitudes on newly emerging issues.[13]

Another analysis of the data from this study found, rather unexpectedly, that the effects of service in the armed forces during the Vietnam War were "non-existent to negligible."[14] This striking contrast to the effects of protest participation was attributed to the differences in recruitment. Being a protester was a voluntary act, but serving in the armed forces was largely a consequence of being drafted or of enlisting as a reaction to the high probability of being drafted. Furthermore, the protesters came from a relatively homogeneous background, whereas those who served in the military came from varied backgrounds. Attitude crystallization and reinforcement concerning the two types of experience also differed; responses to military service were more varied, attitudes regarding it were less crystallized, and responses to everyday military experiences were more closely supervised (by superior officers). Thus, military service during the Vietnam War failed to result in the creation of a generation-unit.[15]

Social Capital, Civic Engagement, and Political Participation

Have the social capital and civic involvement of citizens, both of which sustain a democratic system of government, declined in the United States? Robert Putnam argues that since the 1960s, there has been a "strange disappearance" of social capital and civic engagement in the United States. This change has reverberated throughout the political system, for "the performance of government and other social institutions is powerfully influenced by social capital."[16] He defines social capital as "the features of social life—networks, norms, and trust—that enable participants to act together more effectively"; civic engagement refers to "people's connections with the life of their communities, not only with politics."[17] Putnam views these connections, which enable citizens to cooperate effectively in their efforts to attain shared goals, as essential to the well-being of a democratic political system.[18] He argues that it is only "to the extent that the norms, networks, and trust link substantial sectors of the community and span underlying social cleavages . . . [that] the enhanced cooperation is likely to serve broader interests and to be widely welcomed."[19] His focus is on those forms of social capital that contribute to a civil society and serve collective goals; he argues that it is those forms which have been declining in the United States.

Putnam distinguishes between social capital, which refers to individuals' relationships with others, and political participation, which refers to individuals' relations with political institutions."[20] The decline in civic engagement impacts political participation. The relationship between civic engagement and political participation can vary in both direction and degree, depending on the type of political participation. For example, civic engagement as measured by positive identification with, and involvement in the activity of, a political party has decreased over time, but the proportion of citizens who contribute to political candidates, organizations, and causes has increased.

How can social capital be measured? One indicator of the social networks component of social capital is the extent to which Americans are members of community organizations such as the Parent-Teacher Association, the League of Women Voters, and various service clubs, labor unions, and sports clubs. Evidence from national surveys indicates that memberships in most types of community organizations have declined significantly since the mid-1960s.[21] Furthermore, comparisons of time budgets collected from samples of the American adult population in 1965, 1975, and 1985 suggest that informal socializing has decreased significantly.[22] The second component of social capital includes levels of social and political trust. Both have also decreased significantly in that period.

The third component of social capital is the pattern of norms in society. Putnam does not discuss measures of social norms in his analysis of the disappearance of social capital in the United States, but in his study of successful governing in Italy he emphasizes the importance of the norm of reciprocity. Social trust is engendered by norms of reciprocity and can result from civic engagement. A norm of generalized reciprocity is based on short-term altruism combined with long-term self-interest. Thus if through private acts or governmental programs we assist those who have experienced a natural disaster such as a flood, tornado, or hurricane or who have lost their jobs or cannot pay their medical bills, we anticipate that if we in the future need similar assistance it will be forthcoming. Putnam argues that communities where such a norm is present can more easily solve community problems.[23] We can infer that successful problem-solving methods include the work of effective governmental institutions as well as citizens' political engagement.

Scholars have debated both Putnam's theory and the credibility of evidence used to support hypotheses derived from it. The basic issue in this controversy is whether social capital has declined. If we agree that it has, then what caused the decline, and what are its implications for political participation?

Putnam examines alternative explanations for the decline of social capital in the United States. They include changed economic conditions and changes in the nation's economic structure, time pressures that limit individuals' civic engagement, higher levels of residential mobility, increased employment of women outside the home, the increase in two-career families, higher levels of divorce and more single-parent families, suburbanization (which is alleged to result in social fragmentation), the social upheavals associated with the social and political movements of the 1960s and 1970s, rebellion against formal authority, and social isolation resulting from television and other technological changes. Putnam concludes that the socially isolating effects of television viewing are to blame for the decline in social capital, for the generational change in civic engagement coincided with the introduction of television in an increasing number of American homes.[24] He also blames television and the electronic media (such as electronic games) for the creation of a "mean world" perception among viewers.

Putnam's blaming television for the decline in social capital and civic engagement has not gone unchallenged. Scholars point out that the evidence is not conclusive and raise a number of issues. Is it the number of hours spent watching television or the content of the programs watched that is detrimental to the formation of social capital? The existence of a correlation among declines in social trust, political trust, civic engagement, and political participation does not demonstrate a causal relationship among them. In a study using data collected in 1990, Pippa Norris found that those who spent more hours watching television were less likely to engage in a variety of forms of political activity. When exposure to different types of content was examined, however, it was found that those who viewed programs with political content (such as network news or public affairs programs) were more likely to be politically active. After controlling for socio-economic factors (such as level of educational attainment, age, employment status, and family income), the viewing of news and public affairs programs was related to four forms of political participation (voting, making a campaign contribution, involvement in informal community activities to solve a local problem, and political activity, measured by a political activism scale). Norris concluded that watching television news was related to social engagement but not to any form of political participation.

Thus the research by Norris presents mixed results. It does support Putnam's thesis that higher levels of television watching (in terms of hours spent) are related to lower levels of civic engagement and a decline in social capital. Those who spend more time watching programs with political content are more likely to engage in some types of political activity. However, the research is based on cross-sectional analysis of data, and reported viewing patterns at one point in time are related only to political behavior at that point in time.[25] Putnam's thesis is that the effect occurs across time; television viewing in childhood and early adulthood affects later patterns of social capital formation and civic engagement.

Whether a decline in participation in local civic associations has actually occurred is also a matter of debate. Even if it has, does that mean that there has been a decline in civic participation? Among the middle class, civic participation may now include involvement in professional and business organizations at the regional, state, and national levels, workplace or workplace-related organizations, charitable and issue-related organizations, and sports clubs and other recreational groups.[26]

Participation and Representation

In assessing the effects of political participation, we should ask whether and how participation affects the nature of representation in a democratic polity. Any attempt to answer this question is complicated by the fact that there are at least four types of representation. The first may be called *descriptive representation*—a resemblance to or reflection of the sociodemographic characteristics of those who are represented. For example, the rules governing the selection of delegates to the 1972 national nominating convention of the Democratic Party required that young people, women, and minorities be represented in "reasonable proportion" to their numbers in a state's population. Subsequently, the party rules were revised to call for equal numbers of men and women in each state and territorial delegation, but all other requirements for the representation of demographically described groups were dropped (although state party committees were directed to make a "positive effort" to ensure that any Democrat who wished to participate in the delegate selection process would be able to do so). The incongruity of requiring equal representation by gender but not by other demographic categories is evident.[27]

The second type of representation may be called *representation of political views,* in which the attitudes, beliefs, and policy preferences of a constituency are congruent with the attitudes, beliefs, and policy preferences of its representative, or with the representative's decisions.[28] It is usually assumed that a legislator votes in accordance with the views of the majority in the represented district. However, defining the "majority" is not always easy. Is it a majority of those who voted in the last election or of those who will vote in the next election? Is it the majority of those who voted in the primary election or the majority of those who voted in the general election? And how does a legislator represent constituents' views when the majority of the electorate has no opinion on an issue, as sometimes happens?

Constituents can express their political views in two ways. The voters can elect a representative who shares their views, or the constituents can make their views known to their representative following the election—typically, when the representative is about to vote on some bill. In either case, the views represented are a function of who participates.[29] If half the voters in a district favor allowing formal prayers in schools and half of them oppose it, but two-thirds of those in favor vote while only one-third of those opposed vote, the *effective majority* supports formal prayers in schools. Similarly, if constituents communicate their views to their representative after the election, the views of those who write the letters, make the phone calls, or meet with the representative will have the most influence.

There can be a conflict between descriptive representation and representation of political views.[30] The delegates to the 1972 Democratic convention, selected according to rules that emphasized reflection of demographic characteristics, were found to be less representative of the policy views of Democrats (as expressed by Democratic respondents in public opinion polls) than were the delegates to subsequent party conventions, when descriptive representation in terms of demographic categories was no longer required (except, as noted, for gender).[31]

The third type of representation, *collective representation,* focuses not on the congruence of views between individual public officials and their constituencies but on the congruence between the distribution of policy preferences among the electorate and the distribution in the representative body as a whole. The assumption is that congruence need not exist between the policy views of a particular representative and those of a particular district so long as the district's views are represented somewhere in the legislative body.[32] In this definition of representation, emphasis is placed on participatory actions by members of the political electorate that affect a number of representatives, not just the representatives of one particular constituency. Actions such as contributing to the campaign committee of another congressional district's candidate, to a political action committee, or to a party's congressional campaign committee could have significant effects on who serves and what distribution of views is reflected in the institution. This pattern of contributing money to fund political campaigns has become increasingly prevalent in the United States since the early 1970s. Again, the distribution of representatives' attitudes, beliefs, and policy preferences will reflect the views of those who in some way contributed to the election of any member of the representative body (or who tried to influence the representatives once they attained the office), not necessarily the views of the total potential electorate.

A study based on data obtained by interviewing samples of House members, their electoral opponents, and their constituents found an improvement in the accurate representation of views on three issues when considered from an institutional perspective.[33] A similar conclusion was reached in a study based on roll call data from the Ninety-fifth Congress (1977–1978) and data from interviews with a sample of representatives and their opponents. When adequacy of representation was evaluated in terms of collective satisfaction with the outcome, however, it was found that collective representation did not provide greater satisfaction than did representation considered in terms of each individual member's representation of the constituency's views.[34]

The fourth type of representation is *trusteeship*—acting for others, on their behalf. In a classic statement of this view, Edmund Burke, a member of the British House of Commons in the eighteenth century, defended the actions of legislators, such as himself, in voting for policies they believed were in the best interest of their constituents even when those policies were not the ones preferred by their constituents.[35] Hanna Pitkin is a latter-day exponent of this view:

The representative must act independently; his action must involve discretion and judgment; he must be the one who acts. The represented must also be (conceived as) capable of independent action and judgment, not merely being taken care of. . . . The representative must act in such a way that there is no conflict, or if it occurs an explanation is called for. He must not be found persistently at odds with the wishes of the represented without good reasons in terms of their interest, without a good explanation of why their wishes are not in accord with their interest.[36]

This view of representation also suggests that active participation is necessary. Representatives' perceptions of their constituencies are shaped both by their own prior beliefs and attitudes and by the activities of members of their constituencies.[37]

Participation and Policy Outcomes

An important question in the study of participation is what impact it has on policy outcomes. The increased openness of the American political system to participation by young people, minorities, and women has given rise to a number of studies of the descriptive representativeness of holders of various elective and appointive offices. But as already noted, descriptive representation does not necessarily lead to accurate representation of policy preferences or to the election of representatives who act on behalf of their constituents' interests. Indeed, citizens with similar demographic characteristics can be expected to have different preferences on many issues. For example, if only because of their other group attachments (such as those related to employment, gender, and religion), not all citizens in the age group thirty-five to fifty-five have the same views on issues such as the level of government financial support for public education, the granting of tax credits to families for tuition payments to private schools, or giving vouchers to families for private schools—the tuition, in effect, being paid by the taxpayers.

The passive view of representation underlying descriptive representation is based on at least two assumptions: (1) demographic characteristics largely determine political socialization experiences; and (2) when differentially socialized individuals have discretion in decision making, their decisions will tend to be of particular benefit to, or particularly in the interest of, members of their own demographic group—defined by, for example, race or gender. On most issues, however, division along demographic lines is less likely to occur than is division on some other basis, such as a general philosophical view in support of an active government rather than a preference for limited governmental activity. Nevertheless, the political strategies pursued by a candidate for elective office frequently must take into account the possible reaction of groups in the electorate to various aspects of the candidate's hypothetical descriptive representative. For example, when John F. Kennedy, a Catholic, ran for president, the question of whether he would be particularly responsive to the interest of the Catholic Church and the opinions of its leaders was a major issue. Kennedy faced that issue in a campaign speech he delivered on September 12, 1960:

I believe in an America where the separation of Church and State is absolute—where no Catholic prelate would tell the President (should he be a Catholic) how to act, and no Protestant minister would tell his parishioners for whom to vote—where no church or church school is granted any public funds or political preference—and where no man is denied public office merely because his religion differs from the President who might appoint him or the people who might elect him.[38]

In examining the impact of participation and type of representation on policy outcomes, researchers can track their relationships over time; they can also compare these relationships across jurisdictions that vary in terms of participation patterns or representational styles. Examples of the first type of analysis are the studies of the impact of black elected and appointed officials. Only since the 1960s have African-American citizens been elected or appointed to public office in substantial numbers in many areas of the United States. Several studies of the impact of black mayors in both southern and nonsouthern jurisdictions suggest that their election has had an effect on the policy outcomes of city governments. Some research, using gross expenditure patterns in the analysis of policy outcomes, has concluded that, although the level of black representation on the city council has no effect, the presence of black mayors does make a difference, for it is associated with more spending on social welfare and less spending on amenities, physical plant, and—according to some studies—protective services such as fire and police. These effects may vary with the type of city government system (for example, strong mayor versus weak mayor).[39] But gross expenditure patterns may be too crude a measure; the amount spent on public education, for example, may not change, but the expenditure may be more equitably distributed among the schools in the school system. Representation by blacks has been shown to be correlated with an increase in the employment of blacks in the state bureaucracy.[40] Black representation on school boards has been found to lead to a reduction of racial differences in some school system outputs, although this effect is weakened when controls are applied for the level of black resources in the jurisdiction.[41] The latter study suggests that a set of conditions can be specified as being necessary for the translation of descriptive representation into policy outcomes:

1. Some members of the demographic group must be in a decision-making position.

2. Some issues must be important to members of the group.

3. These issues must be on the decision-making body's agenda.

4. The group's representatives on the decision-making body must hold the same issue position as the majority or dominant plurality within the group or must believe it necessary to act as though they have the same policy preferences.

5. The group's representatives on the decision-making body must be able to influence the decisions made.

6. The policies adopted must be appropriately implemented.

If one or more of these conditions is not met, as often happens, descriptive representation does not have a policy impact.

Some studies of the relationships among participation, representation, and policy outcomes use surrogate indicators of participation levels, and the type of representation is simply assumed. For example, studies of voting-participation levels may use the percentage of the voting-age population in a particular category—such as percent female, percent with Spanish surnames, or percent nonwhite —as the measure of participation, but such a measure is valid only if turnout rates are the same among all groups. That assumption obviously deviates from reality, but estimates of the different turnout rates of groups are not available with regard to many types of elections.

The second type of analysis is the cross-jurisdictional study, an example of which illustrates the methodological problems frequently involved in this kind of research. To examine Mississippi state legislators' support for redistributive social welfare policies, the researchers constructed an index of legislators' voting patterns based on twenty-eight roll calls, all of them concerning policies that would shift benefits to less affluent citizens of Mississippi. They then investigated the relationship between that index and the proportion of the voting-age population that was black in the state's legislative districts. They found that the relationship was curvilinear: support for redistributive policies was high in districts where less than 15 percent of the voting-age population was black; it decreased in districts with higher proportions of blacks of voting age, reached its lowest level in districts whose voting-age population was 25 to 35 percent black, increased in districts that were up to 49.9 percent black, and then decreased again.[42] This puzzling pattern can presumably be explained only by differences with regard to whose interests are represented in different types of districts. Other research has found that when state electorates are disproportionately representative of citizens of higher socioeconomic status, state policies are more likely to favor their economic interests.[43]

Several issues concerning descriptive representation have been subjects of debate and research. For example, does use of a district system or an at-large electoral system make a difference in who gets elected to city councils, school boards, or state legislatures, or are socioeconomic factors, such as the education and income level of the voters, more important? Although there is some support for the latter point of view,[44] there is also persuasive evidence that the electoral system has a significant, perhaps even determining, impact on the extent of descriptive representation.[45] Other factors that may affect policy outcomes are the strength of organizations (social, economic, cultural, political) in the community or the constituency, the extent of organizational memberships, and the skill of organization leaders.[46]

As already pointed out, descriptive representation may not result in accurate representation of constituents' preferences or interests because a group's representatives may not share or may be reluctant to advocate the group's views, particularly if a majority of the other public officials on the council, commission, or board are not receptive to them.[47] (Of course, even if the group's representatives do share the policy positions of a majority of the group and do advocate them, those positions may not be supported by a majority of the representative body.) Another issue in the debate is whether descriptive representation on the basis of race is necessary in order for individuals to be represented effectively. In redrawing state legislative and congressional districts, several state legislatures created districts in which the majority was of a minority race. Many of these districts were not compact. In 1996 in *Shaw v. Hunt,* the Supreme Court ruled that the drawing of legislative districts in which a majority of constituents were of a minority race could be considered a violation of the Equal Protection Clause of the Fourteenth Amendment. In order for the district to be acceptable, the state would have to demonstrate that the redistricting plan was narrowly drafted to meet a compelling state interest.[48]

Although representatives may not share their constituents' policy preferences, they may work to promote those preferences by attempting to enact appropriate legislation. Two researchers examined the data from a sample of districts to ascertain the relationship among constituency preferences, perceptions of those preferences by the district's congressional representatives, and the representatives' own preference, in three policy areas: civil rights, social welfare, and foreign policy. Their results provide evidence concerning the extent of representation as congruence of views and representation as acting in the best interests of the constituents. There was a high degree of correspondence between constituents' preferences and representatives' perceptions of those preferences in the area of civil rights, but a much lower correspondence in the other two areas. The correlation between the representatives' own preferences and their constituents' preferences was only moderate for civil rights policy, weak for social welfare, and almost zero for foreign policy.[49] Thus, at that time (1958), representation by congruence of views could occur only for civil rights policy, but it might be argued that, in the other policy areas, the representatives' views, although not similar to those of their constituents, were nevertheless in accordance with their "best interests," in which case representation should be of the fourth type—acting as trustee.

The general public does not have well-informed attitudes on many issues. Foreign policy issues are generally less salient to most citizens than are domestic issues, and even within the domestic policy areas, issues vary in their salience. Citizens also differ in the degree of their concern with the issues that are salient to them. Hence, what may be important for the quality of representation is that those for whom a particular issue is salient and who care most about it are able, through one or more forms of participation, to bring the issue to the attention of their representatives and that the representatives take account of views on this issue in formulating, enacting, and implementing public policy.

Voting is not the only way that citizens exert influence over policy. They may resort to less conventional methods of participation, such as protest marches and other types of public demonstration to put issues on the policy agendas of otherwise unreceptive decision makers.[50] Once an issue is on the policy agenda, activities other than voting may indicate to decision makers what the parameters of acceptable decisions are to those who are most concerned with it. For example, citizens who are active in a campaign can significantly affect the perceptions of others, mobilizing some of them to work for or against a candidate and to participate in attempts to influence policy outcomes in other ways. The campaign activities of an anti-abortion group opposed to incumbent senators in Iowa in 1978 and 1980 and the actions of supporters of Democratic candidates in the 1998 mid-term elections in Georgia, South Carolina, and California demonstrated that such activities can have a decisive effect on close elections (see Chapter 4). The activities of a passionate minority can thus make clear to a representative the strategic costs and benefits of pursuing certain policy options, even if these activities do not dictate a specific policy stand.

The impact of participation on policy outcomes can also be assessed in terms of the differences in policy preferences between those who vote and those who do not. Since 1952, voters have tended to be more conservative than nonvoters on economic issues, though the magnitude of the difference has decreased since the late 1960s. On many noneconomic issues—notably, racial, public order, and life-style concerns—the views of voters and nonvoters are relatively homogeneous. However, on issues such as housing and social integration, abortion, and women's rights, voters tend to be more liberal than nonvoters.[51] A substantial body of research has been concerned with examining the extent to which primary election voters, as compared with either nonvoters or general election voters, are representative of the electorate. This research indicates that primary voters are not in all respects representative of the eligible electorate. Primary election voters tend to be representative of party followers, although primary voters are of higher socioeconomic status, older, and less likely to be members of minority groups.[52]

It is pertinent to ask whether the problems that are most important to nonvoters get on the policy agenda at all. One historian has concluded that the class bias in voting participation "imbalances the operation of the participation-response system, so that the interests of the electorally inactive remain invisible. . . . Persistently low turnout among working-class citizens relieves elected officeholders of even the likelihood of a retrospective electoral sanctions.[53] Even if the issues relevant to nonvoters are included on the policy agenda, they may not get very much attention.

The political history of the South provides ample evidence of the effects of political and social change on participation patterns; the increase in black political participation has had an impact on the characteristics of representatives and representation as well as on policy outcomes. This increase was stimulated in part by federal laws, such as the Civil Rights Act of 1964 and the Voting Rights Act of 1965, both of which opened access to political participation for many black citizens who had previously been denied the right to vote and not allowed to serve in elected office or on appointive boards and commissions.

That blacks have made use of the opportunity to participate is demonstrated by voter registration data. Black registration in the South increased from 29 percent of the black voting-age population in 1960 to 62 percent in 1970[54] and 65 percent in 1996.[55] The increased access of minorities to the voting booth after the implementation of the Voting Rights Act of 1965 is reflected in their increased representation in public office—both elective and appointive. That increased representation has significantly affected the policy agendas and policy outputs of federal and state governments.[56]

To what extent have blacks used means of participation other than voting, and what have been the effects of participation, whatever the type, on public- and private-sector social and economic policies? James Button's in-depth study demonstrates the significant impact that changes in black political participation have had on public- and private sector policies in six southern communities from the late 1950s to the mid-1980s.[57] However, Button points out that the extent and effects of black participation in stimulating change varied with the nature of the community (size, proportion of blacks, and political culture—Old South versus New South) and with the kind of policy. The policy effects were less significant in the private sector than in the public sector, but the presence of black elected officials did have an impact on private-sector employment. Collective action by blacks, such as protest demonstrations, boycotts, and sit-ins, had a significant impact on employment patterns in the 1960s and a lesser impact in the 1970s. Button concludes that black political participation did contribute to gains in political power for blacks but that improvements in social and economic conditions have been "more difficult and less apparent."[58] Municipal services also improved significantly as a result of increased black participation, but the degree of improvement varied with the type of community and the kind of municipal service.[59]

Earl Black and Merle Black have found evidence that the southern electorate has changed significantly as a consequence of both increased black political participation and other changes (increased urbanization and the development of an urban middle class, generational replacement, and increased employment of women outside the home). However, they conclude from their assessment of public policy that although southern state governments provide more services than in the past, as a rule they tax lightly, regulate mainly where the public interest is so compelling that governmental intervention cannot be avoided, and spend comparatively little except when there are unmistakable direct benefits for the middle and upper-middle classes. In general, southern governments give scant attention and few tangible benefits to those in the bottom half of the socioeconomic structure.[60]

The impact of increased black participation in southern politics appears to vary with the level of government and, within each level, with a host of factors, such as the proportion of the electorate that is black and the type of dominant political culture.

The Changing Nature of Citizenship and Its Implications for Political Participation

Michael Schudson identifies three distinct patterns of citizenship in the United States.[61] The politics of assent dominated the postcolonial era; gentlemen governed and ordinary citizens were expected to support those who governed. In the 1820s the Jacksonian era ushered in mass democracy; citizens identified with and ruled through political parties. At the beginning of the twentieth century, reformers attacked the domination of politics by political parties; their ideal was the informed, rational citizen. The concept of an informed, rational citizen implies a breadth and depth of knowledge; but on many policy issues, many citizens lack both the information sources and the time available to search for relevant information. This concept also presumes a level of background information necessary for evaluating new information that for many citizens may be unrealistic. However, mediating institutions such as social networks, political parties, interest groups, and the mass media may provide cues as to both the issues that are important and the issue positions that are most consistent with citizens' self-interest and collective interests.

Schudson views citizenship in the current political era, which is influenced largely by New Deal and post–New Deal politics and policies, as the era of the rights-bearing citizen. This type of citizenship is supported by impersonal, bureaucratic forms of authority, whose expertise is based on knowledge and information and focuses on citizens' legal rights. Thus, according to Schudson, the kind of knowledge citizens need has changed over time from knowledge of relative social position in the postcolonial era, to knowledge gained from the political rhetoric generated by political parties and acceptance of the legitimacy of rulers conferred by electoral outcomes in the mass democracy era, to knowledge of citizens' entitlements and rights, as well as forms of victimization, in the current political era. Schudson argues that the locus of political authority shifted from shared, generally religious values located in the community in the postcolonial era to the political parties and elections in the mass democracy era; the present focus is on individual rights guaranteed by the courts and by bureaucratic processes that foster administrative fairness. Schudson concludes that the concept of the informed, active citizen has been replaced by the concept of the rights-bearing citizen.

However, it can be argued that rather than the replacement of one concept of citizenship by another, there are multiple perceptions of the type of citizenship existing at any one point in time. The nature of the situations in which citizens confront the political system influences which concept of "citizen" guides their behavior.

Summary

The evidence considered in this chapter suggests that participation, whether in the political or the nonpolitical areas of life, tends to influence individuals' attitudes and beliefs in the direction of more positive orientations toward both themselves and the political system. Patterns of participation also affect the representation of citizens' views in the political system. Representation can be of four types: descriptive representation (correspondence with the sociodemographic characteristics of those who are represented), representation of political views (congruence between a representative's attitudes, beliefs, and policy preferences and those of the members of the representative's constituency), collective representation (congruence between the electorate's policy preferences and those of the representative body), and trusteeship, in which the representative acts on behalf of those who are represented. Participation in all its forms impacts both what is put on the policy agenda and the outcomes of governmental decision making.

The effectiveness of participation cannot be inferred merely from the numbers of citizens who participate. Effectiveness is also dependent on both the quality of the participatory activity and the context within which the participation occurs. Indeed, one of the necessary conditions for policy impact may be to change the context; for example, replacing those who serve in elected office may ensure more receptiveness to the policy demands of those who are represented.

Notes

1. Further research is needed on a number of topics relating to who participates with what effect, such as: To what extent do people with disabilities participate in politics and what has been the impact of their participation on government policies? An example of the type of research that is needed is "Disability and Voter Turnout in the 1998 Election," paper presented by Lisa Schur, Todd Shields, Douglas Kruse, and Kay Schrimer at the annual meeting of the American Political Science Association, Atlanta, September 1999.

2. Carole Pateman, *Participation and Democratic Theory* (Cambridge: Cambridge University Press, 1970), 14.

3. Ibid., 42–43.

4. Abraham Maslow, "A Theory of Human Motivation," *Psychological Review* 50 (1943): 370–396.

5. Gabriel A. Almond and Sidney Verba, *The Civic Culture: Political Attitudes and Democracy in Five Nations* (Princeton: Princeton University Press, 1963), 330–332.

6. Ibid., 331, Table 3.

7. Ibid., 217, and 346–355.

8. J. Maxwell Elden, "Political Efficacy at Work: The Connection between More Autonomous Forms of Workforce Organization and a More Participatory Politics," *American Political Science Review* 75 (1981): 43–58; Harold Sheppard and Neal Herrick, *Where Have All the Robots Gone?* (New York: Free Press, 1972); and William C. Torbet and Malcolm Rogers, *Being for the Most Part Puppets* (Cambridge: Schenkman, 1972).

9. Jeanne N. Knutson, *The Human Basis of the Polity* (Chicago: Aldine-Atherton, 1972), 236, Table 4.50; and 342, Appendix D, part 1.

10. Edward Greenberg, "Industrial Self-Management and Political Attitudes," *American Political Science Review* 75 (1981): 29–42.

11. M. Kent Jennings and Richard G. Niemi, *Generations and Politics: A Panel Study of Young Adults and Their Parents* (Princeton: Princeton University Press, 1981); *Youth-Parent Socialization Panel Study, 1965–1982. Wave III Codebook*, pt. 2, *Youth Data*. 3d ed. (Ann Arbor, Mich.: Inter-university Consortium for Political and Social Research, December 1991).

12. Karl Mannheim, "The Problem of Generations," in *The New Pilgrims,* ed. Philip G. Altbach and Robert S. Laufer (New York: McKay, 1972), 119–120.

13. Jennings and Niemi, *Generations and Politics,* chap. 11.

14. M. Kent Jennings and Gregory B. Markus, "The Effects of Military Service on Political Attitudes: A Panel Study," *American Political Science Review* 71 (1977): 131–147; and Jennings and Niemi, *Generations and Politics,* 378–379.

15. Jennings and Niemi, *Generations and Politics,* 378–379. Differences might be found between those who served in Vietnam and those who did not, or between those who served in combat units in Vietnam and those who served in support units, but the sample is too small to permit analysis of the effects of different patterns of service in Vietnam.

16. Robert D. Putnam, "Tuning In, Tuning Out: The Strange Disappearance of Social Capital in America," *PS: Political Science & Politics* 28 (1995): 664–688.

17. Robert D. Putnam, "The Strange Disappearance of Civic America," *American Prospect,* no. 24 (Winter 1996). (http://epn.org/prospect/24/24putn.html) See also the discussion of social capital in chapter 2.

18. Robert D. Putnam, *Making Democracy Work: Civic Traditions in Modern Italy* (Princeton: Princeton University Press, 1993), 167.

19. Putnam, "Tuning In, Tuning Out," 665.

20. Ibid.

21. Ibid.

22. See, for example, John P. Robinson and Geoffrey Godbey, *Time for Life: The Surprising Ways Americans Use Their Time* (University Park: Pennsylvania State University Press, 1997).

23. Putnam, *Making Democracy Work*, 171–172.
24. Putnam, "Tuning In, Tuning Out," 667–680.
25. Pippa Norris, "Does Television Erode Social Capital? A Reply to Putnam," *PS: Political Science & Politics* 29 (September 1996): 474–480. Putnam's argument has given rise to a vast body of research on social capital. See, for example, the series of articles edited by Jeffrey J. Mondak in the special issue of *Political Psychology*, vol. 19 (1998).
26. Michael Schudson, *The Good Citizen* (New York: Free Press, 1998), 298–300.
27. David E. Price, *Bring Back the Parties* (Washington, D.C.: CQ Press, 1984), 231–232. For a more sanguine view of the consequences of party reform, see William Crotty, *Party Reform* (New York: Longman, 1983).
28. Heinz Eulau and Paul D. Karps, "The Puzzle of Representation: Specifying Components of Responsiveness," *Legislative Studies Quarterly* (1977): 233–254.
29. Aage Clausen, *How Congressmen Decide: A Policy Focus* (New York: St. Martin's, 1973), 131–133. Which party the representative is from and who the particular representative is makes a difference. Patterns of roll call votes differ even when a change in representative means only that a different person from the same party has been elected. See ibid., chap. 6; and Lewis A. Froman Jr., *Congressmen and Their Constituencies* (Chicago: Rand McNally, 1963), chap. 4.
30. Austin Ranney, *Curing the Mischiefs of Faction* (Berkeley: University of California Press, 1975), 111–115; and Jeanne J. Kirkpatrick, *The New Presidential Elite* (New York: Russell Sage Foundation, 1976), chap. 10. See also John S. Jackson III, J. C. Brown, and Barbara Leavitt Brown, "Recruitment, Representation, and Political Values: The 1976 Democratic National Convention Delegates," *American Politics Quarterly* 6 (1978): 187–212; and John S. Jackson III, Barbara Leavitt Brown, and David Bositis, "Herbert McClosky and Friends Revisited: 1980 Democratic and Republican Elites Compared to the Mass Public," *American Politics Quarterly* 10 (1982): 158–180.
31. Kirkpatrick, *New Presidential Elite*, chap. 10.
32. Robert Weisberg, "Collective vs. Dyadic Representation," *American Political Science Review* 72 (1978): 535–547.
33. Ibid., 541, Table 3.
34. Patricia A. Hurley, "Collective Representation Reappraised," *Legislative Studies Quarterly* 7 (1982): 119–136.
35. Edmund Burke, "Speech to the Electors of Bristol at the Conclusion of the Poll, 3 November 1774," in *Selected Prose of Edmund Burke*, ed. Philip Magnus (London: Falcon Press, 1948), 29–31.
36. Hanna Pitkin, *The Concept of Representation* (Berkeley: University of California Press, 1967), 209–210.
37. For reviews of research on representative institutions relating to legislative-constituency connections, see Melissa P. Collie, "Voting Behavior in Legislatures," *Legislative Studies Quarterly* 9 (1984): 3–50; Malcom Jewell, "Legislative Constituency Relations and the Representative Process," *Legislative Studies Quarterly* 8 (1983): 303–338; Lynn Ragsdale, "Responsiveness and Legislative Elections: Toward a Comparative Study," *Legislative Studies Quarterly* 8 (1983): 339–379; and Eric M. Uslaner, "Legislative Behavior: The Study of Representation," in *Political Behavior Annual*, vol. 1, ed. Samuel Long (Boulder, Colo.: Westview Press, 1986). See also Richard F. Fenno Jr., *Home Style: House Members in Their Districts* (Boston: Little, Brown, 1978); David R. Mayhew, *Congress: The Electoral Connection* (New Haven: Yale University Press, 1974); Morris P. Fiorina, *Congress: Keystone of the Washington Establishment*, 2d ed. (New Haven: Yale University Press, 1989), chap. 4; and Morris P. Fiorina, *Representatives, Roll Calls, and Constituencies* (Lexington, Mass.: Lexington Books, 1974).
38. Quoted in Theodore H. White, *The Making of the President 1960* (New York: Atheneum, 1961), 260.
39. David Campbell and Joe R. Feagin, "Black Politics in the South: A Descriptive Analysis," *Journal of Politics* 37 (1975): 129–159; William R. Keech, *The Impact*

of Negro Voting (Chicago: Rand McNally, 1968); Charles H. Levine, *Racial Conflicts and the American Mayor* (Lexington, Mass.: Lexington Books, 1974); William E. Nelson Jr. and Philip J. Meranto, *Electing Black Mayors* (Columbus: Ohio State University Press, 1977); Chuck Stone, *Black Political Power in America* (New York: Dell, 1971); and Susan Welch and Albert K. Karnig, *Black Representation and Urban Policy* (Chicago: University of Chicago Press, 1980).

40. Kenneth J. Meier, "Affirmative Action: Constraints and Policy Impact," in *Race, Sex, and Policy Problems,* ed. Marian L. Palley and Michael B. Preston (Lexington, Mass.: Lexington Books, 1979).

41. Kenneth J. Meier and Robert F. England, "Black Representation and Educational Policy: Are They Related?" *American Political Science Review* 78 (1984): 392–403. The six candidates that follow are generalized from this study.

42. Charles S. Bullock III and Susan A. MacManus, "Policy Responsiveness to the Black Electorate," *American Politics Quarterly* 9 (1981): 357–368; see especially 360–361. For discussions of district characteristics and legislative voting patterns at the national level, see Michael W. Combs, John R. Hibbing, and Susan Welch, "Black Constituents and Congressional Roll Call Votes," *Western Political Quarterly* 37 (1984): 424–434; and Charles S. Bullock III, "Congressional Voting and the Mobilization of a Black Electorate in the South," *Journal of Politics* 43 (1981): 662–682.

43. Kim Quaile Hill and Jan E. Leighley, "The Policy Consequences of Class Bias in State Electorates," *American Journal of Political Science* 36 (1992): 351–365.

44. Leonard Cole, "Electing Blacks to Municipal Office: Structural and Social Determinants," *Urban Affairs Quarterly* 10 (1974): 17–39; Susan A. MacManus, "City Council Election Procedures and Minority Representation: Are They Related?" *Social Science Quarterly* 59 (1978): 153–161; and Albert K. Karnig, "Black Resources and City Council Representation," *Journal of Politics* 41 (1979): 134–139.

45. Richard L. Engstrom and Michael D. MacDonald, "The Election of Blacks to City Councils: Clarifying the Impact of Electoral Arrangements on the Seats/Population Relationships," *American Political Science Review* 75 (1981): 344–355; Keech, *Impact of Negro Voting;* Albert Karnig, "Black Representation on City Councils: The Impact of District Election and Socio-Economic Factors," *Urban Affairs Quarterly* 12 (1976): 223–256; Mary Herring and John Forbes, "The Overrepresentation of a White Minority: Detroit's At-large City Council, 1961–1989," *Social Science Quarterly* 75 (1994): 431–445.

46. Keech, *Impact of Negro Voting;* Donald R. Matthews and James W. Prothro, *Negroes and the New Southern Politics* (New York: Harcourt, Brace and World, 1966), chaps. 7 and 8; and Meier, "Affirmative Action."

47. Keech, *Impact of Negro Voting.*

48. *Shaw v. Hunt,* 116 Sup.Ct. 1894, 135 L. Ed. 2d 207 (1996).

49. Warren E. Miller and Donald E. Stokes, "Constituency Influence in Congress," *American Political Science Review* 57 (1963): 45–56. For a reanalysis of the data pertaining to civil rights, see Charles F. Cnudde and Donald J. McCrone, "The Linkage between Constituency Attitudes and Congressional Voting Behavior: A Causal Model," *American Political Science Review* 60 (1966): 66–72.

50. For a discussion of the effectiveness of protest marches and other types of public demonstrations in forcing a southern city to deal with certain issues in the early and mid-1960s, see Keech, *Impact of Negro Voting,* 83–87.

51. Stephen D. Shaffer, "Policy Differences between Voters and Non-Voters in American Elections," *Western Political Quarterly* 35 (1982): 496–510. See also Raymond E. Wolfinger and Steven J. Rosenstone, *Who Votes?* (New Haven: Yale University Press, 1980), 111; and Paul R. Abramson, John H. Aldrich, and David W. Rohde, *Change and Continuity in the 1996 and 1998 Elections* (Washington, D.C.: CQ Press, 1999), 86–90 and chap. 6. In his study of a Wisconsin primary, Ranney found that nonvoters differed from voters on only two of twenty-one issues; see Austin Ranney, "The Representativeness of Primary Electorates," *Mid-*

west Journal of Political Science 12 (1968): 224–238. See also Austin Ranney and Leon Epstein, "The Two Electorates: Voters and Non-Voters in a Wisconsin Primary," *Journal of Politics* 28 (1966): 589–616.

52. The differences between primary election voters and various comparison groups are examined in Larry M. Bartels, *Presidential Primaries and the Dynamics of Public Choice* (Princeton: Princeton University Press, 1988); John Geer, "The Representativeness of Presidential Primary Electorates," *American Journal of Political Science* 32 (1988): 929–945; and Barbara Norrander, "Ideological Representativeness of Primary Voters," *American Journal of Political Science* 33 (1989): 570–587.

53. Paul Kleppner, *Who Voted?* (New York: Praeger, 1982), 161–162.

54. Harold W. Stanley, *Voter Mobilization and the Politics of Race* (New York: Praeger, 1987), 6.

55. Lynn M. Casper and Loretta E. Bass, "Voting and Registration in the Election of November 1996," Bureau of the Census, *Current Population Reports,* ser. P-20, no. 504 (Washington, D.C.: Government Printing Office, July 1998), 2, Table 2.

56. Paula D. McClain and Joseph Stewart Jr., *Can We All Get Along?,* 2d ed. (Boulder, Colo.: Westview Press, 1998), chap. 4.

57. James W. Button, *Blacks and Social Change* (Princeton: Princeton University Press, 1989).

58. Ibid., 207.

59. Ibid., 213–218.

60. Earl Black and Merle Black, *Politics and Society in the South* (Cambridge: Harvard University Press, 1987), 193.

61. Michael Schudson, *Good Citizen.*

Appendix

Appendix.   Variables Used in the Data Analysis

American National Election Studies Cumulative File, 1948–1996, and 1998 American National Election Study

Variable	ANES Cumulative File, 1948–1996	1998 ANES File
Persuade Question wording: "During the campaign, did you talk to any people and try to show them why they should vote for [*1984 and after*, added "or against"] one of the parties or candidates?" Coding: 0 = no; 1 = yes.	VCF0717	V980361
Meeting Question wording: "Did you go to any political meetings, rallies, [*1984 and after*, added "speeches"; *1978–1982*, added "fund-raising"] dinners, or things like that in support of a particular candidate?" Coding: 0 = no; 1 = yes.	VCF0718	V980363
Work Question wording: "Did you do any (other) work for one of the parties or candidates?" Coding: 0 = no; 1 = yes.	VCF0719	V980364
Button Question wordings: *1956, 1960, 1962–1982:* "Did you wear a campaign button or put a campaign sticker on your car?" *1984 and after:* "Did you wear a campaign button, put a campaign sticker on your car, or place a sign in your window or in front of your house?" Coding: 0 = no; 1 = yes.	VCF0720	V980362
Money Question was asked a variety of ways over time. The variable measures whether respondent gave money to a candidate or a party. See ANES Cumulative File Codebook, 1948–1996, and 1998 ANES File Codebook. Coding: 0 = no; 1 = yes.	VCF0721	Sum of V980367 and V980365
Interest in public affairs/follow public affairs Question wordings: *1960, 1962:* "We'd also like to know how much attention you pay to what's going on in politics generally. I mean from day to day, when there isn't any big election campaign going on, would you say you follow politics very closely, fairly closely, or not much at all?" *1964 and after:* "Some people seem to follow [*1964*, substituted "think about"] what's going on in government and public affairs most of the time, whether there's an election going on or not. Others aren't that interested. Would you say you follow what's going on in government and public affairs most of the time, some of the time, only now and then, or hardly at all?" Coding: 1 = hardly at all; 2 = only now and then; 3 = some of the time; 4 = most of the time.	VCF0313	V980340

(*Continued on next page*)

(*Continued*)

Variable	ANES Cumulative File, 1948–1996	1998 ANES File
Interest in current campaign Question wording: "Some people don't pay much attention to political campaigns. How about you, would you say that you have been/were very much interested, somewhat interested, or not much interested in following the political campaigns this year?" Coding: 1 = not much interested; 2 = somewhat interested; 3 = very much interested.	VCF0310	V980201
Care who wins presidential election Question wording: "Generally speaking, would you say that you personally care a good deal which party [*1992, 1996,* substituted "who"] wins the presidential election this fall, or that you don't care very much which party wins?" Coding: 1 = don't care very much or don't know, pro-con, depends, and other; 2 = care a good deal.	VCF0311	—
Care who wins House election Question wording: "How much would you say that you personally cared about the way the elections to the House of Representatives came out?" Coding: 1 = not very much, not at all, don't know, pro-con, depends, other; 2 = very much, pretty much.	VCF0312	V980222
Number of campaign acts performed Sum of the scores assigned to Persuade, Meeting, Work, and Button. Coding: 0 = none; 1 = 1; 2 = 2; 3 = 3; 4 = 4.	Sum of VCF0717– VCF0720	Sum of V980361– V980364
Voted in current election Question wordings: *All years except 1948, 1962:* "In talking to people about the election we [*1972 and after,* added "often"] find that a lot of people weren't able to vote because they weren't registered or they were sick or they just didn't have time. *Additions, 1964–1970:* "How about you, did you vote in the election this time, or did something keep you from voting?" *1972–1976:* "How about you, did you vote in the election this fall?" *1978 and after:* "How about you, did you vote in the election this November?" See ANES Cumulative File Codebook, 1948–1996, for question wording in 1948 and 1962. Coding: 0 = no; 1 = yes.	VCF0702	V980303
Civic duty Item wording: "If a person doesn't [*1988:* "If people don't"] care how an election comes out he [*1980, 1984,* "then that person"]; [*1988, 1992,* "they"] should not vote in it." Coding: 1 = agree; 2 = disagree.	VCF0616	—

(*Continued on next page*)

(Continued)

Variable	ANES Cumulative File, 1948–1996	1998 ANES File
Too complicated Item wording: "Sometimes government and politics seems so complicated that a person like me can't really understand what's going on."		
Coding: 1 = agree; 2 = disagree. *1988–1998:* Response categories "agree strongly," "agree somewhat," and "neither agree nor disagree" were coded as 1; "disagree" and "disagree strongly" were coded as 2.	VCF0614	V980523
External efficacy index Item wordings: *VCF0609 and V980524 (1952–1988, 1992):* "I don't think public officials care much what people like me think." *(1990, 1994, and after):* "Public officials don't care much what people like me think." *VCF0610 and V980525:* "People like me don't have any say about what the government does."	Sum of VCF0609 and VCF0613	Sum of V980524 and V980525
Coding: 0 = low; 1 = medium; 2 = high.		
Party identification Question wording: "Generally speaking, do you usually think of yourself as a Republican, a Democrat, an Independent, or what?" [If Republican or Democrat]: "Would you call yourself a strong ["Republican" or "Democrat"] or a not very strong ["Republican" or "Democrat"]? [If Independent, other, or no preference]: "Do you think of yourself as closer to the Republican or the Democratic Party?"	VCF0301	V980339
Coding: 1 = Strong Democrat; 2 = Weak Democrat; 3 = Independent Democrat; 4 = Independent; 5 = Independent Republican; 6 = Weak Republican; 7 = Strong Republican.		
Strength of party identification		
Coding: 1 = Independent; 2 = Independent who usually votes for candidates of one party or the other; 3 = weakly identify with one party; 4 = strongly identify with one party.	Recode of VCF0301	Recode of V980339
Belief in government attentiveness Question wording: *VCF0622 and V980521:* "Over the years, how much do you feel the government pays attention to what people think when it decides what to do?"	Sum of VCF0622 and VCF0624	Sum of V980521 and V980522
Coding: 1 = not much; 2 = some; 3 = a good deal. *VCF0624 and V980522:* "How much do you feel that having elections makes the government pay attention to what the people think?"		
Coding: Ranges from 1 = low to 5 = high.		

(Continued on next page)

(*Continued*)

Variable	ANES Cumulative File, 1948–1996	1998 ANES File
Expected closeness of election Question wording: "Do you think the presidential race will be close or will one candidate win by quite a bit?" Coding: 1 = win by quite a bit; 2 = close race.	VCF0714	—
Trust Index constructed from responses to four trust questions: "How much of the time do you think you can trust the government in Washington to do what is right— just about always, most of the time, or only some of the time?" "Would you say the government is pretty much run by a few big interests looking out for themselves, or that it is run for the benefit of all?" "Do you think that people in the government waste a lot of money we pay in taxes, waste some of it, or don't waste very much of it?" "Do you think that quite a few of the people running the government are [*1958–1972, added* "a little"] crooked, not very many are, or do you think hardly any of them are crooked [*1958–1972, added* "at all"]?" Coding: Ranges from 0 = no trust to 5 = high trust.	VCF0656	Constructed from V980526– V980529
Region Coding: 1 = 11 states of the Confederacy; 0 = other states.	VCF0113	—
Age in years	VCF0101	V980572
Family income in percentiles Coding: 1 = 0–16 percentile; 2 = 17–33 percentile; 3 = 34–67 percentile; 4 = 68–95 percentile; 5 = 96–100 percentile.	VCF0114	V980652
Gender Coding: 1 = male; 2 = female.	VCF0104	V980672
Educational attainment level Coding: 1 = grade school; 2 = grades 9–12; 3 = grade 12; 4 = some college; 5 = college degree.	VCF0140A	V980577
Marital status Coding: 1 = married and living with spouse; 2 = never married; 3 = divorced; 4 = separated; 5 = widowed; 6 or 7 = partners.	VCF0147	V980573
Race Coding: 1 = white; 2 = black.	VCF0105	V980673

(*Continued on next page*)

(*Continued*)

Variable	ANES Cumulative File, 1948–1996	1998 ANES File
News media index Sum of use or nonuse of four types of media (newspapers, radio, television, and magazines) to follow political news during the campaign. Coding: 1 = no media; 2 = one; 3 = two; 4 = three; 5 = all four.	VCF0728	—

1976 American National Election Study

Nationally oriented activities
    In the preceding two or three years,

Has written letter to the editor of a magazine or newspaper about some national problem. Coding: 0 = no; 1 = yes.	V763046
Has worked with others or joined an organization trying to do something about some national problem. Coding: 0 = no; 1 = yes.	V763047
Has written letter to congressman or some other national leader. Coding: 0 = no; 1 = yes.	V763048
Has signed a petition either for or against action taken by national government. Coding: 0 = no; 1 = yes.	V763049
Has taken part in a sit-in or other demonstration or protest concerned with some national problem. Coding: 0 = no; 1 = yes.	V763050
Index of nationally oriented activities: Scores range from 0 = low to 5 = high.	Sum of V763046–V763950

Locally oriented activities
    In the preceding two or three years,

Has attended meetings of school board or city council. Coding: 0 = no; 1 = yes.	V763065
Has written letter to the editor of the local newspaper about some public problem. Coding: 0 = no; 1 = yes.	V763066
Has worked with others or joined an organization in local community to do something about some community problem. Coding: 0 = no; 1 = yes.	V763067

(*Continued on next page*)

(*Continued*)

Nationally oriented activities In the last preceding two or three years,	

Has spoken to, or written to, an official about some local problem. Coding: 0 = no; 1 = yes.	V763068
Has signed a petition for or against action of the local government. Coding: 0 = no; 1 = yes.	V763069
Has taken part in a sit-in or other demonstration or protest concerned with some local problem. Coding: 0 = no; 1 = yes.	V763070
Index of locally oriented activities: Scores range from 0 = low to 6 = high.	Sum of V763065–V763070

SOURCE: The American National Election Studies are conducted by the Center for Political Studies, University of Michigan. The data are made available through the Inter-University Consortium for Political and Social Research. In all calculations, cases with missing data have been deleted from the analysis.

Index